Alejandro García Caturla

A Cuban Composer in the Twentieth Century

Charles W. White

The Scarecrow Press, Inc.
Lanham, Maryland, & Oxford
2003

SCARECROW PRESS, INC.

Published in the United States of America
by Scarecrow Press, Inc.
A Member of the Rowman & Littlefield Publishing Group
4720 Boston Way
Lanham, Maryland 20706
www.scarecrowpress.com

PO Box 317
Oxford
OX2 9RU, UK

British Cataloguing in Publication Information Available

Library of Congress Cataloging-in-Publication Data

White, Charles W., 1929–
    Alejandro García Caturla: a Cuban composer in the twentieth century
/ Charles W. White.
    p. cm.
"Catalog of works" :p.
Includes bibliographical references (p.) and index.
ISBN 0-8108-4381-1 (alk. paper)
1. García Caturla, Alejandro, 1906–1940. 2. Composers—Cuba—
Biography. I. Title.
ML410.G168 W55 2003
780'.92—dc21   2002008914

♾™ The paper used in this publication meets the minimum requirements
of American National Standard for Information Sciences—Permanence of
Paper for Printed Library Materials, ANSI/NISO Z39.48-1992.
Manufactured in the United States of America.

For Olga Caturla de la Maza, poet and mentor,
who inspired this book

"Alma de Horizontes/A Soul for Horizons"

I was born with a soul for horizons
And cannot live between walls,
Above my heart's desire: the dome of space,
I am sustained by arcades of pure distances.

Olga Caturla de la Maza

Contents

Acknowledgments

Above all, I wish to thank Olga Caturla de la Maza and her daughter Elena Maza Borkland for translating most of Caturla's correspondence quoted in this book. Elena translated over four hundred pages of correspondence and articles in Cuban journals; without her arduous work, this book could not have been completed. Olga Caturla (now living in Washington, D.C.) is Alejandro García Caturla's first cousin and grew up with him in Remedios, Cuba. A recognized poet and authority on the history of Caturla's family, Olga Caturla became my mentor throughout the writing of this book and graciously shared with me her well-documented memories of Alejandro, including his family relationships, circle of friends in Remedios, and lifestyle.

Next in importance is Santos Ojeda, whom I wish to thank for providing all of the resource materials (including reviews, photographs, and printed programs) and translations for chapters 14 and 15. Because of his historical role as piano soloist at the premiere of Caturla's *Bembé* with the Orquesta de Conciertos de Caibarién (under Caturla's direction) Santos Ojeda was able to create for me a vivid picture of just how far ahead of his time Caturla was. Santos also helped me realize the significance of Caturla's influence upon the younger generation. The many meetings, phone calls, and correspondence that ensued after our first meeting became a source of great inspiration and reinforced my determination to finish this book.

The person who contributed most about Caturla's judicial career was former Cuban judge Fernando Arsenio Roa (now deceased), whom I met in Miami in 1990. Fernando Arsenio Roa was the judge who replaced Caturla in Remedios immediately after Caturla's assassination.

I wish to thank Cuban-American Roberto A. Nodal, a prolific researcher and writer on Cuban music and musicians, for sharing with me his private library and collection of articles, which were published in *El Huracán*. His parents shared much information with me about the history of Remedios during Caturla's time.[1]

I wish to thank the following libraries, museums, and their respective personnel who so generously gave me their time, encouragement, and high level of expertise: the Connelley Library at La Salle University (Philadelphia); the Otto G. Richter Library at the University of Miami; the New York Public Library at Lincoln Center; the Library of Congress; the Benson Latin American Collection at the University of Texas (Austin); the San Francisco Public Library; the Biblioteca de Cataluña; the Bibliothèque Nationale (Paris); the Instituto de la Música (Havana); and the Museo de la Música Provincial "Alejandro García Caturla" (Remedios). Special thanks are due to Kile Smith, Curator of the Fleisher Collection of Latin American orchestral music at the Free Library of Philadelphia, who never failed to ask how it was going and eventually sponsored a concert of Caturla's music at the Free Library of Philadelphia. I also wish to thank Dr. Daniel Cabedo for his generous hospitality and research assistance during my stay in Barcelona, where he is director general at La Salle University and Univesitat Ramon Llull. Chapter six of this book could not have been completed without his help.

I owe much to the director of Cuba's Instituto de la Música: Alicia Perea Maza who sponsored my first official invitation to visit Havana in 1991. Alicia also arranged my first trip to Caturla's hometown, Remedios, where I visited the Museo de la Música Provincial "Alejandro García Caturla."[2]

Also, I wish to thank María Teresa Linares, director of the Museo Nacional de la Música in Havana, for allowing me to research most of Caturla's unpublished scores and correspondence over a period of six years. Composer Hilario González (now deceased) and musicologists Carmelina Muñoz Albuquerque and José Piñeiro Díaz, staff members at the Museo Nacional de la Música, assisted me on each of my many visits to this archive. Other Cuban musicians and musicologists I wish to thank include Tulio Peramo, Harold Gramatges, Carlos Fariñas, Edgardo Martín, Félix Guerrero, Tamara Martín, Maruja Sánchez (official historian for the Orquesta Filarmónica de La Habana—now deceased), Hector Angulo and Danilo Orozco. A special thanks goes to María Antonieta Henríquez, former director of the Museo Nacional de la Música and recent biographer of Alejandro García Caturla. The many hours I spent with María Antonieta in Remedios and Havana provided me with the rich source of references found in this book.

I wish to thank Ángel Augier (president of the Fundación Nicolás Guillén, now deceased) and Andrea Esteban Carpentier (widow of Alejo Carpentier and director of the Alejo Carpentier Centro in Havana). Long interviews with each of these esteemed directors and literary scholars provided me with valuable resources and permission to publish excerpts of texts Caturla set to music.

A very special thanks goes to Dr. Miguel Martín Farto (historian and author of *Las parrandas remedianas*) and Jesús Pernús Pérez (now deceased), both of whom I met in Remedios. Their intimate knowledge of the history of Remedios and the life and times of Alejandro García Caturla was an invaluable source of information for this book. Thanks to Dr. Martín Farto, I traveled by car to visit each of the Cuban towns and cities in which Caturla lived and worked as a judge and was known as a composer; these included Santa Clara, Caibarién, Vueltas, Ranchuelo, Santiago de Cuba, Palma Soriano, and Quemado de Güines. I was greeted with enthusiasm, good will, and abundant hospitality in each of the official institutions (mainly libraries and museums) I visited in these places.

Translators of texts in Spanish found in this book, other than those already mentioned, whom I also want to thank, include Dr. Noemí Escandel, Patricia Silva, Prof. Roland Morelli, and Raisa Williams. Established scholars who read the working manuscript and encouraged me to complete this book include Howard E. Smither (Prof. Emeritus, University of North Carolina), Prof. Isabelle Cazeaux (Bryn Mawr College), Dr. Eva Badura-Skoda (University of Vienna), and Santos Ojeda (Cuban pianist).

Among the performing artists who participated in the production of this book, I wish to thank, above all, Stephanie Griffin, concert violist and director of the Griffin String Quartet, for recording Caturla's *Preludio* and *Danza a la cubana* on the CD included with this book; all members of the quartet are graduates of the Julliard School of Music. Attending rehearsals of this recording in New York was the most rewarding experience of all my research. Kenneth Marchant, who recorded the solo piano music on this CD, also participated in several programs of Cuban music (including Caturla) in Philadelphia where he was well received. Among vocalists who also participated in these concerts, I wish to thank Jackie Smith and Cuban-American Mayda

Prado; Mayda introduced me to many important musicians in Havana, where she is admired as a concert artist. Lastly, I wish to thank Johannes Kreusch, concert guitarist. His recording _Portraits of Cuba_ (Arte Nova) includes "Tres Imágenes Cubanas—Homenaje a Caturla" by Tulio Peramo provides an important perspective of Caturla's image today.

Among the many scholars I contacted in reference to research for this book, Prof. Malena Kuss remains the most important, because of her expertise on Caturla's opera _Manita en el suelo_. Thanks also goes to Rob Haffley for helping to prepare the computerized music examples.

Among the few musicians who knew Caturla and were still living at the time I began my research is Nicolas Slonimsky. Although my meeting and correspondence with Slonimsky was limited to a short period prior to his death, I wish to give thanks posthumously, especially for the day I spent with him at his house in Los Angeles on 8 June 1990.

Finally, I wish to thank my wife, Polish actress Helena Morawska White, for remaining sanguine during the endless flood of books, papers, phone calls, e-mail, faxes, and unexpected visitors (some from Cuba) into our home during my research. More important, however, was the inspiration of her encouragement and support that made possible the completion of this work.

NOTES

1. Roberto A. Nodal's father was a school teacher and later superintendent of schools in the province of Villa Clara, Cuba; his mother was an elementary school teacher in Remedios, where she taught several of Caturla's children. Roberto received his elementary school education in Remedios.

2. The Museo de la Música Provincial "Alejandro García Caturla" is located at the former residence of the García Caturla family. The Museo consists of nine rooms, each with a different display of Alejandro's personal belongings, including his private library, desk and typewriter, manuscripts of unpublished music and first editions of music he had published in Havana, and photographs, especially those of distinguished musicians he knew and admired, including Henry Cowell, Manuel de Falla, Manuel Ponce, and Augustín Crespo (who was director of the Banda Municipal de Remedios during Caturla's lifetime). Also on display are the suit he was wearing the day he was shot to death (the bullet holes in his suit are visible) and the pistol with which the criminal committed the act.

Noticeably absent in the Museo were any references to Manuela Rodríguez (Caturla's first wife), Catalina Rodríguez (his second wife), and his children.

Introduction

In a recent dissertation on the Mexican composer Silvestre Revueltas, author Carlos Daniel Sánchez-Gutiérrez states: "The life of
Silvestre Revueltas was at once so colorful, intense, prolific, complicated, pathetic, and, in the end, tragic, that it may seem the invention of a nineteenth-century novelist."[1] With the exception of one
word, "pathetic" (which refers to Revueltas's alcoholism), author
Sánchez-Gutiérrez unintentionally described the life of Alejandro
García Caturla. Revueltas and Caturla both died prematurely in
1940, abruptly ending heroic efforts to bring their respective nations
into the mainstream of avant-garde twentieth-century music. In
both cases, their music was eclipsed shortly after their deaths by
new trends in modernism, leaving their visions of a new aesthetic
dormant for almost a half century.

Revueltas and Caturla were modern native-born patriotic zealots
whose mission was to bring about a cultural liberation of their own
people. They did so by assimilating the environments of the towns
in which they lived and worked and transforming them into sources
for a new musical language, one that was syncretic in nature and
highly personal in style.

In contrast to most of their contemporaries, including Carlos
Chávez and Amadeo Roldán, Caturla and Revueltas belong to a small
group of composers described by Cuba's renowned composer Leo
Brouwer as the *"real maravilloso de nuestra América."* Other members of
this group include Charles Ives and Heitor Villa-Lobos. What makes
these composers unique and separates them from their contemporaries is the stark originality that eventually brought a new sound of

national identity to their music. They invented a musical syntax that was syncretic, daring, exotic, humorous, totally liberated from past traditions, and in most cases too far ahead of their times to be understood by contemporary audiences. The spirit common to these composers is complex; it was inspired by their environment, political involvement (they were all political activists, opposed to the status quo), national pride, self-esteem (particularly Caturla), and an exigency to transcend the barriers of Eurocentric influence. These composers were extremely outspoken regarding their opposition to the sociopolitical climate in which they lived, and their artistic ideals served as the driving force behind their music. Caturla was the youngest of the group and the most provocative in his rhetoric. He was also the most competitive by nature; he remained a relentless fighter for his causes, daring, and willing if necessary to take great risks for the sake of progress. Writing to Alejo Carpentier in 1928, for example, Caturla states: "I am prepared for the fight when the three *Danzas* which I consider rather daring are performed. We are expecting the scandal of the century . . . a true dynamic orgy."[2] Such rhetoric is typical of Caturla's assertiveness when it came to promoting his own music; yet, he was self-conscious as a composer and critical of virtually all of his peers. As a result, Caturla faced a colossal struggle for acceptance in Cuba, a goal he eventually achieved by promoting his music abroad. None of the composers in this exclusive group fought so courageously against such extreme odds to raise cultural standards in their respective homelands as did Caturla.

Although it may be said that Caturla is kindred in spirit to these composers, that is not to say he consciously aligned himself with this small group, or isolated himself from other groups of composers.[3] To the contrary, Caturla's affiliation with Henry Cowell's Pan American Association of Composers (PAAC) brought him into contact with a vast network of international figures and musical organizations. In Cuba, Caturla was at the forefront of contemporary music organizations and active as critic, performer, teacher, composer, and conductor dedicated to the promotion of his own music and that of other avant-garde composers as part of an overall mission to raise cultural standards throughout his homeland.

The stark originality and new sound of national identity in the works of the "real maravilloso" composers separated them from their contemporaries and also separated Caturla from the rest of the group. While each of them marked distinctive changes in the musical landscape of their respective nations, Caturla—along with

Amadeo Roldán—initiated a whole new Afro-Cuban movement in the domain of art (or concert) music.

The main purpose of this book is to present a new perspective of Caturla based on recent and exhaustive research intended to follow his footsteps throughout Cuba, Barcelona, Madrid, and Paris, the pursuit of which occupied me for over a decade.

Another purpose of this book is to rectify some of the misconceptions by previous writers, critics, and musicians who misunderstood Caturla's music or wrongly compared him to nineteenth-century models. What emerges is a new perspective of Caturla that not only establishes him as the most *innovative* Cuban composer of the first half of the twentieth century and one of the pioneers of Latin American music during his time, but also a great humanitarian. I hope this perspective will give new meaning to Alejo Carpentier's statement: "Alejandro García Caturla was the richest and most generous musical temperament that has appeared on the island."[4]

CUBA IN CATURLA'S TIME

Cuban culture is a "mulato" in many of its forms, a product of dynamic hybridization (*mestizaje*), under specific historical and social conditions, of seeds of the "West" and the "non-West."

Gerardo Mosquera, "Modernidad y Africanía"

After decades of political reforms, massive migrations to Cuba by Spanish families, civil wars that brought death to more than two hundred thousand Cubans and Spaniards, and occupations by U.S. forces (1898), the first Cuban Congress took over their Republic from U.S. authorities on 20 May 1902. Shortly thereafter the first president of the new Republic (Estrada Palma, Thomás) was caught up in corruption and brought down by Cuban revolutionaries in 1906—the year Alejandro García Caturla was born. The ensuing thirty-four years that span Alejandro García Caturla's life were no less turbulent in his native land. During that time, Cuba replaced its president fourteen times; it was an era of nationalistic fervor and political unrest that reached a climax in 1933 with the fall of General Gerardo Machado, Cuba's first dictator.[5] This historical event brought about profound changes in every aspect of Cuban life, including labor issues affecting the lower working class, mainly Afro-Cubans, whom Caturla defended so aggressively in his courtrooms.[6]

CATURLA'S FAMILY HERITAGE

"Alejandrito" (as Caturla was affectionately called by his family and close friends) came from a highly distinguished family of judges, lawyers, doctors, and landowners. The Caturlas were a Spanish family steeped in traditions of their old colonial town of Remedios, deep in the interior[7] of the island. The environment in which the young Alejandro grew up was dominated by the influential position of his family, one that placed him in a privileged social position. As a result he and his younger brother Othón inherited an influential role in local politics and were expected to uphold family traditions regarding civic responsibility.

Caturla's bourgeois family background influenced his tastes and view of society throughout his life. American jazz, Broadway musicals, and European theater and opera were just as much a part of Caturla's world as the annual *parrandas* in the streets of Remedios. Caturla loved the good life but never indulged himself at the expense of others or to the detriment of his ideals.[8] At home, Caturla yearned for the atmosphere of the big cities abroad that he visited. He modeled his study at the house of his parents in Remedios after those of the artists he met in Madrid; he later added to his study photographs of Villa-Lobos and Henry Cowell, a bust of Cuba's José Martí, and a relief of José Miguel Gómez, former president of Cuba (1909–13), referred to by Caturla as "the unforgettable *Tiburón*" (shark). Writing from Havana to his close friend and confidant Lorenzo Martín y Garatea (whom he nicknamed "Lordi," and whose brother Sebastián was Caturla's chauffeur from time to time), Caturla reflected on his bourgeois inclinations: "I continue to be very happy in this city. Decidedly, Remedios . . . engenders the neurotic. . . . I don't produce with the solidity and constancy [in Remedios] as I do in other cities such as Havana, Paris . . . and I am sorry, it shouldn't be that way."[9]

CATURLA COMPROMISES HIS FAMILY LINEAGE

Caturla's rebirth at age seventeen, when he became a member of an Afro-Cuban family by common-law marriage, marked a break with family lineage and tradition, but did not eradicate his inherent bourgeois roots—it simply reaffirmed his fierce sense of independence.

Caturla's first Afro-Cuban common-law wife, Manuela Rodríguez, never took part in his public social life, and there is no evidence that

Manuela enjoyed any social interaction with the Caturla family. Caturla's open bondage to a family of African descent was considered a scandal in Remedios. Caturla and Manuela were never officially married in a church or civil ceremony. The same is true of Caturla's relationship with Catalina, Manuela's younger sister.[10] By the time Manuela Rodríguez died, Caturla was already infatuated with Catalina. He wrote cards to her from Santander, Spain, en route to Barcelona. Caturla also lavished Catalina with presents when he returned to Remedios from his first trip abroad. Catalina Rodríguez was more physically attractive than Manuela and was known for her ability to sing and dance. Manuela, on the other hand, was homely, quiet, church-going, and exclusively dedicated to her children. It was a natural transition when, upon Manuela's death from typhoid fever in 1938, Catalina replaced her as Caturla's common-law wife and stepmother to Caturla's eight children by Manuela. Catalina was the mother of Caturla's last three children.

CATURLA'S CULTURAL HERITAGE

The town of Remedios, one of the oldest in Cuba, dates back as far as 1514 but was not officially established until 1692. Rich in natural resources, Remedios became a center for sugarcane, coffee, and cattle. Plantation life during the Spanish colonial era prospered, bringing with it a large community of African slaves who did the manual labor. And in true Spanish colonial tradition, one of the oldest and most beautiful churches in Cuba, San Juan Bautista, was built there in 1692.

Following the Spanish colonial period, the municipal park in Remedios was planned and dedicated to the great Cuban liberator José Martí. Built just to the side of the San Juan Bautista church, the Parque José Martí was eventually surrounded by elegant buildings, including the grand colonial-style house built in 1875 by Don José de Caturla Rojas (Alejandro García Caturla's grandfather), with the church of Buen Viaje on the opposite side of the park. The Parque José Martí in Remedios became an important hub of cultural activities, mainly because of performances by the Banda Municipal de Remedios, traditional activities related to the *parrandas* (carnivals celebrating historical events of Remedios), and Sunday afternoon promenades for the townspeople. Many Remedianos heard the strains of Alejandro's music coming from the *casa de Caturla* on the Parque José Martí square during his lifetime.

Cultural institutions in Remedios such as Teatro Miguel Bru (built by one of Caturla's uncles), places of cultural activities such as La Tertulia, and music activities related to the churches of San Juan Bautista and Buen Viaje also became part of Caturla's cultural heritage. However, the most penetrating aspect of Caturla's cultural heritage is not of Hispanic origin; it stems from the presence of a large African community that surrounded Remedios and the sounds of their ceremonial drums (as, for instance, the popular *bembés*) that little "Alejandrito" heard throughout his childhood.

By the time of Caturla's birth, Remedios had reached a population of 18,766 and, unfortunately, was known for its racial discrimination—a condition Caturla fiercely opposed throughout his life. Ironically, the year of Caturla's birth (1906), a small-scale reproduction of the Statue of Liberty was erected in Remedios, between the front of the Buen Viaje church and Parque José Martí.[11]

Most of the townspeople in Remedios, including local musicians, resented Caturla's progressive attitude concerning social change and cultural standards. For example, his plans to establish a chamber orchestra in Remedios (an idea eventually adopted by the neighboring town of Caibarién), dedicated to the performance of contemporary music, were misunderstood and eventually abandoned. As a result, many of his other plans to improve cultural standards in Remedios were foiled by the very people who, after his success abroad, officially hailed him as the town's *hijo eminente y distinguido* (eminent and distinguished son). Of all the bitter disappointments Caturla was to experience, those inflicted upon him by the townspeople of Remedios must have been the most painful. It seems ironic that the bronze plaque commemorating his tragic death, which designates the exact location where he was shot in Remedios, was placed there by the neighboring townspeople of Caibarién.

CATURLA'S DILEMMA: MUSIC AS A CAUSE FOR THE EXPRESSION OF HIS IDEOLOGY

Unlike Amadeo Roldán, with whom his name is usually linked, Alejandro García Caturla is Cuba's first native-born modernist composer. Caturla expressed the despair, hopes, and ideology of a new era of nationalism in Cuban music with more depth and magnitude than any other Cuban composer of his time. Caturla was not "in search of the Cuban soul," he *was* the Cuban soul, and proved it by sacrificing everything, including his life, for the cause of his people—a cause committed to social justice and cultural liberation from stagnant local traditions and Eurocentric influences. Consequently, Caturla's music became a discourse for his cause, a circumstance that placed his creative process in a dilemma. The nature of Caturla's dilemma is complex, for it relates to the collective contexts of his ideology and aesthetics. A consideration of the following aspects of Caturla's sociopolitical (external) and musical (internal) circumstances may provide a rationale for understanding his dilemma:

1. early reactions against the "social and spiritual elite" in Remedios (including his parental family)
2. patriotic commitment to the rebellious "Spirit of '23" movement of nationalism
3. relationship of his creative process to the multiple and constantly changing environments of North America (jazz) and Europe (neoclassicism)
4. early collaborations with and influences of Alejo Carpentier (*Dos poemas afrocubanos*) and Henry Cowell (Pan American Association of Composers [PAAC])
5. obsession to be on the cutting edge of the latest music of the avant-garde
6. anxiety to surpass Roldán's footsteps in developing a new style of Afro-Cuban symphonic music
7. struggle to invent musical forms that would distinguish his new style of Afro-Cuban music from traditional Cuban and European forms
8. resolve to gain acceptance of Cuban contemporary music (including his own) abroad
9. resistance to his new Afro-Cuban music in Cuba and failure to establish himself as a resident composer and musician in Havana
10. break with family tradition by establishing a common-law marriage to an Afro-Cuban woman
11. frustrations of balancing the duality of his domestic and professional life as judge and musician
12. rejection of his plans to upgrade musical standards in Remedios

13. failure to sustain his Orquesta de Conciertos de Caibarién
14. surviving the economic hardships of Cuba and surviving as a composer by having his music performed and published abroad.

Perhaps the most compelling aspect of Caturla's dilemma is his common-law marriage, which not only breached family tradition, forever compromising his personal lifestyle, but symbolized the emancipation of class distinction by a new generation. No other Cuban composer of that time understood the dichotomy between Afro-Cubans and Cubans of Spanish descent with such intimacy as Caturla, and no other Cuban composer of that time expressed the spirit of Afro-Cubans in music so naturally and with such authenticity as Caturla. In an attempt to explain the complexity of Caturla's creative disposition, Spanish musicologist Adolfo Salazar, who knew Caturla personally, offers the following perspective:

> I think the reader must understand by now the problems which are presented by a composer like Caturla—American of Spanish race and with a background of Latin culture who wants to orient himself to American indigenous culture in general and in particular that of Cuba—and he solves this in a narrow way—he chooses music that is not Spanish, European, or native but imported from Africa.[12]

All of the above aspects of Caturla's circumstances (including Salazar's perspective) influenced his creative process. Needless to say, Caturla's iconoclastic approach to issues of social class and the use of music as a discourse for his cause placed him in direct conflict with his peers and challenged established musical standards, wherever he was living.

CONFLICTS AND COMPLEXITIES RELATED TO CATURLA'S DILEMMA AS A COMPOSER

The Duality of Caturla's Life: Fighting Corruption and Composing Music

During the initial stages of his judicial career in Remedios, most of Caturla's energy was spent on trying to find ways to emulate the latest musical trends in Havana. Inevitably, the duality of his life as a lawyer and musician in Remedios brought about a conflict, one that was never fully resolved. Caturla could not escape the necessity of supporting his children as a lawyer, nor could he satisfy his quest for a full-time career in music. In the end he combined both careers, each conflicting with and stimulating the other; what each career had in common with the other was Caturla's heroic drive to bring Cuba out of the past and into the future.

Fearless in his pursuit of justice, Caturla's life was often in jeopardy. As a result his spirit was fatalistic, yet exigent. Caturla's mockery of death itself is reflected in his *Canto de los cafetales* (*"Mamá, la muerte me está rondando"* [Mama, death is hanging around]), composed shortly after an attempt was made on his life in Palma Soriano.

Undoubtedly, the nature of Caturla's duties as a judge in the rural districts of Cuba influenced his creative process. The pain and misery of the lower working class that Caturla witnessed in his courtroom is dramatically expressed, for example, in *Comparsa* (*Primera suite cubana* II), a carnival street dance that he transformed into an ironic dirge. Other music by Caturla, such as his four songs on texts by Nicolás Guillén, is more explicit. These songs clearly reflect Caturla's intention to jolt the listener with a new musical language that captures the contempt and protest against social injustice expressed in Guillén's folk poetry. In both cases, Caturla's use of music as a discourse for his cause is apparent.

Caturla complained bitterly about his isolation from the mainstream music in Havana and his fate of becoming a rural judge. Nevertheless, he enriched his creative spirit by gathering source materials from local folk and ceremonial musicians (particularly those involved with *bembé* rituals) wherever he was assigned. Writing to José Antonio Portuondo in 1935, Caturla stated: "I have many themes and much data written down from Palma [Palma Soriano]. It is probable that I might do a Palman symphony or something like it."[13] In fact, Caturla finished most of his opera *Manita en el suelo*, a virtual thematic catalog of Afro-Cuban themes and rhythms gathered from the countryside, in Palma Soriano.

During his tenure as a judge, Caturla reached out of his courtroom to modernize musical life and stimulate social reform wherever he was assigned. For example, he conducted the new music of Henry Cowell, Gershwin, Stravinsky, and other modern composers in concert band arrangements he made for his own Orquesta de Conciertos de Caibarién. Piano recitals and lectures on contemporary music were also part of his musical activities in the small towns of Cuba where he served as judge. Among the many ways Caturla stimulated social reform was the publication of *Atalaya,* a progressive journal in Remedios that cried out against the tyranny of Gerardo Machado ("Students Unite").

All of Caturla's musical activities reflect his use of music as a discourse for his cause. However, it was Caturla's integrity and strictness as a judge, his important legal briefs, sentences, and projects for reforming the criminal code, particularly in respect to juvenile delinquency, that influenced social reform, not his music. Shortly before his death, for example, Caturla was so well known as "a worthy judge . . . immersed in truth and justice" that the prisoners in Santa Clara appealed to him to reform the deplorable conditions of life in prison. The Santa Clara prisoners saw Caturla as their only hope for relief, and as their only means of salvation. On the other hand, musicians in the same town saw Caturla the composer quite differently; as was the case in Remedios, the musicians in Santa Clara rejected Caturla's proposal to present a concert of contemporary music (including his own) by his Orquesta de Conciertos de Caibarién.

Caturla's Struggle for Self-Identity as an Innovative Composer in Havana

Unlike his professional life in the interior, Caturla's professional life in Havana was directed solely to music, including journalism and executiveships in national and international musical organizations; he never served as a judge in Havana. By the time Caturla completed his studies at the university, he was better known in Havana as a musician than a promising young lawyer. Caturla's image as a musician in Havana varied from that of a dilettante vocalist at popular matinee concerts to a serious young composer, playing viola with the Filarmónica under the baton of Pedro Sanjuán.

Caturla's reaction to Havana's musical environment was, for the most part, severely critical. For example, he found the music of Jorge Ankermann "weak," Sánchez de Fuentes's music "a pestilence," the Alberto Falcón Orchestra (Havana) "pompier," Roldán "lacking in sincerity and emotion," "'Frenchification' of his music," and Gonzalo Roig's censure of Cuban composers who "work the Negro part of our music" ridiculous. Caturla also criticized Pedro Sanjuán by saying he "denaturalized himself by composing a hybrid of our 'Afro-Cuban' music," and pointed out to many in Havana Sanjuán's faltering success abroad. One of Caturla's most stinging criticisms of Cuban composers in Havana appeared in his letter to Henry Cowell of 1934: "Insipid and superficial Lecuona; adulterated Sánchez de Fuentes—bad music—poor Cuba!" Havana's Pro Arte Musical Sociedad concerts of traditional European music also came under Caturla's critical fire, despite the fact that he solicited many of the celebrities they hosted to sponsor his music abroad; by 1930 Caturla simply stated, "Pro Arte Musical does not relate to my ideals or my music."[14]

Simultaneously, during his student years, Caturla was influenced by progressive intellectuals in Havana whom he met, including the Minoristas—Fernando Ortiz, José Antonio Fernández de Castro (editor of *Diario de la Marina*), and Alejo Carpentier (later arrested for his activities in the Minoristas)—and others.[15] While a student at the university, Caturla reacted to Havana's musical environment by forming his progressive Jazz Band Caribe, featuring the latest hot steps of North American jazz, from ragtime to the Charleston.

Following his student years at the university and subsequent assignments to the interior of Cuba as a judge, Caturla's longing to live in Havana intensified. In the meantime, his determination to continue his musical career in Havana necessitated endless trips to the capital from the interior. Caught between two worlds, Caturla repeatedly implored his father to support his move to Havana. The following quote from a letter to his father is typical of Caturla's urgency concerning this matter:

> Staying in Remedios I am cut off, removed from the *only nucleus of art there is in Cuba* [Havana]. . . . I will accept living in conditions much reduced from those I have always been accustomed to, but I will do so with pleasure so that my art may not die. [italics mine][16]

Although Caturla's father was completely sympathetic to his son's artistic ambitions, he was unable to finance Alejandro's residency in Havana. Despite these circumstances, which were compounded by the fact that he had a family to support, Caturla succeeded in becoming a vital part of Havana's contemporary musical life. As a result, his perception of national and international cultural standards changed from that of a provincial composer to one of international sophistication in a relatively short time. Simultaneously (but through independent efforts), Caturla and Amadeo Roldán changed the direction of Cuban classical music by combining contemporary European and

North American techniques with Afro-Cuban musical sources—an ideal Caturla defended in his article "Posibilidades sinfónicas de la música Afrocubana" of 1929. Ultimately, Caturla's music was admired and performed more frequently abroad—thanks to his own initiative and collaboration with Henry Cowell's PAAC—than in the Cuban cities he loved most: Remedios and Havana.

CATURLA'S PERCEPTION OF HIMSELF AS A COMPOSER

Caturla's transition from dilettante musician to an innovative composer of Afro-Cuban music began in 1925 with the publication in Havana of his *Danza Lucumí* for piano solo. By 1927 Caturla simply invented a new identity for himself by proclaiming to Fernando Ortiz that his status as a musician was that of a composer of "Afrocuban" music. Caturla described his Afro-Cuban music as "fresh and authentic" (to Cowell) and a "blow to the detractors of Afrocuban rhythms" (to Carpentier). From this point on, Caturla was adamant in his references about himself as a worthy composer of Afro-Cuban music. Caturla's articles—"Posibilidades sinfónicas de la música Afrocubana" (1929) and "Realidad de la utilización sinfónica del instrumental Cubana" (1933)—written in defense of his and Roldán's new genre of symphonic music based on Afro-Cuban musical elements—reflect his sense of mission and commitment to that cause. By 1930, Caturla found it quite natural to present himself abroad in the same context. Writing to the Afro-American poet Langston Hughes that same year, Caturla stated: "I am a Cuban composer of the new generation . . . all the serious, mature works I have done and published until now, all belong to Afrocubanismo."[17]

Following his recognition abroad at the 1929 Barcelona Festivales Sinfónicos Ibero-Americanos, subsequent success in Paris of his *Dos poemas afrocubanos* and *Bembé*, and becoming an honorary executive in Henry Cowell's PAAC, Caturla's self-image changed dramatically. Caturla not only perceived himself as a torchbearer of avant-garde music (thanks to Carpentier), but a composer with a patriotic duty to compose music that would place Cuba side by side with other nations on the international stage of contemporary classical music. His self-image was supported by Antonio and María Muñoz de Quevedo who, along with Carpentier, were among the few in Havana to recognize the "telluric force" (Carpentier) buried in the music of the young lawyer from Remedios.

Filled with confidence related to the success of his music abroad, Caturla saw himself as a leader in the field of contemporary Cuban classical music and a "true and deserving" composer. Subsequently, he demanded from Roldán performances of his music by the Orquesta Filarmónica de La Habana and viewed performances of his Afro-Cuban music in Cuba as events of national significance. For example, following a performance in Havana by Roldán of his *La Rumba*, Caturla chided the local musical critics for ignoring this concert, accusing them of lacking loyalty to their own country.

Caturla did not belong to any "school" of composers nor did he follow any specific system as a composer. As a result, he felt that he was unfairly judged by "eyes impassioned with creeds and schools" and subsequently complained that "there is a conspiracy to silence and annul me." Writing to Francisco Curt Lange the year before he was assassinated, Caturla stated: "Roldán and I were always orphans with no guide. Because of that, we had to construct everything for ourselves from A to Z."[18] As you will see in subsequent chapters, Caturla's studies with Pedro Sanjuán and Nadia Boulanger were disastrous. And his visit to Spain did not result in any musical influence by Spanish composers whom he met and admired, such as Manuel de Falla. The same held true in Paris.

While Caturla gained recognition at home for the success of his music abroad, he was self-conscious and insecure as a fledgling composer in international circles; as a member of Cowell's PAAC, he constantly looked for approval of his music by well-known composers abroad. "In order to establish myself, I need an opinion as authoritative as yours," wrote Caturla to Edgard Varèse.[19] Subsequently, Caturla wrote to Adolfo Salazar, Manuel de Falla, Manuel Ponce, Carlos Chávez, Henry Cowell, Nicolas Slonimsky, and other musicians, soliciting their opinion of his music.

At home, Caturla's disposition as a composer was far from self-conscious and insecure, though he was faced with a more challenging set of circumstances. Caturla thought of himself as the foremost Cuban composer of the younger generation, including Roldán. Writing to Antonio Quevedo, Caturla stated: "At the age of only twenty-four I already have my main work published, due largely to the two trips I have made to Europe, which gives me an advantage over him [Roldán]."[20] Caturla defended this posture with an avalanche of critical reviews, shamelessly bragging about his success abroad. And when letters arrived from abroad by well-known composers, such as Charles Ives, Henry Cowell, and Nicolas Slonimsky, confirming his talent, Caturla immediately spread the news throughout Havana and Remedios. Caturla's position as staff member of Quevedo's music journal *Musicalia* also became a means by which he spread news of his success abroad.

Realizing that his future in Cuba as a composer was hopeless, Caturla wrote to Antonio Quevedo from Remedios saying he was sending his recent compositions abroad, because, "you as well as I, know how little atmosphere there is for them in Havana and the limited possibilities of having them performed." Caturla closed this letter by ratifying his plans for another trip abroad, a venture that never developed. Despite the dismal aspects of his future in Cuba, Caturla's positive self-image was based on his success abroad, where he foresaw a brighter future. This disposition is reflected in a letter to Slonimsky: "Your article about me in the Jan.–Feb. issue of *Modern Music* is simply wonderful. You may enjoy the glory of having said of me only the truth, which many here . . . persistently deny. *When history does me justice . . . your name will be next to mine*" [italics mine].[21] Caturla informed the musical circles in Havana and Remedios that his fame was spreading internationally, and he hoped his music would soon be heard over the radio in Cuba (particularly Remedios).

One must not be misled by the actions of the young impetuous Caturla. He was able to honor the esteem held in Cuba for Sánchez de Fuentes without admiring his music; he forgave Gonzalo Roig his shortsightedness about Afro-Cuban music as an integral part of Cuban national music; he was inspired by Roldán's early footsteps into the world of Afro-Cuban symphonic music, which he consistently and proudly acknowledged; and he flattered Sanjuán: "If I conduct in Cuba I would love to conduct the Rondo and Babaluayé [from Sanjuán's Afro-Cuban Suite *Liturgia Negra*] of yours because both works fit my nervous temperament very well."[22]

CATURLA'S REACTION TO HIS MUSICAL ENVIRONMENTS

Caturla's reaction to the musical environments in which he lived is complex; it varies according to time and place. However, there is a pattern of rebelliousness that characterizes his reactions. Caturla confronted the musical status quo wherever he was with demands for higher, more progressive, standards, while striving to be at the cutting edge of the latest international trends himself. His drive to be out front, ahead of his colleagues, has roots connected to his precocious childhood, when he was always the center of attention; but this same drive also relates to his conscience and pride as a "Cuban composer of the new generation."

Caturla's reaction to the musical environment of his hometown Remedios and the surrounding provinces is a case in point. He was radical in his approach to upgrading the cultural standards of this old colonial town, known for its ultraconservative traditions. Because of this, his long task of trying to impose new cultural standards in Remedios, Caibarién, and the surrounding provinces was finally broken down by intense resistance of local townspeople who were intimidated by his aggressiveness and suspicious of his taste for music of the avant-garde. Nevertheless, Remedios and Caibarién became central to his creative process and survival as a composer; by sheer necessity Caturla transformed the municipal bands in each of these towns into concert orchestras for which he provided some of his most brilliant transcriptions and rearrangements of his own music, and the music of others as well.

During Caturla's lifetime, the musical environment of Havana blossomed for a decade, beginning with the formation of the Orquesta Filarmónica de La Habana in 1923 and ending with the fall of Cuba's dictator Gerardo Machado in 1933. During that time, Caturla participated in a wide variety of musical activities in Havana, each depending on his disposition at the time. For example, when the "battle of the orchestras" in Havana came about in 1923, Caturla reacted by rebelling against the older, more traditional, Sinfónica to join the new, more progressive, Filarmónica; eventually, he reacted against the new Filarmónica by criticizing the director, Pedro Sanjuán, among other things, for being too conservative.

The musical environment of Havana that inspired Caturla most were those few circles that promoted contemporary music; his connections with such circles were made mainly through Alejo Carpentier and Antonio and María Muñoz de Quevedo. Carpentier's preoccupation with European contemporary music at that time, particularly the French avant-gardists, had an enormous impact upon him. As a result, Caturla's aesthetic was influenced by the music of such composers as Stravinsky, Ravel, Debussy, Honneger, Milhaud, Satie, and Schoenberg, changing his concept of style dramatically. Caturla reacted to Carpentier's influence by adapting traditional Cuban forms (*danza* and bolero) to the avant-garde music of Paris. Elements of avant-garde music such as tone clusters, bitonality, whole-tone and pentatonic scales, parallel chord progressions, and frequent changes of meter can be found in his compositions from 1925 on. Caturla's short-lived experiment with European neoclassicism in 1927 was not a "sterile anachronism."[23] Unlike European neoclassicism, Caturla did not favor a return to eighteenth-century practices and functions; he transformed classical genres (sonata, minuet, gigue, waltz) into new Cuban music, with no regard to form. The apex of Caturla's freestyle approach to neoclassicism may be found in his 1927 Preludio Corto No. 1, which was written as an homage to Erik Satie. Composed without bar lines, this nondevelopmental miniature for piano relates directly to the bohemian, ironic, and at times banal aesthetic of Satie, whose music, for the moment, had much to do with Caturla's changing identity.

The musical world that Caturla responded to most positively was that of Henry Cowell: his New Music Society[24] and the Pan American Association of Composers (PAAC). Once he made connections with Cowell (1928) and realized the potential for future performances and publications of his music, Caturla established a warm friendship with Cowell, which lasted to the end of his life. Caturla also became an honorary executive in PAAC until it collapsed in the mid-1930s under the weight of the Great Depression.

The duality of Caturla's personality is complex, and an awareness of his disposition may help explain the thorny path he followed as he waged his own musical revolution. Caturla stood up against the musical establishment of his times and those who did not understand his motives or agree with his aesthetics. "I am prepared to fight," wrote Caturla to Carpentier in reference to having his "rather daring" *Tres Danzas Cubanas* performed in Havana.[25]

Caturla's actions and music—parallel to the Afro-Cuban music of Roldán—tended to polarize Havana's musical elite into groups for or against the concept of African musical elements as integral aspects of a true Cuban national music.

No other Cuban composer of his, or any other time, was so abrasive, outspoken, intrepid, determined, critical of everyone around him, and at odds with the world in which he lived as Caturla. According to Cuban composer Edgardo Martín, Caturla was "wild, super-intelligent, indulged in music primitivism and revolted in all matters, not only music."[26] At the same time, one finds in Caturla an idealist—a romantic with dreams of a better future for Cuba—a docile father, with a keen sense of humor—a sentimentalist who loved to play Argentine tangos and ragtime music, and sing popular Cuban music and Italian opera—a compassionate man, deeply concerned about the youth in the communities where he lived—and above all, a young Cuban composer with an obsession to succeed, at any cost, in bringing Cuba out of its stereotyped musical past into a new era of nationalism in music based on Afro-Cuban sources.

QUOTES FROM SELECTED INTERVIEWS

He often laughed, he was a friendly person. Another trait of his personality is that he spoke in a calm way, low voice (when he lived in Havana he took singing lessons with Professor Bovi). . . . He was a very active person. He adored his mother. Also he was a perfectionist and an idealist, very easy to understand. In addition he was very straight in his profession and his work. He was interested in all types of arts.

I remember how eagerly Alejandro awaited correspondence from abroad, particularly from Henry Cowell and Nicolas Slonimsky, whom he admired so much.

Bertha García Caturla[27]

Alejandro used to run over to my house when he received new recordings of modern music from abroad and excitedly play them for us. And when he discovered a new harmony, usually very dissonant, he would play that chord on our piano with electrifying excitement, proudly exclaiming about its unique quality.

He was extremely handsome. Tall, black hair, and eyes that were slightly crossed and of different colors, one slightly green, the other blue. His baritone voice was beautiful. Many young girls in Remedios were attracted to him. He wrote to some of them when he went abroad in the late 1920s (1928 and 1929). He was very high strung, and had a nervous habit of tapping rhythms with his fingertips, and he always walked quickly, as if in a hurry. He enjoyed swimming and was a judge at some of the swimming contests at Caibarién where we always went during the summer.

He adored his mother, Diana Caturla, who often played music with him at the piano when he was just a child. And later, when family tensions ran high because of his decision to live with Manuela Rodríguez, an Afro-Cuban domestic working for the

Caturla family, it was his mother, above all, who supported him throughout his crisis.

Olga Caturla de la Maza[28]

The García family were really blue bloods. They kept the doors to their great house on José Martí square closed. Alejandro was elegant—well educated. He always wore a white suit and walked with a high chin and a serious expression on his face. I remember seeing Alejandro banging large clusters of notes at the piano with his forearm, creating noisy dissonance while making loud exclamations.

Dr. Chalon Rodríguez[29]

At the time of the Orquesta de Conciertos I was barely fourteen; but I still carry the awe and the warmest memories of that extraordinary genius who was Alejandro. He opened for me a horizon in my formative years which has resonated throughout my career.

The members of Caturla's Orquesta de Conciertos de Caibarién were inspired by his progressive ideals. They stood in awe of his determination to upgrade cultural standards in the small towns of Cuba by presenting concerts of international contemporary classical music, performed by local musicians. For them, Caturla's countenance engendered a spirit of renewal and strengthening of pride in Cuban culture at a time when the island was faced with some of its most depressing economic times and political unrest. For those in Cuba who misunderstood Caturla's mission with the Orquesta de Conciertos de Caibarién, his concerts of contemporary music, including his own, were regarded as scandalous.

Santos Ojeda[30]

We both were students in the School of Law, University of Havana. He was rather tall (5′11″), broad shouldered, of feline movements, frank face, large mouth, long arms and very long fingers. I also was a country boy, from Cárdenas, some 150 kilometers from San Juan de los Remedios, in another province. He belonged to an old and distinguished family, and it was not long that we learned him to be an accomplished pianist. He played with "passion" in small concerts in Havana, very specially some Cuban music, not the one of Cervantes or Sánchez de Fuentes, but his own. It was the music of the Cuban Blacks, which we were then beginning to appreciate. I was sort of secretary to Fernando Ortiz, the noted Cuban Africanolist [*sic*], then heading the Cuban-Hispanic Cultural Institute and having a law office with another elderly lawyer: Jiménez-Lanier, from Remedios. All things then played together for García Caturla to appear in some modest concerts in which he played his own music with startling success. . . . [Alejandro García Caturla came from] A very distinguished Cuban family, but he was always alone or in the company of a striking Negro Cuban Lady, something that at that time was rather strange in Cuba, where slavery came to an end in 1888 and 23% of the population was as you say here "colored." His white family got along well with the first wife (colored), and when she died he married her sister. They had children. By that time Maestro Pedro Sanjuán, the conductor of the Havana Symphonic Orchestra, had come to know García Caturla, was thinking very highly of his music and was teaching him some important points.

Herminio Portell-Vila[31]

During that time (1933–40) all judges in Cuba faced terrible conditions. The courts were overloaded, the work was endless and the pay was often postponed. Alejandro was a highly respected judge; one whose reputation for strictness and concern with juvenile delinquency spread throughout the whole island. He was also known to go out of his way in his courtroom to treat the lower working class with respect and dignity. Many of Caturla's peers in law saw him as an eccentric because of his personal lifestyle and for some, his black wife and mestizo children were targets of ridicule.

Alejandro was very outspoken about police corruption and judges "on the take." He was despised by many local petty politicians, judges and policemen and his life was threatened several times by criminals at large. Because of this, and an awareness of his own uncompromising position of strictness and righteousness, Alejandro had a strong premonition of his own premature death.

Fernando Arsenio Roa[32]

NOTES

1. Sánchez-Gutiérrez, "The Cooked and the Raw," 9.

2. Henríquez, *Correspondencia,* 3 de noviembre 1928, 41.

3. Caturla did not come in personal contact with any of these composers; however, he did corresponded with Charles Ives, whose fourth symphony he wrote about in the Havana music journal *Musicalia.*

4. Carpentier, *La música en Cuba*, 290.

5. "In 1923 'nationalism' was the battle cry beginning to rally such diverse characters as President Zayas, hacendado [landowner] José Tarafa, young students—and intellectual, Fernando Ortiz . . . this emerging nationalism was not offensive, but defensive. It was not basically anti-American; it was essentially pro-Cuban. . . . [S]ide by side another more violent and radical nationalism was growing in Cuba. Rooted in passion more than in statistic, expressed in anger more than in legal arguments, this second nationalism was voiced by students, intellectuals, and leftist elements who were responding to a broad anti-Yankee feeling which was sweeping Latin America at the time" (Aguilar, *Cuba 1933*, 46–47).

6. By the time of Caturla's birth, Cuba was becoming the most densely populated country of the Antilles. Because the need for migrant workers on the sugar and coffee plantations was so great, over 150,000 Negroes, including Haitians and Jamaicans, were brought to Cuba after 1912; most of them did not return to their native land. At that time very few Negroes were in professional positions, and many who fought in the great war of independence were denied pensions. Such grievances led to the Negro revolution of 1912 that temporarily shut down the huge profit-making plantation revenues before it was crushed. The aftermath of these circumstances produced a Negro scene in Cuba that was complicated and thrived in an ambiguous religious, social, and moral atmosphere. Much of the Negro difficulties derived from the difficulties met by all Negroes in dealing with freedom after generations of slavery. See Thomas, *Cuba*, 499–522.

7. "Interior" is a term used by Cubans to describe areas inside the country, that is, not along the shore.

8. When the economy of Cuba dropped in the 1930s, Caturla wrote to his prosperous neighbor, Modesto Gutiérrez Heredia, with whom he previously traveled to Paris: "I see that this year you won't be passing through Broadway nor will I be eating the chicken salads at Childs in New York . . . but next year . . . surely we will be able to go once more to the theatre on 56th Street to hear *Show Boat* or to the Grand Opera of Paris for the Coq d'or" (Henríquez, *Correspondencia*, 11 de junio 1930, 137–38).

9. Henríquez, *Correspondencia*, 15 de enero 1930, 107.

10. In reference to the matter of Caturla's common-law relationship to the Rodríguez sisters, Manuela and Catalina, Caturla's first cousin, Olga Caturla de la Maza, gave me the following testimony in a written document dated 6 March 1998. This testimony of Olga Caturla's was written in reference to an earlier version of the acknowledgments of this book:

> Now I will tell you about something I have given a lot of thought. You say in the acknowledgments: "His second wife, Catalina Rodríguez de García Caturla." It makes her his legal wife, which in Castro's regime was accepted, when she claimed to be his legal widow. But there are two arguments against this being the truth. (1) His own words, the morning of the day when he was

killed, in his letter asking for permission to bear firearms, he wrote: Civil Status: Single (not married). (2) In 1987, in Miami, when Bertha [Caturla's sister] was still very sound of mind, I asked her: "Was Alejandro married to Manuela and Catalina?" [Bertha replied,] "He never got married. But he inscribed their children as his own, and gave them his name. For that reason, when our mother died, and my father gave each of us our part of her inheritance, he gave Alejandro's part to his children, for they were his legal heirs." Based on these facts, I consider it would be worthwhile to give second thoughts to writing "Catalina Rodríguez de García Caturla" because, whatever his motives, Alejandro never gave her his name. That is a fact. She is Catalina Rodríguez. Indeed he loved her and Manuela, and the children he had with them. They had a tremendous impact on his life and music. But he did not marry them.

11. By 1919 the population of Remedios expanded by 33.4 percent to a total of 25,043. The neighboring town of Caibarién expanded in that same time period by 52 percent to a total of 14,583. Today, the population of Remedios stands at approximately 44,752 residents, most of whom are Afro-Cubans.

The Remedios Statue of Liberty was made by the Italian sculptor Carlos Nicoli. It was dedicated to the Cubans who lost their lives during the great war of liberation from Spain.

12. Salazar, "La obra musical de Alejandro García Caturla," 20.

13. Henríquez, *Correspondencia*, 14 de noviembre 1935, 272.

14. On Ankermann: Henríquez, *Correspondencia*, Caturla to Alejo Carpentier, 3 September 1927, 23. On Sánchez de Fuentez: Henríquez, *Correspondencia*, Caturla to Antonio Quevedo, 2 November 1928, 39. On the Alberto Falcón Orchestra: Henríquez, *Correspondencia*, Caturla to Alejo Carpentier, 3 November 1928, 41. On Roldán: Henríquez, *Correspondencia*, Caturla to Antonio Quevedo, 29 August 1930, 143, and 12 February 1931, 180. On Roig: Henríquez, *Correspondencia*, Caturla to Antonio Quevedo, 12 November 1939, 294. On Sanjuán: Henríquez, *Correspondencia*, Caturla to Antonio Quevedo, 29 August 1930, 143. On Lecuona and Sánchez de Fuentes: Caturla to Cowell, 12 December 1934, from García Caturla, "Correspondencia inédita." On Pro Arte Musical: Henríquez, *Correspondencia*, Caturla to Lorenzo ("Lordi") Martín y Garatea, 12 January 1930, 106.

15. Like Roldán, Caturla's new Afro-Cuban music was esteemed by the Minoristas, some of whom were editors of *Revista de Avance*, a politically daring publication that later served as a model for Caturla's progressive periodical *Atalaya*.

16. Henríquez, *Correspondencia*, 22 de marzo 1931, 186–87.

17. To Ortiz: Henríquez, *Correspondencia*, 12 September 1927, 25. To Cowell, 3 February 1931, from García Caturla, "Correspondencia inédita." To Carpentier: Henríquez, *Correspondencia*, 19 April 1927, 16. To Hughes: Henríquez, *Correspondencia*, 4 January 1930, 132.

18. Letters quoted in this paragraph are all from Henríquez, *Correspondencia*, and addressed to Francisco Curt Lange. On being unfairly judged: 17

May 1939, 285. On the "conspiracy to silence": 5 November 1939, 292. On himself as an "orphan": 29 August 1939, 291.

19. Henríquez, *Correspondencia,* 27 de diciembre 1930, 160.

20. Henríquez, *Correspondencia,* 29 de agosto 1930, 143.

21. To Antonio Quevedo: Henríquez, *Correspondencia,* 20 September 1930, 143. To Slonimsky: Henríquez, *Correspondencia,* 8 February 1940, 295.

22. Henríquez, *Correspondencia,* 26 de septiembre 1929, 66–67.

23. Stevens, Halsey, symposium paper, "Critical Years in European Musical History, 1915–1925," 224.

24. Henry Cowell is internationally known for a movement he simply called "New Music." Cowell's New Music consisted of a variety of musical activities: (1) the New Music Society, (2) *New Music Quarterly,* a journal, and (3) the New Music concerts sponsored by his New Music Society.

25. Henríquez, *Correspondencia,* 3 de noviembre 1928, 41.

26. From an interview with Edgardo Martín; Havana, Cuba, 25 October 1992.

27. Letter to the author dated 29 July 1989 from Caturla's oldest sister, Bertha. By "profession," Bertha refers here to Caturla's career as a judge. Bertha passed away in the summer of 1995.

28. From an interview with Olga Caturla de la Maza, 15 September 1990.

29. From an interview with Dr. Chalon Rodríguez, 20 November 1990; he was living in Washington, D.C., at the time. Dr. Rodríguez was one of Caturla's peers from Remedios.

30. Letter to the author dated 4 August 1990. Born in Caibarién, Cuba, Santos Ojeda's talent as a brilliant child prodigy was brought to Caturla's attention; he selected Ojeda to perform as piano soloist with his newly formed Orquesta de Conciertos de Caibarién in 1932.

31. Letter to the author dated 21 March 1991.

32. From interviews in 1991–93 with Fernando Arsenio Roa, then residing in Miami, Florida.

Chapter One

Family Background and Early Musical Influences

Alejandro García Caturla, one of the most innovative Cuban composers of the twentieth century, was born on 7 March 1906 in Remedios in the province of Las Villas, Cuba. Caturla was the first of four children of Silvino García Balmaseda and Diana de Caturla: he had two sisters, Laudelina and Bertha, and a brother, Othón.

Caturla's grandfather, Alejandro García Carrillo, was killed in action during the "big war" of independence from Spain (1868–78), leaving his widow, Concepción Balmaseda, to give birth to their only child, Silvino, shortly thereafter (1879). Thus, Silvino never knew his father, a fact that may have intensified his natural love for and commitment to his own children, particularly the first-born son, Alejandro, named after his grandfather. Like his father, Silvino served under General Francisco Carrillo Morales, captain of the fourth corps of the Ejército Libertador. Owing to his outstanding achievements in this organization, Silvino was awarded the title Comandante del Ejército Libertador Cubano, an honor that was ratified by General Máximo Gómez, commander of the Ejército Libertador. After the war of independence (1895–99), Silvino became a successful Procurador Público, which entitled him to officially assist attorneys and judges. He also acquired accounts as financial adviser to prominent Remedians and became a prosperous landowner. An educated and righteous man, an excellent husband, father, and citizen, Silvino was held in high esteem and at one time was president of La Tertulia, a highly respected social club in Remedios.

Diana's family background is also related to military honor and prestige. Her grandfather, José de Caturla of Valencia, served as a

1

captain in the Spanish army during the Napoleonic wars and eventually, after numerous battles and heroic deeds, rose to the rank of brigadier general. Later he was sent to Cuba as governor of the district of Las Villas where he married Dolores de Rojas and retired in Remedios. Their son, Don José de Caturla Rojas, became a prominent attorney, was elected mayor of Remedios, and became wealthy from sugar plantation profits. He married Laudelina García. Diana's parents were related to Silvino's family, making Diana and Silvino cousins. Diana and Silvino were married at the church of San Juan Bautista in 1905 in accordance with the social and religious conventions of Remedios at that time.

All of the García Caturla children except Othón were born in a house on Calle San Juan de los Mercaderes and baptized at the church of San Juan Bautista. In 1920 Silvino bought the spacious, elegant colonial residence on the Plaza de Armas, facing the Parque José Martí in the center of Remedios, previously owned by his in-laws.[1] This distinctive building, with its large carriage doors, arched columns, and beautiful hanging lamps at the front portal, was familiar to all in Remedios and the surrounding towns during Caturla's lifetime. It stands as a reminder of colonial times and a symbol of the class distinction that existed during Caturla's lifetime.

Growing up in Remedios, Caturla was surrounded by a family circle of highly distinguished judges, lawyers, doctors, and landowners. They were a Spanish family steeped in traditions of their hometown and influential in local politics. The family circle included Judge Marcelo Caturla, a member of the Supreme Court in Havana, and Federico Laredo Bru, who eventually became president of Cuba in 1936.[2] The privileged class into which Caturla was born carried with it a commitment to nurture the culture and society of Remedios, a commitment that he cherished and attempted to carry out with great pride, but one that was doomed to failure from the very beginning. As you will see, the enthusiasm with which Caturla asserted his progressive artistic ideals antagonized most of the townspeople in Remedios, and his youthful ambition to bring about major changes in the cultural life of such a conservative town was naïve.

MUSICAL INFLUENCES AT HOME

Among the many musical influences Caturla experienced prior to any formal music studies, the most significant, perhaps, was the singing of his Afro-Cuban nannies, particularly Bárbara Sánchez who taught him melodies of *Lucumí* and *Ñáñingo* origin. "Avive," as Caturla was later to call her, was but a young girl herself when she first tended his cradle, and to an extent, grew up with him. Many years after his death she remembered that when he was a little boy she used to hold his hand as they walked to church to sing in the choir of the Franciscan priest Fray (Father) Pedro Galdeano. And when they were together at home, the little "Alejandrito" loved to hear her sing the following song of *Lucumí* origin: "Orile, orile / Babalú já / Pero dame la cadena / que me voy mea adorná [Orile, orile / Babalú já / But give me the necklace / so I can dress up]," often imploring her to repeat it over and over. Avive also remembered how responsive he was to music of the *parrandas* (traditional carnival seasons in Remedios) and later, in an interview, emphasized how this music excited the little Alejandro:

> Alejandrito always said to me, when he was little, to take him to the parrandas, and he became like a fool listening to the music. Listen, can you believe that the first thing the boy played on the piano was a song from the neighborhood of El Carmen that says, "Evacua Sansarí / Evacua / Evacua Sansarí / Evacua." It was a little rumba from that time that really stuck with you.[3]

Altogether, the Caturla family was very musical. Caturla's mother, Diana, her sister Olga, and her brother Marcelo, known for playing the Cuban *danzón*, were competent, amateur pianists. All of the García Caturla children played musical instruments (piano or guitar) and sang. Next to Alejandro, his brother, Othón, was the most gifted, excelling as a pianist. Othón often accompanied Alejandro's singing at home and later at public concerts. There was usually much music making at family gatherings, and it was on just such occasions that the young (twelve years old then) Caturla, with the help of his brother and sisters, would put together musical entertainment of singing and piano playing that they called "Teatro Caturla."

One of Caturla's closest musical companions in the family was his first cousin María del Carmen de Caturla y Alvarez, known as "Mamilla." A gifted singer, she and Caturla met often at her house to make music and prepare for benefit concerts in surrounding towns such as Camajuaní, Vueltas, Caibarién, and others.[4]

Caturla's other musical companions in the family were his uncle Edgardo (a dentist in Remedios at that time), a true opera buff, and his uncle Gaston, a lawyer and founder of the Teatro Miguel Bru in

Remedios. Edgardo influenced Caturla's passion for opera, and together with Silvino, they attended operas at the Teatro Atenas in Caibarién (*Il Trovatore* and *Thäis* in 1917), Teatro La Caridad in Santa Clara (*Madame Butterfly* and *Äida* in 1918), and—beginning in 1920—at the Teatro Nacional in Havana where they heard the great Enrique Caruso in *Tosca* that year. The intensity of Caturla's passion for opera was such that he attended over fifteen performances in Havana in 1920 alone and reportedly was familiar with the scores of at least forty standard operas.

Keeping up with the latest trends of popular and classical music by way of radio broadcasts (by 1923 Remedios could receive over twenty radio stations from Havana), phonograph records, books, periodicals, and musical scores was another, less personal way in which the young Caturla's musical nature was influenced at home. Such popular trends as ragtime music and fox-trots like the Charleston were just as familiar to him as the latest Cuban *danzón* or criollo-bolero.

FORMAL STUDIES: ACADEMIC AND MUSICAL

Caturla's elementary schooling was administered by Rosa Molina, an established pedagogue in Remedios who tutored him at home; she reported that his I.Q. and speed of learning were extraordinary. Later he attended the Instituto de Segunda Enseñanza de Santa Clara where he received his *Título de Bachiller en Letras y Ciencias* on 9 September 1922.[5]

Music lessons for Caturla were first undertaken at the Fernando Estrems school of solfeggio and piano in the city of Santa Clara when he was eight years old. The following year Caturla continued his formal music studies in Remedios with María Montalván de Valdés, an accomplished and well-established local musician. A precocious child, Caturla studied piano with María, solfeggio and music theory with her husband, Juan F. Valdés, and violin with América Ruiz, also of Remedios.[6] Much of Caturla's versatility as a musician can be attributed to the music making he experienced in the studios of these outstanding musicians who recognized his unusual talent.

During the same period, Caturla joined the choir at the Buen Viaje church. The choir was directed by Fray Pedro Galdeano, who was known as a colorful personality and was active in directing secular as well as religious choral music in the community.[7]

"MÚSICA POBRE"—COMMUNITY MUSICAL INFLUENCES

Caturla's early musical life in public relates to a number of diverse musical experiences in Remedios, all of which contributed to the character of his compositional style. The two most important community musical activities in which he was engaged were the *parrandas* and the Sunday afternoon concerts by the Banda Municipal de Remedios in the Parque José Martí. The *parrandas* occurred annually throughout his life during the Christmas season. Music of the *parrandas*—the authentic *música pobre* of Remedios—brought together music from every sector of society in Remedios, regardless of race or economic status.[8] This meant the mixing of musical instruments in a variety of ways. For example the *piquete repique*—a small *conjunto* ("performance group" or "ensemble of musicians") consisting typically of pairs of trumpets, clarinets, trombones, one *bombardino* and one *timbal de agarre*—could be heard playing popular music, such as rumbas and polkas. Other instrumental groups used folk instruments such as guitars, *tres,* maracas, *güiro, cencerro* (cowbell), and bongos to accompany *danzónes, guajiras,* and other forms of popular vocal music. Caturla participated in the annual *parrandas* in Remedios by singing, dancing, and playing an instrument of some kind. Undoubtedly, Caturla absorbed the ethnic mixture of timbre, rhythm, and melody heard during the *parrandas,* mixtures that eventually became a trademark of his style.

Caturla's relationship to the Banda Municipal de Remedios was singular. He did not become a member of this band, nor did he conduct it; there is no evidence that he was influenced by the conservative music they played (arrangements of Italian overtures were popular at the time). However, the Banda Municipal eventually became Caturla's most important musical resource in Remedios for the performance of arrangements of his own music and that of other composers (such as George Gershwin's *Rhapsody in Blue*). From an early age, Caturla became familiar with the sonorities and instrumentation of the Banda Municipal at their traditional Sunday afternoon concerts in Remedios. His mastery of integrating band instruments in later compositions (such as *Primera suite cubana,* 1931) can no doubt be traced back to these experiences.

Caturla was able to establish an important musical relationship with Augustín Crespo, director of the Banda Municipal de Remedios, because Caturla's music teachers, María Montalván de Valdés and Juan F. Valdés, were Crespo's parents-in-law.[9] In time, Crespo and Caturla collaborated in programming concerts that included Caturla's own music and developed plans for the future of music education in Remedios. They also worked together on some of the administrative aspects of funding the band's budget. However, as time went on, their relationship was often strained because of Caturla's efforts to modernize the band's concert programs and influence music education in the city to include the most advanced contemporary music from abroad.

Other community musical experiences that influenced Caturla at an early age relate to the neighboring cities of Santa Clara, the capital of Las Villas Province (later renamed Villa Clara Province), and Caibarién, a prosperous seaport town and district center for the Institución Hispana-Cubana. As previously mentioned, Caturla attended opera in both of these cities, but he also heard music by Mexican, Latin American, and Spanish musicians passing through on their tours.

Added to these varied and rich musical experiences in his community, the young Caturla absorbed yet another musical tradition of the region: the African *bembé*.[10] As he traveled throughout Cuba later in life, Caturla listened to the chants and rhythms of *bembé* ceremonies in all the cities he visited; attending these rituals became part of his lifestyle. One of Caturla's most famous compositions, *Bembé-Mouvement Afro-Cubain*, became a musical symbol of his artistic ideals.

MUSICAL IMAGE IN THE COMMUNITY

At age eleven, Caturla was piano accompanist for the visiting Italian operetta company La Sociale in productions of *Eva* (Franz Lehar) and *Elixir de amor* (Gaetano Donizetti) at Teatro Miguel Bru; he also performed in concerts at La Tertulia, usually as part of a cultural program that included poetry readings and singing. Caturla was sought after at parties and social gatherings for his singing and playing popular music on the piano in his own arrangements. By age fifteen he published *I Will Love You Forever,* a waltz for piano; he also played piano for the silent movies in Remedios and formed the Jazz Band Remedios. In short, during Caturla's boyhood and adolescence, he became known in Remedios as a musical "bon vivant."[11]

FAMILY CRISIS

Sometime during the period between his graduation from the Instituto de Segunda Enseñanza de Santa Clara and his move to Havana in 1923 to study law, Caturla developed an intimate relationship with Manuela Rodríguez, an Afro-Cuban girl who was employed by his uncle Edgardo de Caturla. When she became pregnant, her mother, Quirina Rodríguez, confronted Caturla's father, Silvino, with the facts. Siding with Quirina, who engaged in intense conflicts with Silvino, Caturla moved out of his parent's house to live with Manuela, her younger sister Catalina, and their mother. By the time Caturla was seventeen, Manuela had given birth to the first of their eight children, Alejandro, named after his grandfather and born on 29 December 1923.[12]

Despite Caturla's "concubinary relations" (as his younger brother, Othón, described it), ties to his parents and the Caturla family circle in Remedios were never broken. As the eldest son he inherited a privileged role in the family, one that he may have taken for granted. However, at the same time he compromised this status by openly establishing his own family life out of wedlock with an Afro-Cuban woman. Apparently Caturla became a master of balancing human circumstances, inasmuch as he was able to divide his life in such a way as to accommodate his own priorities while satisfying two totally different kinds of domestic lifestyles. Thus, needs related to his private personal family life were fulfilled at Manuela's house, while the life his parents wanted to provide for him—which included music—was fulfilled at the García Caturla residence. The openness of his relationship with Manuela became the talk of Remedios; their relationship ended his bourgeois lifestyle at home and marked the beginning of a new life among lower working class Afro-Cubans. It also marked the beginning of a lifelong struggle to support his own family.[13]

All of these circumstances combined to create a formidable scandal in Remedios, one that stained Caturla's reputation for the remainder of his life. In breaking with family tradition by publicly committing himself to a relationship that would compromise his ethnic heritage, Caturla launched a fierce personal revolution against the social conventions of his time. It was the starting point of a lifelong stream of actions that would identify him as a nonconformist, a trait of his character that eventually turned up in his strictness as a judge and daring syncretic style as a composer.

Even though Caturla's ties with his family were never completely broken, the indignities and financial burden that fell upon the García Caturla family as a result of his relationship with Manuela and her family were far-reaching. In the end, Caturla's parents continued to support him, and his father insisted he study law at the University of Havana. Although Caturla yielded to his father's decision, his studies of law at the University of Havana were from the very beginning secondary to his pursuit of a career in music.

NOTES

1. The house was built by Caturla's grandfather in 1875. Silvino acquired the house when his brother-in-law Edgardo, who inherited the house, sold it to him. This structure still stands as one of the most prominent buildings in Remedios and today houses the Museo de la Música Provincial "Alejandro García Caturla."

2. Caturla's aunt—his mother's sister Sylvia—was married to Federico Laredo Bru's younger brother.

3. See María Helena Capote, "Por las calles de Remedios en busca de Caturla." "Alejandrito siempre me decía, así chiquitica, que lo llevara a las Parrandas, y se ponía como bobo oyendo la música. Oigame y usted puede creer que el niño lo primero que tocó en el piano fue una canción del Barrio de El Carmen que dice: 'Evacua Sansarí / Evacua / Evacua Sansarí/ Evacua.' Era una rumbita muy pegajosa en aquella época."

4. Mamilla also participated frequently in music making at the home of Carmen Valdés and Augustín Crespo, who praised the beauty of her voice. She later became an outstanding soloist in various choral societies in Remedios. I had the good fortune to meet and interview this remarkable person in Remedios shortly before her death in July 1994.

5. Following the great war of independence, Remedios developed its own local school system administered by people of a pedagogical vocation, but not necessarily with teaching degrees. By 1923, the Colegio Mario Pando (named after its founder) opened its doors to accept children at primary and secondary levels. Known for its excellence, this school became affiliated with the Instituto de Segunda Enseñanza in the capital city of Santa Clara. Most of the faculty of the Colegio Mario Pando held university degrees. (This information was submitted to me by Mr. Roberto Nodal, Sr., former administrator of education in Remedios, now living in the U.S.)

6. María Montalván came from a family of musicians who had contributed much to the musical tradition in Remedios, including performing

church music, training musicians, and organizing bands. Her parents were successful in preparing María for a position as church organist in Remedios, and her brother José María became the director of the Municipal Band in Caibarién. Later she studied classical piano with Manuel Jiménez, a well-known concert pianist and teacher. María Montalván's husband, Juan, was an accomplished cellist who formed several string ensembles and organized the Banda Municipal in Remedios.

7. "The Franciscan priest Fray Pedro Galendo [*sic*] eventually returned to Spain where he died in Madrid. He was friendly to [my father] and his children, who were influenced somewhat by his knowledge of music." From an interview on 15 October 1991 with Francisco Rodríguez Caturla, one of Caturla's surviving sons, now living in Havana.

8. This tradition dates back as far as the early nineteenth century and is still practiced today. Each district (*barrio*) in Remedios—El Carmen and El Salvador—is represented in the *parranda* by its own musicians, dancers, and artists, whose lavish floats and large portable lanterns (*faroles*) carried on poles are paraded around the town square. All participants, young and old, wear costumes and join in the singing and dancing during the parade. Lavish fireworks are set off in the square to bring the event to a climax, during which the crowd dances, usually improvising their own rumba. It is worth mentioning that Cuba's great ethnologist of the times, Fernando Ortiz, considered the *parrandas* of Remedios "*unas de la más atrayentes de la República* [one of the great attractions of the Republic]," one that engendered "*numerosos germenes de cultura artística* [many buds of artistic culture]." For a descriptive and detailed history of the *parrandas* see Martín Farto, *Las parrandas remedianas*.

9. The Valdés's daughter, Carmen, married Augustín Crespo, who was the director of the Banda Municipal de Remedios during Caturla's lifetime. Crespo and Carmen Valdés played together in Havana (piano and saxophone) for a short period prior to his appointment as director of the band. Caturla and Carmen Valdés performed a one-piano four-hand arrangement of Gershwin's *Rhapsody in Blue* at La Tertulia in Remedios (exact date not given; this information is from my interview with María de Carmen de Caturla ["Mamilla"] in Remedios, 28 May 1994).

10. The small colonial town of Remedios included one of the largest communities of African Cubans in the district of Villa Clara, many of whom were descendants of slaves. When a *bembé* ceremony took place, sounds of the ceremonial drums could be heard throughout Remedios—a fact I personally verified in 1993 when I attended a demonstration of *bembé* drumming in Remedios performed by Afro-Cubans from the region.

11. This information is based on interviews with Caturla's first cousins Olga Caturla de la Maza and "Mamilla" (mentioned above).

12. Among the few close relatives who understood Caturla's precocious nature was his aunt Olga, whom he affectionately called "Tata." An excellent

pianist herself, she adored Caturla and acted as a liaison to his parents and other family members during the initial stages of his crisis related to Manuela Rodríguez.

13. The Cuban economy reached a peak of sugarcane profits in 1920, the year that Caturla's father purchased the colonial house on the Parque José Martí square. However, following a surge of inflation, the bottom dropped out and by 1921, the failing economy brought about much misery and suffering throughout the island. For details see Aguilar, *Cuba 1933*, 43.

Chapter Two

Havana:
The University Years

The *Minuet* by Caturla, a young Cuban composer for whom the future has reserved a glorious place, was a pleasant piece, full of harmony and very inspired.

Enrique Fernández Ros, *La Noche*

STUDENT LIFE IN HAVANA

By the summer of 1923 Silvino García saw to it that his son Alejandro was registered in the *facultad de derecho* (school of law) at the University of Havana. When Caturla began his studies at the university, the García Caturla family moved to Havana where his mother, Diana, set up housekeeping at an apartment close to her brother Marcelo (a member of the Supreme Court in Havana) and sister Porcia.[1] The younger children were enrolled in high school at the Instituto de La Habana. During his student years at the university, Caturla brought Manuela and their infant son to Havana, providing separate accommodations for them. He proudly presented his infant son to his aunt Porcia and others among his closest family and friends in Havana. Family gatherings in Havana were frequent and it was through his uncle Marcelo that Caturla made many important social connections.

Caturla's enrollment at the University of Havana in 1923 coincided with Cuba's first "University Revolution," which took place in January of that year when "the students forcibly occupied the University and demanded the dismissal of professors whom they considered

11

anachronistic, inefficient, or corrupt; the modernization of textbooks, autonomy for the University and free education for all."[2] Thus Caturla became part of the famous nationalist "Spirit of '23," a movement that, as previously noted, had far-reaching political consequences.

CHANGING TIMES—EXPANDING IDEALS

While studying at the university, Caturla was influenced by the "Grupo Minorista," the most revolutionary young intellectual group in Havana. Composed mainly of writers (including editors of the progressive *Revista de Avance*), artists, poets, and musicians, they aspired to awaken a new sense of nationalism in the arts—a type of nationalism that recognized the multiethnic culture of the island. Their quest coincided with the emergence of "Afro-Cubanismo"—a movement stimulated by the research of Fernando Ortiz (1881–1969). Ortiz's research was committed to establishing an ethnic identity of the island that recognized African culture as an integral part of its national profile.[3] The Minoristas identified fully with the ideals of Afro-Cubanismo, a term that eventually symbolized a dividing line between conservative and progressive sectors of Cuban society at that time.

Inspired by the avant-garde of Paris, the Minoristas experimented with new art forms. To paraphrase Alejo Carpentier: Stravinsky's *Le Sacre du Printemps* became for the Minoristas a banner of cultural revolution. While the cubists and atonalists of Europe sought excitement in a culture foreign to theirs, the Minoristas turned to the wonder and mystery of African elements buried in their own national culture.[4]

Among the leading Minoristas the young Caturla met were José Zacarias Tallet (whose poem *La Rumba* he later set to music) and Alejo Carpentier, a journalist and music critic who became the greatest Cuban writer of his time. Caturla's close friendship and artistic collaboration with Carpentier lasted to the end of his life. Carpentier was the first one in Havana to recognize the potential talent that Caturla and composer Amadeo Roldán possessed. He later credited them with opening "a wide and proper path in the wilderness of the Afrocuban field." Carpentier also introduced these two young composers to the latest trends in contemporary European music and commissioned them to compose music for his librettos. The music of Caturla and Roldán was hailed by the Minoristas as a symbol of their own aesthetic ideals.

CATURLA'S MUSICAL ACTIVITIES IN HAVANA

Battle of the Orchestras

Among the many musical activities in Havana in which Caturla was engaged by 1923, the most significant was playing violin in Gonzalo Roig's newly formed Orquesta Sinfónica.[5] Becoming a member of Roig's Sinfónica not only put Caturla in touch with Havana's musical elite but provided an opportunity for him to meet, on professional grounds, some of the key players in the future of Cuba's classical symphonic music. Among them was his most formidable peer in Cuba—the one whose innovative musical paths he followed, the one with whom he vied for commissions, and the one by whom he would always measure his success as a composer— Amadeo Roldán.

While active as members of Roig's Orquesta Sinfónica, Caturla and Roldán found themselves directly involved with the notorious "battle of the orchestras." First of the contending orchestras to emerge was Roig's Orquesta Sinfónica de La Habana, Cuba's first resident classical symphony orchestra.[6] The Orquesta Sinfónica was very popular and admired by all who heard it, including Caturla's father who referred to it as "a brilliant Cuban institution." At first Caturla established a very favorable position in Roig's orchestra; however, when it was announced that a new orchestra was forming under the direction of the Spanish conductor Pedro Sanjuán, the more progressive-minded musicians, including Caturla and Roldán, quit the Orquesta Sinfónica to join Sanjuán's new Orquesta Filarmónica. They reasoned that Sanjuán was more advanced aesthetically because he had just arrived from Europe. Caturla's father reportedly said to him: "How can you join a foreigner's movement—you are a Cuban and you want to join a Spanish conductor's group. Havana cannot support two orchestras—who will support the second orchestra?" Caturla's break with the Orquesta Sinfónica was emotional, rude, and rash. Later, after joining the Filarmónica, he apologized to Roig, reestablished their old friendship, and for a short time played in both orchestras.

The programs of the new Filarmónica were not as exciting as Caturla expected, and, he soon realized how difficult it would be to have his own music performed by the new Filarmónica.[7]

The tension among concert audiences that built up as a result of the confrontation between Roig's Sinfónica and Sanjuán's Filarmónica resulted in the notorious "battle of the orchestras." In reality this emotional issue became a question of conservative versus progressive musicians and audiences. Alejo Carpentier summed it up:

> The co-existence of the two rival orchestras gave place to a struggle that reached true violence, to the point of direct aggression between musicians. . . . If a work appeared in the program of the Sinfónica, the Filarmónica interpreted it in its next concert, with the aim of imposing its (superior) quality. . . . Besides, that contest jolted the passiveness of the public, provoking them to side with one orchestra or the other. One was a "Sinfónico" or a "Filarmónico."[8]

As to be expected, Silvino was a "Sinfónico" and took great pride in the fact that Cuba established its own symphony orchestra under a Cuban director, Gonzalo Roig (whom he knew personally). Also to be expected was his bitter disappointment at his son's decision to abandon the Orquesta Sinfónica for the new Orquesta Filarmónica under Pedro Sanjuán. In the end, Caturla complied with his father's demands and apologized to Maestro Roig by writing:

> I am extremely sorry because of the attitude which I took in that famous meeting of the Society [Orquesta Filarmónica] and I blame myself for having acted incorrectly and somehow *out of control*, as if I were a stranger to you who have always treated me with all kinds of courtesies. [italics mine][9]

The Roig incident would be but just one among many that followed in which Caturla would have to pay the consequences of his outspoken temper, but always, after having first made his point. Although he did make up with Maestro Roig, who subsequently conducted his *Minuet*, their musical paths would soon split forever.

Caturla as a Popular Vocalist

Shortly after the inaugural concert of the Orquesta Filarmónica, Caturla appeared with the Orquesta Sinfónica (15 June 1924) under Gonzalo Roig with one of Cuba's most glamorous, popular singers (to whom Alejo Carpentier had paid homage in a review the previous year)—"Rita Montaner: La única." Together, Caturla and Rita sang *Marisa* by Jorge Ankermann as part of a concert of popular Cuban music.[10] Caturla's success was such that he was invited to participate in another *Concierto Típico Cubano*, this time without Rita Montaner, at the Teatro Payret on 10 August 1924. Organized by Gonzalo Roig and Jorge Ankermann, the concert consisted of a program of boleros by Rodrigo Prats, Gonzalo Roig, Jorge Ankermann, Sánchez de Fuentes, and Moisés Simons. On this occasion Caturla sang his own criolla, *Mi amor aquel* (text by Rosario Sansores). Notes on the program included the following passage:

> It is not very easy to find persons such as A. G. Caturla, who have a facility for the art of music, an intense temperament and the qualities that distinguish this gentleman. Caturla has made rapid progress. Having accomplished himself in the difficult field of beautiful tone production as a violinist, and as a baritone with a satisfying voice, well articulated, confident in attack and filled with an attractive stability, he has seen the beginnings of his career complimented by well deserved triumphs.[11]

Freelancing as a Versatile Musician

During his student years in Havana, Caturla earned money by singing on the radio (sometimes with his younger brother, Othón), playing piano for the famous *Podrecca* puppet shows at the Teatro di Piccoli under the direction of Maestro Renzo Massarani, and playing piano music at the silent movies in Havana.[12] Other musical activities in which Caturla was engaged include radio broadcasts on Havana's station PWX with his Jazz Band Caribe, a student band he organized at the university, and participating in Carpentier's *conciertos de música nueva* (concert-lecture) series. Regarding these concerts, Carpentier later wrote: "I gave a lecture on Debussy—a very modern and advanced composer for the Havana of the time—and it was García Caturla who played the long fragments of *Pelléas et Mélisande* at the piano."

Caturla also performed at social gatherings in Havana, as he did in Remedios. Carpentier witnessed one such occasion in Havana; he later wrote about it (to paraphrase Carpentier): Maestro Renzo Massarani announced he would give a first performance of ragtime music at the home of Pedro Sanjuán. Caturla appeared, and after applauding Massarani's performance, quietly and much to everyone's surprise, announced he would play three original ragtime pieces that he had composed the night before. Such assertiveness toward his elders, particularly in matters of being on top of the latest trends in music, became a trademark of Caturla's personality.

Performance and Publications of Caturla's Music in Havana

In addition to singing his own music in Havana at the *Concierto Típico Cubano* concerts (mentioned above), Caturla's tango *La deshilachada* was performed in Havana by the Argentine baritone José Muñiz in 1924. The following year, Caturla's *Minuet* (from *Pequeña suite de conciertos*) was performed at one of Roig's *Sociedad de Conciertos* at the Teatro Nacional. Reviews of the concert were favorable: *El Mundo* said, "[I]t [*Minuet*] consists of a graceful inspiration, of a certain lyrical eloquence, at times melancholic, and powerfully romantic at others. It seems that our compatriot shows great promise." *La Noche* declared, "The *Minuet* by Caturla, a young Cuban composer for whom the future has reserved a glorious place, was a pleasant piece, full of harmony and very inspired."[13]

Caturla's image in Havana as a promising composer and popular performer was enhanced by his own publication of several *danzas* and *danzónes,* including: *El olvido de la canción* (1923), *Danza Cubana No. 3* (1924), *Danza Lucumí,* and *Danzón el Cangrito* (1925).

Formal Academic and Musical Studies

Following his first year at the University of Havana, Caturla began lessons in composition with Pedro Sanjuán, establishing a student-teacher relationship that was doomed from the very beginning. While Sanjuán was impressed by Caturla's talent he found himself strained to the limit by his lack of discipline and irresponsible attitude toward conventional methods of composition. Caturla resisted academic rules by simply composing the way he saw fit. Much to Sanjuán's dismay, he persisted in developing his own peculiar and at times disruptive (particularly in harmony) musical language. After assigning Caturla studies in counterpoint and fugue and reviewing his compositions, Sanjuán described Caturla as "a disaster" to his Spanish friend Antonio Quevedo, who eventually became one of Caturla's most influential supporters.[14]

The direction in which Caturla was headed with his music was far in advance of Pedro Sanjuán's thinking. For example, compositions such as *Poema de ambiente de cubanos* (1925) and *Guajireñas* (1926) use excessive orchestration, reflecting Caturla's efforts to find new sonorities while developing his concept of timbral rhythm. "Skyscraper" chords (altered sevenths, ninths, and elevenths) spread throughout the orchestra are characteristic of *Poema de ambiente de cubanos*, while traditional rhythms of the *guajira* are placed in a context of impressionism in *Guajireñas*.

Sanjuán's rejection of *Poema de ambiente de cubanos* and *Guajireñas* caused Caturla to conform, at least temporarily, to a more disciplined style. The result was two compositions, both of 1926, in which there is a total absence of Cuban musical elements. The first was *Allegro noble*, the first movement of an unfinished violin concerto; the second was *Preludio* for string quartet (later arranged for string orchestra). Cast in a free rondo-variation form, *Allegro noble* demonstrates Caturla's ability to exploit tonal and virtuosic possibilities of the violin. The main theme of *Allegro noble* clearly reflects European influences (see figure 2.1 below). Influences of Schoenberg's breakdown of tonality are apparent in *Preludio*, a tranquil movement of great beauty, demonstrating the young composer's mastery of part-writing for strings. Sanjuán was never to see the score of *Allegro noble*, a composition that was discovered after Caturla's death. Apparently, Sanjuán was pleased with Caturla's *Preludio* for strings, which he later conducted with the Orquesta Filarmónica in Havana.

Figure 2.1.   *Allegro noble*, mm. 1–8.

While studying at the university, Caturla also undertook vocal lessons with the Italian maestro Arturo Bovi, conductor of the opera at
the Teatro Nacional in Havana.[15] Caturla took great pride in his success as a popular singer, describing his voice as *baritonante atenorada.*

TOWARD A CONFLUENCE OF STYLES:
THE FORMATIVE YEARS, 1923–26

During his adolescence, Caturla absorbed, performed, improvised,
and composed every type of music available to him. As a result there
is no consistency in his style or single model he followed. His ability
to simultaneously compose music of such contrast in style as *Danza
Lucumí* and *Berceuse* (*"Para el cariño más puro de vida, de Papá* [For the
most pure heart of my life, from Papa]") of 1925 or *Pieza en forma de
Giga* (string quartet) and songs such as *Labios queridos* (*Berceuse a lo
guajiro*) and *Una lágrima* of 1926 cast him as an iconoclast. Caturla followed his own intuition, always with an ear for the latest developments. Nevertheless, Caturla was a self-conscious composer, always
on the defense of modernizing Cuban music, yet never abandoning
the sentimental traditional music of Cuba he treasured so much.
Caturla's songs *Labios queridos* (*Berceuse a lo guajiro*) and *Una lágrima*
(criolla-ballada) are prime examples of this type of music.

Caturla's catalog of works for this period (1923–26) almost reached
one hundred compositions (including arrangements of his own
pieces). These compositions include music for piano, film, band, voice
(accompanied songs, operetta), chamber music (including a septet for
saxophones and pieces for string quartet), orchestral music, tangos,
ragtime, jazz fragments, and waltzes. At least 60 percent of this music
is based on popular criollo music he knew from early childhood such
as the *danza, danzón,* criollo-bolero, and bolero types. Caturla's
danzónes El olvido de la canción and *Ay, mamá, yo te vi bailando* of 1923
and the bolero *Bajo mis besos* of 1924 demonstrate his ability to emulate colorful dance band sonorities commonly used by *danzeros*
(*danzón* players) in a highly imaginative and daring (dissonant) style.
Most of these adolescent *danzónes* may be classified as "salon" music
intended to amuse his family and friends.[16] At the same time, however, Caturla composed *Danzas Cubanas: No quiero juego con tu marido*
and *La viciosa* (1924), both of which reflect his familiarity with the traditional music of early Cuban composers such as Manuel Saumell,
Ignacio Cervantes, and Laureano Fuentes. Other *danzas* for piano

from the same period, such as *Danza Negra* and *Danza Lucumí* (1925), break with traditional form and harmonic content. Of particular interest is Caturla's earliest composition based on the Cuban *Son*, *Pieza en forma de son* for string quartet. Abstract and dissonant in style, yet undeniably Cuban in rhythmic content, *Pieza en forma de son* clearly sets the path for Caturla's lifelong obsession with the Cuban *Son*.[17]

The broad diversity of musical form and inconsistency of style found in Caturla's early music sets him apart from all of his Latin contemporaries, including Roldán.

CATURLA'S MUSICAL PEERS IN HAVANA

During his student years at the university, Caturla kept up with every musical event of any significance and knew, personally, most of the leading professional musicians in Havana. Of the many musical impressions and influences he experienced in Havana during his student years, those engendered by Alejo Carpentier, Amadeo Roldán, and Ernesto Lecuona had a far-reaching effect upon his creative process.

The Influence of Alejo Carpentier

Caturla's music first showed signs of contemporary musical influences from abroad after he met Alejo Carpentier in Havana in 1924. Carpentier's preoccupation with European contemporary music, particularly the French avant-gardists, had an enormous impact upon Caturla. As a result, his aesthetic was influenced by such avant-garde composers as Stravinsky, Ravel, Debussy, Honneger, Milhaud, Satie, and Schoenberg, changing his concept of musical style.

An early example of this change may be seen in *Escenas infantiles*, a set of ten miniatures for piano, composed shortly after he met Carpentier. In essence these miniatures, with descriptive titles such as *El baile del gnomo Pinocho, Fuegos artificiales de juguete,* and *Doctor Gradus ad Parnassum*, are parodies of Debussy's *Children's Corner Suite* for piano. *Escenas infantiles* represent Caturla's first stage of utilizing in his music avant-garde elements such as tone clusters, bitonality, freely invented scales, parallel chord progressions, and frequent changes of meter.[18] From 1925 on, these elements, which Caturla quickly adapted to traditional Cuban musical forms such as the *danza* and bolero, became a trademark of his compositional style. Caturla's bolero *Ansia* of 1925 is an example of just how rash he could be in such adaptations. Dedicated to Carpentier, *Ansia* (for voice and piano to his own text) is filled with unconventional harmonic progressions, textures that emulate a small *conjunto*, and mocking musical gestures that classify it as a musical burlesque (see figure 2.2 below).

Carpentier's influence took another turn in 1926, with Caturla's outbreak of neoclassic chamber music. Music by Caturla such as *Concierto de cámara* and pieces for string quartet demonstrate his ability to adapt such classical forms as prelude, minuet, vals, pavane, and gigue to contemporary harmony and Cuban rhythms. However, Caturla never really accepted the tenets of European neoclassicism and soon abandoned such excursions in his music.

The Influence of Amadeo Roldán

The beginning of Roldán's influence upon Caturla is marked by the world premiere of Roldán's *Obertura sobre temas cubanos* by the Orquesta Filarmónica in Havana under the baton of Pedro Sanjuán on 29 November 1925. Roldán's inclusion of Afro-Cuban percussion instruments in the orchestration of this music caused a sensation. Carpentier wrote a glowing review in the Havana periodical *Social* in which he hailed Roldán's new work as a landmark in Cuban music, one that, because of its Afro-Cuban elements, was nothing less than a musical revolution.[19]

Figure 2.2.   *Ansia*, mm. 1–10

Following Roldán's direction, Caturla composed *Obertura Cubana* (initially entitled *Rumba*) based on Cuban themes. Unlike Roldán's *Obertura sobre temas cubanos*, Caturla's *Obertura Cubana* does not call for Afro-Cuban percussion instruments.[20]

Roldán's leadership in organizing chamber music concerts in Havana is another instance of his influence upon Caturla. For example, Caturla's pieces for string quartet (mentioned above) were intended for Roldán's quartet, then participating in Carpentier's *conciertos música nueva* concert-lectures in Havana.

Overall, Roldán's influence upon Caturla was that of an innovator of new Cuban symphonic music, practitioner in advancing performances of contemporary music, and a pedagogue dedicated to improving performance standards of classical music in Havana. Carpentier summarized the importance of their meeting:

> In being contemporaries, by having appeared at the same moment, by having shared contiguous ideas, Amadeo Roldán and Alejandro García Caturla represent two inseparable figures in the history of Cuban music. Nevertheless, a question of tendencies and chronology should not make us forget that their natures were absolutely different and that, although they worked in parallel areas, their works offer diametrically opposed characteristics.[21]

The Influence of Ernesto Lecuona

The success and subsequent commodification of Lecuona's popular Afro-Cuban song and dance music was well established by the time Caturla entered the university.[22] Clearly, the influence of Lecuona's music was, for Caturla, aesthetic, not literal. Lecuona's piano music with Afro-Cuban titles such as *Danza Lucumí* and *Danza Negra* offered Caturla a new genre to modernize with musical elements of the avant-garde. As a result, Caturla's style of the Cuban *danza* is just the opposite of Lecuona's. For example, in Caturla's *Danza Lucumí* of 1925 (for piano solo), traditional binary form is dropped in favor of a short theme with variations, dissonance replaces consonant harmony, and the fragmented melodic-rhythmic theme is abstract in nature.

Carpentier's review of Caturla's *Danza Lucumí* appeared in the April (1925) issue of *Social*. He described it with such phrases as "understanding the marvelous richness of Cuban national folklore, [Caturla] has taken care to use its most typical rhythmic and melodic *ekenebtis* of our national production enriching it with a new harmonic vestment brimming with color, somewhat rough at times, but perfectly well adapted to the character of the composition" (see figure 2.3 below). Caturla's *Danza Negra* of the same period exceeds Lecuona's grand piano style. Composed in traditional three-part form, *Danza Negra* exploits the full sonority of the piano with chordal textures that are at times impractical for one player. Like other compositions for piano solo that followed, *Danza Negra* was probably conceived as orchestral music (see figure 2.4 below).

NEW DIRECTIONS

Because of his pursuit of music and the rapid pace at which he completed his law degree (including courses in English), his classmates in the student yearbook of 1926 characterized Caturla as follows:

> It is not necessary to introduce this perpetual motion because all of you have seen him dancing and jumping from his piano bench. If as a student he never found himself among the upper ranks of his class, as a pianist he is one of the best and some of his compositions are worthy of notice. We hope that his judicial arguments will be filled with melodious notes.[23]

Underlying this public image of Caturla was one tied to an artistic life of a struggling, determined vanguardist composer. Following his graduation, the exciting days of directing his Jazz Band Caribe, playing in the theaters around Havana (like Roldán), singing at popular concerts, playing in the orchestras of Roig and Sanjuán, and a

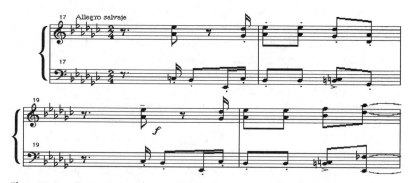

Figure 2.3. *Danza Lucumí*, mm. 17–24

Figure 2.3. *Continued*

Figure 2.4. *Danza Negra, mm. 97–104.*

host of other musical activities came to an end. Caturla's vision now was to bring about a renewal of musical standards in Remedios based on his rich and varied experiences in Havana. His first step was a lecture called *"Diferencias entre la escuela antigua y moderna"* ("Differences between the old and modern schools"), presented in Remedios in 1926. As you will see in subsequent chapters, Caturla relentlessly pursued his vision, one that was never realized. As a result, he turned to his friends in Havana (particularly Carpentier) to help negotiate performances of his music by the Filarmónica. His vision of developing a musical utopia in Remedios would soon dissolve into hopes of establishing himself in Havana as a composer, conductor, and teacher dedicated to the cause of contemporary Cuban concert music.

NOTES

1. Caturla's father, Silvino, remained in Remedios to maintain the family business but commuted to Havana on weekends.

2. Aguilar, *Cuba 1933*, 73.

3. Among conservatives in Havana who rejected the acceptance of African elements as far as Cuban national music was concerned were Eduardo Sánchez de Fuentez, Gonzalo Roig, and others in their circle. Theorizing that Cuban folk music retained certain Indian elements of the ancient Siboneys, their purist (i.e., non-African) view became known as *Siboneyismo.* Fernando Ortiz criticized the racist aspects of this movement: "Just as the affirmation of an original and transcendent 'Indianism' in the music of Cuba was a preposterous idea, equally so was the negative attitude toward the black influence" (see Ortiz, *La africania de la música folklórica de Cuba*, 104).

4. Carpentier, *La música en Cuba*, 278.

5. During an interview (in Havana in 1992), Cuban musicologist Hilario Gonzalez told me that Roldán and Caturla performed together in the orchestra that Gonzalo Roig assembled for the performance of José Maury's opera *La Esclava* prior to the emergence of the Orquesta Sinfónica. It is worth mentioning that the year Caturla joined Roig's Orquesta Sinfónica (1923), he published in Havana his *danzón El olvido de la canción*. Above the title is printed: *"Dedicado a mi amigo, el SR. GONZALO ROIG."*

6. The Orquesta Sinfónica was founded in 1922 by Gonzalo Roig (born in Havana, 20 July 1891, died 13 June 1970), Ernesto Lecuona, and César Pérez Sentenat.

7. The inaugural concert of the Orquesta Sinfónica took place at the Teatro Nacional on 29 October 1922. The program included *Overture from*

Oberon by C. M. von Weber, *Scenes Pittoresques* by J. Massenet, *Piano Concerto No. 2 in G Minor* by C. Saint-Säens (with Ernesto Lecuona, soloist), and other compositions by Rheinberg, Bach, and Wagner. The inaugural concert of the Orquesta Filarmónica took place on 8 June 1924 at the Teatro Nacional. The program included Beethoven's *Egmont Overture*, Mendelssohn's *Symphony No. 4*, and Liszt's *Les Preludes*.

    8. Carpentier, *La música en Cuba*, 280.

    9. Cañizares, *Gonzalo Roig*, 60–61.

    10. The complete program was as follows: Nicolai-Obertura, *Las Alegres Comadres de Windsor*; Schubert, *Sinfonía No. 8*; Marín Varona, *Dame un Beso* with Rita Montaner and Dulce María Verdes, sopranos; Alberto Villalón, *Un Falso Amor* with A. G. Caturla and Tomasita Nuñez, soloists; Jorge Anker-mann, *Marisa* with A. G. Caturla and Rita Montaner, soloists; and C. Anker-mann, *Cuba*.

    11. *Datos sobre Alex,* 9–13. Caturla's father kept a diary of his son's concerts, printed programs, and reviews. This file is at the Museo de la Música Provincial "Alejandro García Caturla" in Remedios, Cuba.

    12. Caturla played for such American favorites as Tom Mix, William Hart, Rudolf Valentino, Mary Walcamp, and others. Caturla composed two film scores in 1923: *Recuerdos del Sheik* (Rudolf Valentino) and *Kaleidoscopio*.

    13. José Calero, *El Mundo,* 20 de abril 1925. Enrique Fernández Ros, *La Noche,* 20 de abril 1925.

    14. It was through Pedro Sanjuán that Caturla met Antonio and María Muñoz de Quevedo in Havana. Although Caturla did not study music with them in a formal sense, Caturla spent many hours at their home, playing and discussing contemporary music and sharing his latest compositional ideas with them. Caturla met many of Havana's leading musicians at their home, which was frequently a gathering place for Havana's musical elite. The Queve-dos recognized Caturla's genius and supported him throughout his life.

    15. Maestro Arturo Bovi, together with another Italian musician, Tina Farelli, established the Havana *academia de canto* in 1912. Bovi and Farelli offered vocal lessons and organized choruses for the opera.

    16. The following titles of *danzónes* composed by Caturla in 1923 are typical of these whimsical and humorous salon pieces: *Ay, mamá, yo te vi bailando* (Hey, Babe, I saw you dancing), *El saxofón de Cuco* (Cuco was the nickname of a saxophonist friend), and *Tócala con limón* (reference to playing a joke: someone displays a lemon as the saxophonist plays). Of particular interest is the 1924 *danzón, Mi mamá no quiere que yo baile el son* (My mama does not want me to dance the *Son*), which by its very title makes a social statement. The *Son* was the most important type of Afro-Cuban music to emerge at this time. The title of Caturla's *danzón* reflects his disposition toward those Cubans who, because of their racial attitudes, felt threatened socially by the pervasiveness of such *Son* bands as the Sexteto Habanero (later Septeto Habanero).

17. During the 1920s, the *Son* swept through Havana and broke many racial barriers by bringing black music and black musicians into employment at white middle- and upper-class social and private functions. In 1925 and 1926 the Sexteto Habanero won first prize at the *Concurso de Sones* and became the first such group to have hit records in Cuba (many of which became "standards" in the *Son* repertoire).

18. Caturla's personal dedication for each of the *Escenas infantiles* to family, friends, and teachers in Remedios reveals his eagerness to share his recent discoveries of new music with them. These dedications reveal episodes of his private life that were taking place at the time. For example:

No. 1—(*Baladita del niño en la cuna*)—"I dedicate this little piece to that child that will be born soon, sent to me by God."

No. 2—(*El baile del gnomo Pinocho*)—"This is for my brother Othón who hates modernism."

No. 3—(*El scherzito de la lluvia en los cristales*)—"This is for my friend Rolondo, who feels sad when the rain prevents him from going out for wine and women."

No. 5—(*Fuegos artificiales de juguete*)—"These fireworks are for my esteemed friend Augustín J. Crespo, who now is well acquainted with Ravel, Stravinsky, and Debussy."

No. 6—(*Balada del amor bandolero*)—"This is for Rita, my bandoleer love." [Reference to Rita Montaner]

No. 7.—(*Doctor Gradus ad Parnassum*)—"To my very esteemed teacher, Mrs. María Montalván de Valdés, with all my consideration."

No. 8—(*Alba Radiante!!! Sol, Sol!!!*)—"And this is dedicated to that little one who is everything for me in my life." (Composed in 1925, after the birth of his first son.)

No. 9—(*El caballo encantado*)—"For Mr. Vittorio Podrecca and his Piccoli, inspired by the Thousand and One Nights tale." (Composed in 1925. Caturla learned much new music from the director of the Teatro di Piccoli, Maestro Renzo Massarani, whose repertoire for his shows included such interesting music as Ottorino Respighi's La Cenicienta [Massarani was a student of Respighi in Rome], Blanco y Negro, Massarani's own composition in playful counterpoint, and other contemporary music.)

19. Carpentier would later write in his *La música en Cuba* that Roldán's *Obertura sobre temas cubanos* was "the most important event in Cuban musical history" (281). Roldán was the first to use Afro-Cuban rhythm instruments (*güiro* and timbales) in Cuban classical symphonic music.

20. Caturla did not introduce Afro-Cuban percussion instruments into his orchestral music until *Liturgia* in 1928.

21. Carpentier, *La música en Cuba*, 290.

22. Caturla borrowed one of Lecuona's most popular titles, *Palomita blanca* (White dove), for one of his early *danzónes*, which he dedicated to his closest friend in Remedios, Lorenzo "Lordi" Martín y Garatea. Composed in traditional form and harmonic language, Caturla's *Palomita blanca* is typical of his early salon style.

23. Taken from the 1926 yearbook of Caturla's class at the University of Havana. Former Judge Fernando Arsenio Roa, a friend and classmate of Caturla's, made this reference available to me.

Chapter Three

Emergence of a New Image: Lawyer-Composer

I am a musician composer . . . my specialty is Afrocuban music.

Caturla to Fernando Ortiz

CHALLENGES AND CONFLICTS OF DUAL CAREERS IN REMEDIOS

Upon graduating from the University of Havana on 22 January 1927 with the title of *Doctor en Derecho Civil* (doctor of civil law), Caturla began his new life as a lawyer in Remedios. Although he had the full support of his father, who provided employment and business connections, circumstances were not easy because he still had a family to support, one that grew steadily. Manuela was soon to bear their second child, another son, born on 12 February 1927, whom they named after Caturla's father, Silvino. Family tensions eased as Caturla's mother and aunt "Tata" softened the reality of his circumstances, eventually making Sunday visits of Caturla's small children to the García Caturla residence a regular family occasion. However, there would never be a normal in-law relationship between his parents and Manuela's family, a circumstance that was noticed by the townspeople of Remedios.

Caturla had yielded to his father's insistence that he pursue a degree in law (but privately resolved to pursue a career in music at the same time) only because he found himself caught between the differences of two families—his own and the one he shared with Manuela Rodríguez. Family legend has it that, upon graduating from the university, Caturla handed over his law degree to his father, indicating his preference for a career in music. However, his hopes for a career in music were compromised because of the worsening economy in Cuba, and he soon took on duties as a local lawyer in Remedios. At the same time, he was appointed municipal judge in Placetas by the district government in Santa Clara.[1] Thus, Caturla's career in the field of law was from the very beginning twofold: lawyer and judge.

Caturla wrote to Carpentier that he was "forced to be a hick" and that "something must give in the conflict between my profession and that of musician-composer"[2] This would be the first in a long stream of complaints over his discontent in Remedios and despair at not being able to sustain himself as a professional musician.

Determined to resolve this conflict by establishing himself as a professional musician and composer, Caturla's ambition intensified. As a result, 1927 was to become one of his most prolific and innovative creative periods, culminating with the completion of *Obertura Cubana*, Caturla's first major Afro-Cuban symphonic work. In the meantime, Caturla participated in a variety of civic cultural events in the region, this time in a more serious role as a career musician than in earlier days.[3] His involvement with the musical life of Remedios was directed mainly to reorganizing the Academy of Music in Remedios, finding ways to improve the material circumstances of the municipal band, and trying at one point to organize his own chamber orchestra. However, his greatest hopes for professional recognition were in having his music performed in Havana. Caturla relied upon Carpentier to negotiate performances of his music by Sanjuán and the Orquesta Filarmónica, a mission that ended with limited results; he also continued sending Carpentier copies of his latest chamber music and solicited him for publicity in the Havana press.[4]

SYNTHESIZING NEW MUSICAL SOURCES

Among the scores Caturla sent to Carpentier were *Pieza en forma de danza Cubana*, to be played by Roldan's string quartet (as part of Carpentier's New Music concerts), and *Preludio* (previously mentioned), arranged for string orchestra and intended for Sanjuán's Filarmónica concerts.[5] The dissonant harmonic idiom found in both these compositions reflect Caturla's continuing search for a new musical language—a language that could be adapted to abstract or traditional Cuban musical forms. Caturla clarified this point himself when he remarked to Carpentier that *Pieza en forma de danza Cubana* is actually an old-fashioned *danza Cubana,* run through harmonic procedures that are "very 1927."

By contrast, *Preludio* is singular in its abstract quality resulting from the development of a "cell motive" in the context of bitonal dissonance (see figure 3.1 below). *Preludio* for strings was performed on 29 March 1927 by the Orquesta Filarmónica under Pedro Sanjuán but was not well received. Among the negative reactions was one by the music critic of Havana's *El Sol,* Francisco Ichaso, who likened Caturla's *Preludio* to the music of Arnold Schoenberg (whose progressive music was unappealing to general audiences at that time).

Undaunted by this setback, Caturla focused his attention on the possibilities of forming his own chamber orchestra in Remedios dedicated exclusively to the performance of avant-garde music—including his

Figure 3.1.   *Preludio,* mm. 1–8.

own. He urged Carpentier to spread the news of his proposed chamber orchestra to Roldán and Sanjuán suggesting they could send their music for him to perform in Remedios, with hopes of having their names alongside of his in his first concert. Caturla's plans also included an invitation for Carpentier to give a conference in Remedios on avant-garde music; however, none of these plans materialized.

The most complex mixture of Caturla's new musical sources with traditional and nontraditional Cuban music is to be found among his miniatures for piano of 1927. Composed of a collection of neoclassic forms, some of these miniatures reflect the diversity of his private life and have flirtatious subtitles that may have been intended for Manuela's younger sister, Catalina: _Preludio Corto No. 2, Tu amor era falso_ (Your love was false); _Sonatina, Ojos que te vieron ir . . . cúando te verán volver_ (Eyes that saw you leave . . . when will they see you return); and _Preludio Corto No. 3, Un sueño irrealizable_ (An unattainable dream). Others, without subtitles, were composed for the amusement of his friends in Remedios. They include _Canzonetta, Momento Musical, Pieza en forma de Minuet, Vals, Giga,_ and the whimsical _Monsieur l'agriculteur: Pieza satírica_ (after Satie). Frequent changes of meter, shifting tone clusters, parallel bitonal chord progressions, and fluctuations of rhythm and tempo are characteristic of these experimental pieces that are essentially nondevelopmental in structure. Aesthetically, the most interesting of all these miniatures for piano is _Preludio Corto No. 1,_ subtitled, _"A la excelsa memoria de Erik Satie."_ Inspired by Satie's _Second Nocturne_ (published in _Social_ along with an essay on Satie by Carpentier in the September 1927 issue), Caturla's _Preludio Corto No. 1_ extended the concept of neoclassicism by eliminating the use of bar lines altogether. The resulting freedom of rhythmic expression, combined with a mixture of impressionism, vagueness of tonality, and exploitation of parallel fifths (melodic and harmonic)—unified by a recurring triplet—qualify _Preludio Corto No. 1_ as one of Caturla's most original and poetic compositions for piano.

The diversity of forms and inconsistency of style found throughout Caturla's compositions of 1927 clearly reflect his undisciplined use of new musical sources he found in music of the avant-garde. Caturla saw himself as a pioneer of new Cuban music, and took pride in composing music that is daring and unorthodox. At the same time, he assumed a duty to enlighten his fellow musicians at home on the latest international trends in contemporary music—a self-imposed posture that was naïve, causing him to be resented by most of the local musicians in Remedios. Undoubtedly, Caturla's most experimental music of 1927 may be described as "creations associated with a newly emerging ego identity."

TOWARD A NEW IDENTITY: COMPOSER OF *OBERTURA CUBANA,* AN UNREALIZED MASTERPIECE

Caturla's disappointment in the limited success of *Preludio* at the Filarmónica concerts became a turning point in his career as a composer. He abandoned the abstract style of *Preludio,* which relates more to European than Cuban aesthetics, for a new style of orchestral music based on Afro-Cuban musical elements: the result was *Obertura Cubana.*[6] With the success of Roldán's *Obertura sobre temas cubanos* still in the air (the third performance of which was heard by the Orquesta Filarmónica under Sanjuán on 12 September 1926), Caturla was convinced that his *Obertura Cubana* would be a great success and bring about his "consecration as a musician of some worth," as he put it. Caturla also believed that his new overture would counteract recent lectures by the distinguished Cuban composer Sánchez de Fuentez and others in Havana who denied the influence of African rhythms in Cuban music. Caturla shared these views with Carpentier:

> I have completed a work where I use Cuban rhythms for grand orchestra and have cast it in the form of an Overture. . . . I call it *Obertura Cubana* to differentiate it from Amadeo [Roldán] . . . if Sanjuán were to perform it I'd have a formidable "hit" as a composer *one that would be a blow to those who detest Afrocuban rhythms* because in reality the Overture is composed totally on such rhythms and particularly those from the Villareña region. [italics mine][7]

Unlike Roldán, Caturla's elevation of Afro-Cuban musical elements to the realm of symphonic music became a cause for his personal liberation, and at the same time, an expression of his call for racial equality through music. As a result, Caturla's *Obertura Cubana* is imbued with an exigency reflecting his relentless commitment to that cause. Also, unlike Roldán (now his competitor), Caturla placed the Afro-Cuban musical elements of his *Obertura Cubana* within the context of a complex, eccentric musical language, ignoring past traditions of Cuban orchestral music. In so doing, he formulated, "a priori," an arsenal of rhythmic and thematic Afro-Cuban sources that became a catalog of references for his future compositions.

The main theme of *Obertura Cubana* is one of the most musically eloquent and fertile to be found in all of Caturla's orchestral music (see figure 3.2 below). The relationship of altered pentatonic intervals found therein made possible a seemingly endless flow of rhythmic and melodic permutations of the main theme throughout the whole composition. Orchestral sonorities such as a clarinet obbligato against the opening main theme, muted trumpet solos, unusual doublings of woodwinds and strings, progressions of brass "clusters," and changes of instrumentation that create an independent timbral rhythm—all became a trademark of his orchestral music that followed. The most complex aspect of Caturla's *Obertura Cubana*, however, is its rhythmic content. Aspects of African rhythms such as silent downbeats, cross rhythms (hemiola), polyphonic rhythmic textures, and mixtures of Afro-Cuban rhythmic patterns such as *comparsa, danzón,* rumba, and *Son* are to be found throughout. Overall, *Obertura Cubana* is filled with climaxes reiterating and transforming the main theme to extreme proportions of forceful dynamics and dissonance. *Obertura Cubana* is music intended to confront the establishment in Havana with a new kind of symphonic music that is essentially Afro-Cuban. Introspectively, *Obertura Cubana* may be seen as music of an angry young composer (then twenty-one), determined to openly cry out in protest against racial discrimination, by way of launching a freely invented, syncretic style of music that he described as "Afrocuban."

Caturla implored Carpentier (who attended Sánchez de Fuentes's lectures in Havana) to persist in having Sanjuán perform his "fiercely Afrocuban" *Obertura Cubana* with the Filarmónica the following autumn. However, the circumstances surrounding Carpentier and Sanjuán at that time meant that such plans were doomed. Carpentier was identified as an activist in the Minorista movement, which eventually lead to his arrest and imprisonment (9 July 1927), and Sanjuán was preparing to leave Havana for his first tour in the Unites States. Caturla shelved his *Obertura Cubana* until 1931, when he revised it and took first prize in a national competition for Cuban symphonic music.

SELF-PROMOTION OF A NEW IDENTITY

In the September 1927 issue of the *Diario de la Marina*, Fernando Ortiz (then director of Archivos del Folklore Cubano and recent founder

Figure 3.2. *Obertura Cubana,* mm. 1–4.

of the Institución Hispano-Cubana de Cultura) announced the forth-coming publication of his book *La música Afrocubana.* Eager to gain recognition as a composer of new Afro-Cuban music, Caturla, after reading the above-mentioned announcement, wrote to Ortiz:

> Yesterday I read in the literary section of the *Marina* that you are go-ing to publish a new book on Cuban music specializing naturally, in Afrocuban music. The edition of your book and my creation of a

Poema negro based on folkloric themes have coincided and because of this and the other considerations that I offer in the first paragraph, I have taken a new liberty: to dedicate entirely to you the *Poema negro* alluded to, which will see the light very soon, as I expect to publish it on my own for the benefit of my friends and to send a few copies abroad where I can count on a few others and naturally, to you to whom I dedicate it, and as such, you may ask for as many copies as you wish. . . .

It's little to say that in addition to being a lawyer *I am also a musician-composer, and that my specialty is Afrocuban music,* since I have been dedicating all my attention to this part of our vernacular music. The magazine *Social* published my *Danza Lucumí* in April 1925 and now they are preparing to print one of my latest works for the piano, *Danza del Tambor,* which I have dedicated to Moisés Simons, also one of the most fervent admirers of Afrocuban music. [italics mine][8]

In reply, Ortiz thanked Caturla for his letter, encouraged him to send his music, and offered his hospitality in Havana. Their mutual interest in African aspects of Cuban culture provided a firm basis for friendship. Caturla and Ortiz later met at conferences in Havana contesting Sánchez de Fuentez's anti-African polemics.

In an effort to further promote his image as a specialist of Afro-Cuban music, Caturla assembled a set of *danzas* for solo piano representing his Afro-Cuban style including *Lucumí, Tambor, Negra,* and *Conga.* Caturla's perception of himself as a specialist in Afro-Cuban music is reflected in the following remark he made to Carpentier about *Danza del Tambor:* "As you can see, the title is perfectly justified as the bass is constantly developing the rhythm of the conga drum"[9] (see figure 3.3 below). Caturla's *danzas* in Afro-Cuban style contrast greatly his earlier *danzas* of 1924 (*No quiero juego con tu marido, La viciosa,* and *[Danza] La no. 4*), which are more like intermezzi or caprices in a Latin vein with no Afro-Cuban musical elements. He borrowed money from his father to print two hundred copies of his booklet of Afro-Cuban *danzas,* with the intention of dedicating a new one, based on Afro-Cuban rhythms from Remedios, to Carpentier. Although Caturla found ways to publish *Danzas Lucumí, Negra,* and *Tambor,* the original project, as envisioned, did not materialize. Eventually, *Danzas Lucumí* and *Tambor* were orchestrated to become part of his *Tres Danzas Cubanas* for orchestra published in Paris two years later. Caturla also arranged *Danza del Tambor* as duos: one for violin and piano, and one for cello and piano.

Figure 3.3. *Danza del Tambor,* mm. 1–10.

Other less well-known piano pieces of 1927 that reflect Caturla's use of Afro-Cuban musical elements are *Son en do menor* and *Elegía litúrgica,* the latter of which was dedicated to Catalina, Manuela's younger sister (see figures 3.4 and 3.5 below). The experimental nature of these compositions allow for full reign of dissonant harmony

Figure 3.4 *Son en do menor,* mm. 1–8.

Figure 3.5. *Elegía litúrgia,* **mm. 1–8.**

and complex rhythmic invention. More interesting, however, is Caturla's creative response to musical sources of such contrast as *Son* and African liturgical chant. *Son en do menor* is one of Caturla's earliest attempts to modernize the Cuban *Son.*

HAVANA: REJECTION AND SUBMISSION

As 1927 drew to a close, Caturla was intent upon having his music performed once again by the Filarmónica in Havana. He approached Roldán, who as assistant conductor was directing the orchestra while Sanjuán was on tour in the United States. Caturla had previously shown Roldán his *Poema* (*Poema de verano*), which was yet to be copied and edited, and hoped to have him conduct it at the next Filarmónica concert in December. Self-conscious of his public image as a composer, Caturla wrote to Roldán from Remedios:

> [W]hat the public knows of my music is a bit lightweight and poorly representative of my personality. . . . *Poema [Poema de verano]* . . . is large in dimensions and demonstrates my entire personality, and through it, *the public could know the real me and then hold me in regard as a true composer.* [italics mine][10]

Reminding Roldán that he had only been allowed to have "small dances and short pieces" performed, Caturla, in a typically outspoken manner, augmented his plea by adding he was "already deserving" and that Roldán could and should be entrusted with the opportunity of rewarding his efforts by performing his new *Poema de verano*.

Less than a week later, Caturla informed Roldán that he was "somewhat embarrassed" to say that because of his copyist's illness he would not be able to submit a finished copy of *Poema* in time for the December concert. Regarding a future performance date, Caturla seemed apprehensive about approaching Sanjuán to conduct *Poema de verano* and asked Roldán to intercede for him. In return Caturla presented a violin sonata to Roldán, dedicating it to him with the inclusion of "an effusive handshake." As it turned out, Caturla was unable to produce a finished copy of *Poema de verano* prior to the return of Sanjuán to Havana, and the music was permanently shelved.

Apparently, Sanjuán had not responded to Caturla's correspondence prior to his departure for the United States, a circumstance that Caturla could not accept. He told Carpentier he was a bit sensitive about Sanjuán and planned to confront him with a complaint when he returned. Caturla did so in a letter, sent through Carpentier. In stating his case to Sanjuán (of whom he was highly critical regarding taste and judgment in programming the Filarmónica concerts), Caturla took him to task in a demanding tone that was at once abrasive and self-righteous:

> As a sincere man and 100% truthful, I cannot understand why until now you appear cold, reserved and inattentive to me, as the repeated letters which I have addressed to you as of this date merited at least one answer to all that I have written to you, especially when I know that you write to your other friends.[11]

Caturla also informed Sanjuán in the same letter that he did not expect any favors from him, even though by supporting his friendship and the ideals of the Filarmónica he had suffered "persecution" by "influential artistic elements at home." In what appears to be an effort to have his relationship with Sanjuán and the Filarmónica clarified and rectified once and for all, Caturla drew his letter to a close by writing: "I do wish, fervently, that if you have any reason for complaint against me, to expose it to me so that I may act upon it as a gentleman and friend should."

Sanjuán's response was prompt and diplomatic. After assuring Caturla of his loyal friendship and admiration, he dismissed his breakdown of correspondence by simply saying that other of his friends had also complained about his not writing and that he was very busy. As to Caturla's "persecution" for having defended him and the Filarmónica as friends, Sanjuán responded somewhat ostentatiously:

> [F]rom my heart I appreciate it, but do not forget that for serving the artistic culture of Cuba I have been and continue to be systematically bothered and even slandered. . . .
>
> ¡bon eleve, do not regret having defended a beautiful gesture in honor, not only of a man but, of an idea![12]

After reminding Caturla that the Filarmónica represented a "high artistic ideal," Sanjuán approached the end of his letter by thanking Caturla for his support on behalf of his orchestra.

By the summer of 1927, the political and economic climate of Cuba was extremely strained and uneasy; Caturla described this period in a letter to Sanjuán as "a regrettable error on the part of the government," cautioning "we must be quiet about it since they have the power." Gerardo Machado's closing down the University of Havana and arresting key members of the Grupo Minorista (including Alejo Carpentier) were indications of just how brutal his dictatorship had become. Caturla's life in Remedios during the summer of 1927 was also uneasy. He was intimidated by Carpentier's arrest, and fearful of writing directly to him in prison.

PLANS TO STUDY ABROAD

Upon his release from Havana's Prado jail, Carpentier made careful plans for his self-imposed exile to Paris. By then he had finished his first draft of *Écue-Yamba-O* ("God be praised" in *Ñáñigo* dialect), a novel intended to capture the essence of the black world of Cuba. Prior to his departure for Paris, he also completed several Afro-Cuban poems and ballet librettos, including *La rebambaramba*, which he left for Roldán to set to music. Although Carpentier had promised Caturla some "theatrical interludes," their collaboration was stalled for the time being.

In the meantime, Caturla was unable to establish himself as a professional composer in Havana. His hopes of having the young Orquesta Filarmónica (then scarcely three years old) perform his new music were unrealistic and soon became an incentive for him to travel abroad with the purpose of gaining recognition back home.

Caturla's trip to Paris was planned well in advance, with the intention of traveling with Carpentier. Undoubtedly, they discussed their future abroad, one that coordinated and intensified the direction of their creative paths, both of which were dedicated to the fate of Cuba's future in the arts. As it turned out, Carpentier left Havana in March 1928 for Paris, where Caturla would soon join him.

Besides Carpentier's influence, there can be little doubt that failure to have his music performed by the Filarmónica (subsequent to *Preludio*), disenchantment with Sanjuán, and the musical impasse he faced in Remedios strengthened Caturla's determination to travel abroad. Caturla followed Carpentier to Paris in June 1928, where he remained until the end of October the same year. The main objectives of his sojourn was to study orchestration, revise and reorchestrate his scores for publication and performance abroad, and make contact with as many influential musicians as possible. He could then return home with the traditional European "stamp of approval," a credential that would no doubt enhance the possibilities of having his music performed by the Filarmónica, establish his reputation as a serious composer of symphonic music, and secure his place in the musical world of Havana. Caturla's studies in Paris also offered him the obvious advantage of going beyond Havana by having his music published while he was abroad. In the end Caturla's plan worked, except the part for which he struggled the most: a permanent position in Havana as a professional musician.

CATURLA SOLICITS THE PAN AMERICAN ASSOCIATION OF COMPOSERS

Even though I am a lawyer, in addition I am a musician and composer. I count myself, with pride, among Latin American composers, a Cuban.

Caturla to Carlos Chávez, vice president of PAAC

Precisely at this time, 1928, the newly formed Pan American Association of Composers (PAAC) in New York, headed by Edgard Varèse, and a small group of vice presidents including Carlos Chávez and Henry Cowell, solicited Cuban composers to submit their music for review and performance. PAAC's contact in Cuba was the editor of *Diario de la Marina* (Cuba's oldest newspaper), José Fernández de

Castro who, in collaboration with Alejo Carpentier, suggested the names of Caturla and Amadeo Roldán.[13] Once informed that his name was submitted to PAAC, Caturla was eager to make this connection and wrote to José Fernández de Castro. In his letter, Caturla advised Fernández de Castro that he was prepared to send his music directly to PAAC. Caturla ended his letter by pressing Fernández de Castro to publish an article about himself in *Revista de Avance* (of which Fernández de Castro was a coeditor) written by Alejo Carpentier.[14] With no word from Fernández de Castro, Caturla simply preempted him by writing directly to PAAC in care of Carlos Chávez. Caturla seized the opportunity to further his own cause as an upcoming composer by telling Chávez about performances of his music by the Orquesta Filarmónica (*Preludio*) and Roig's Orquesta Sinfónica (*Minuet antico*). In closing his letter to Chávez, Caturla offered to send examples of his latest compositions. While Caturla did not hear from Chávez before he left to join Carpentier in Paris, he did later submit to PAAC the original piano versions of *Danza del Tambor* and *Danza Lucumí* that were performed in New York less than one year later.[15] Caturla's letter to Chávez may be seen as his first attempt to export his music from the island. However, it was not until his mission to study abroad had been completed that he stepped into an international sphere that would forever influence his life as a composer.

NOTES

1. For details, see Henríquez, *Correspondencia,* 59–60.

2. Henríquez, *Correspondencia*, 25 de diciembre 1927, 9; 15 de febrero 1927, 10.

3. These events included his high school reunion in Santa Clara at which time he presented a formidable piano recital of classics and publicly praised his colleague Joaquín Molín for honoring the Cuban composer Valdés Costa (1898–1930). Caturla also performed Gershwin's *Rhapsody in Blue* with the Banda Municipal de Remedios (12 August 1927) and presented his *Ave Maria* (dedicated to his mother) in Remedios. Caturla's *Ave Maria* is a dismal piece, filled with dissonance, unexplainable chord progressions, and unconventional voicings; it does not reflect any influence of the traditional church music he learned earlier in Fray Pedro Galdeano's choir.

4. Carpentier was writing for a number of journals in Havana, including *Social, Carteles,* and *Diario de la Marina.*

5. Both compositions became part of *Piezas para cuarteto de cuerdas,* a set of eight pieces for string quartet. Some of these compositions used old European forms (minuet, waltz, gigue) dressed in new harmonies—a neoclassic trend that was then in vogue in Paris (Debussy, Ravel, Satie, etc.).

6. Caturla's *Obertura Cubana* (1927) was originally entitled *Rumba (Movimiento sinfónico)*; he later changed it to *Obertura Cubana.* The original 1927 version was revised in 1931. *Obertura Cubana* may be the result of Caturla's intention to compose a "Symphony on Sones and Rumbas."

7. Henríquez, *Correspondencia,* 19 de marzo 1927, 17.

8. Henríquez, *Correspondencia,* 12 de septiembre, 24–25. Caturla was also to dedicate one of his finest compositions, *Comparsa: Negro Dance,* to Fernando Ortiz. Arranged for piano and published in Henry Cowell's *New Music Quarterly,* this composition was originally part of the orchestral score for an unfinished ballet, *Olilé (El velorio),* which was composed between 1929 and 1930.

Caturla's *Danza del Tambor* was eventually published in *Social* in 1930; his efforts to have Carpentier negotiate the publication of *Danza del Tambor* at that time (1927) were hopeless because Carpentier was in prison for his activities as a Minorista.

9. Henríquez, *Correspondencia,* 19 de abril 1927, 17.

10. Henríquez, *Correspondencia,* 7 de noviembre 1927, 26–27.

11. Henríquez, *Correspondencia,* 31 de enero 1928, 32.

12. Henríquez, *Correspondencia,* 2 de febrero 1928, 317.

13. Caturla and Roldán each became executive members of PAAC. Varèse left New York for Paris at the end of 1928 at which time Henry Cowell became president of PAAC; Amadeo Roldán was appointed as regional representative of the West Indies for PAAC, a connection that resulted in the performance of contemporary music in Havana by Roldán and other PAAC members with the Havana Philharmonic, Havana Chamber Orchestra, and the National Theatre Orchestra. See Deane L. Root, *Yearbook,* 69.

14. Henríquez, *Correspondencia,* 23 de marzo 1928, 36. There is no evidence of a reply by José Fernández de Castro, and an article about Caturla did not appear in *Revista de Avance.* Meanwhile, Caturla acquired the address of PAAC in *Musicalia,* the newly established music journal of Antonio and María Muñoz de Quevedo in Havana, and wrote directly to Carlos Chávez.

15. The music of Roldán and Caturla was performed at the first concert of PAAC in New York on 12 March 1929 at Birchard Hall (113 West 57th Street). Caturla's *Dos Danzas* (*Danza del Tambor* and *Danza Lucumí*) for piano were performed by Stephanie Schehatowitsch, pianist, and Roldán's *Dos canciones populares cubanas* was sung by Martha Whittemore.

Chapter Four

Paris: Studies Abroad

[T]he music which I will compose in the future is not intended to take the "Prix de Rome" nor does it follow anyone's footsteps but comes from the creative impulses of my free inspiration which is perhaps disorganized but essentially mine.

Caturla to María Muñoz de Quevedo

By the end of February 1928 Caturla's strained relations with Sanjuán eased but still left him in a position of having to further prove himself as a composer. Roldán and Sanjuán frequently performed their music with the Filarmónica during the 1927 season, a fact that no doubt increased Caturla's longing to see his music on the same programs. He was hoping Sanjuán would conduct his *Tres Danzas Cubanas* that May and urged Carpentier to "prepare the success" by publishing the original piano version of *Danza del Tambor* (the first of the *Tres Danzas*) in the April issue of *Social*. Apparently Carpentier did not have time to take any action; he was probably involved with the final stages of his departure for Paris. As a result, *Danza del Tambor* was postponed for publication in *Social* until the January issue of 1930, and Sanjuán did not conduct Caturla's music that season.

Accompanied by Modesto Gutiérrez Heredia and other well-to-do family friends from Remedios, Caturla departed for Paris, via New York, aboard the SS *Leviathan* on 16 June 1928.[1] En route to Paris, Caturla took in a performance of the spectacular Hammerstein-Kern musical *Show Boat* at Radio City Music Hall in New York. Later, while at sea, Caturla arranged for the ship's dance orchestra to play some of his music—much to the delight of the passengers.

Upon arrival in Paris, Caturla found his own way to Hotel de Maine, a sort of bohemian headquarters for Cubans and other Latin artists abroad. When Carpentier reacted with surprise at this, Caturla reportedly quipped with his characteristic irony, "I studied the station plan (metro map)."

During his first days abroad, Caturla indulged in the exciting life of Paris. He experienced everything from the exuberance of cafés and theaters (he had hopes of seeing Josephine Baker), to attending concerts, ballets (including Diaghilev's Ballet Russe), and jazz clubs. As Carpentier noticed, Caturla also satisfied his palate with exotic gourmet food in a restaurant at Montparnasse, including wild boar filet, smoked eels, sea urchin, and Alsatian or Russian dishes.

Thanks to Carpentier, Caturla met important composers and writers who were then in Paris, including Sergey Prokofiev, Manuel María Ponce, Jacques Maritain, and Maurice Jaubert, and such surrealist poets as Robert Desnos, Georges Sadoul, and Luis Aragón.

Much of Caturla's time in Paris was spent at the elegant Paris residence of Justo Pastor Gutiérrez Heredia (Modesto Gutiérrez Heredia's brother), where he often appeared at social gatherings for Cubans in Paris. Caturla delighted the guests by singing, playing the piano, and accompanying others. He often played his favorite Spanish composers Albeniz and Granados as well as parodies of popular music (including tunes from *Show Boat*) and excerpts of his latest original compositions. Before the summer was out, Caturla spent a short time at the fashionable spa in Aix-les-Bains with the Gutiérrez Heredia family, catching yet another glimpse of the good life abroad.

In the following letter to his mother, Caturla revealed just how cosmopolitan he had become in such a short time:

Paris, June 27, 1928
My dearest Mamá . . .
   After attending the Russian ballet on Saturday I went to the Folies-Bergère on Sunday afternoon but was unlucky because Josephine Baker did not appear since she was in Vienna and then Sunday night I went with Carpentier and friends to the artists café in Montparnasse called *La Coupole*. The day before yesterday I bought a ticket for the Spanish ballet directed by La Argentina, a Spanish ballerina who is the most serious in her class and nationality I have seen and will perform at the Teatro Femina on the Champs Élysées . . . and I

saw two new Spanish ballets: *El contrabandista* and *Sonatina*, the last one by a student of de Falla, Halffter and in addition other music of Albeniz and Granados including the celebrated Córdoba and Danza española which I played so often. Last night I went with Carpentier to the theater of the Champs Élysées . . . to see the Jazz Opera Johnny dirige el baile [Ernst Kreneck]. . . . Tonight I won't leave the neighborhood since tomorrow is the second concert by Cortot with the Orchestra de la École Normale and since I already have my seat (40 francs) I don't want to spend any money today and besides there isn't anything interesting in the theaters unless Desnos, a writer friend of Carpentier's comes to take me to the Jewish theater which it is said is very interesting.[2]

The diversity of Caturla's musical interests are well documented in the above letter and consistent with his broad interests and activities in music at home. His apparent interest in Josephine Baker is not surprising because her rave reviews and place in the *art nègre* movement in Paris were well known to him through the Cuban press (*Diario de la Marina, Social*, etc.). Josephine Baker's controversial *step afro-américaine* became a sign of the times, one that Caturla related to aesthetically and had already expressed in his Afro-Cuban style of music.

STUDIES WITH NADIA BOULANGER

Once Caturla settled down in Paris, Carpentier made arrangements for him to study with Nadia Boulanger, a renowned teacher of composition. From the very beginning, it must have been clear to Mlle. Boulanger that Caturla had no intention of following strict academic rules (just as it was with his previous teacher, Pedro Sanjuán). Writing to María Muñoz de Quevedo from Paris, Caturla clarified his disposition:

I have come to Paris as a simple student without bothering the politicians nor taken a cent from Cuba. Since I was not in the spirit of the conservatory I have presented myself to Nadia Boulanger as a young man who knows something of the profession to which he aspires but cannot be burdened with theory nor compositional formulae because the music which I have composed and the music which I will compose in the future is not intended to take the "Prix de Rome" nor does it follow anyone's footsteps but comes from the creative impulses of my free inspiration which is perhaps disorganized but essentially mine.[3]

Among other things, Caturla worked on orchestrating *Tres Danzas Cubanas* as part of his studies with Nadia Boulanger. His lessons caused her no end of frustration: "Nadia says I make her pull her hair out," wrote Caturla to his father. However, Mlle. Boulanger's intuition was such that she was able to guide him along the creative paths he so desperately wanted to follow *his way*; she summed up her work with Caturla in the following statement to Carpentier: "Seldom have I had to deal with such a gifted student. Because of this, I do not want to change him: I make him compose and analyze scores with my advice. That's all. He is a natural force."[4]

Caturla was quick to see through the superficial world of would-be composers in Paris at that time, and wrote to the Quevedos:

> Life in Paris is very fatiguing; there is much to see and much not to see. The concerts with some exceptions do not vary from the instrumental virtuoso and the Fifth Symphony. I'm a little tired of so many national geniuses and although in Cuba we also have many we don't take them so seriously as they do here. I'm dying to return to the back yard and to work in my own environment. . . .
>
> The composers seen at close range lose some of their prestige. There they are at their table surrounded by scores taking crumbs from people whom you would not expect. Nadia once discovered that Oratorio by composer X which had been premiered with great success was totally "influenced" by a cantata of Buxtehude and that even the disposition of the voices, the tonality and the rhythmic order coincided. Critics concealed such plagiarism to preserve national honor if the composer was French. Fame here owes much to friendships and 5 o'-clock teas. If you have a comfortable house with good heat, wines and good cigars and some agreeable and discreet visitors—success will come immediately———
>
> In Paris I have seen young musical talents fall into desperation and misery while many sponsored by wealthy aristocratic widows triumphed in the salons and evening concerts. Every day musicians from everywhere in the world arrive in Paris—especially Americans—who come "to perfect their studies" without even knowing their solfège and in two or three years happily spend their scholarships which have been given to them—God knows how—by the government of their country. Some fall in the École Normale de Musique some in the National Conservatory where they don't even pass from the first grades. Life at the café—the gallant running around the Boulevards—if not the cold or

rain, inhibit all action of the foreigners. When they return, the local media must be mobilized and a group of friends will organize the expected welcoming. Now we have consecrated genius and themes for
the chronicles.[5]

Caturla's frank exposure and typically bold criticism of student
life in Paris sharply contrasts the other side of life he experienced in
Paris which he described so vividly in the above letter to his
mother.

LITURGIA: A MUSICAL COLLAGE

Caturla's most significant project while studying with Nadia
Boulanger that summer was a musical setting of Alejo Carpentier's poem *Liturgia*, an evocation of Afro-Cuban initiation rites of
the *Ñáñigos*.[6] *Liturgia* was Caturla's first collaboration with Carpentier, followed by *Dos poemas afrocubanos* the following year and
later the puppet opera *Manita en el suelo*. The juxtaposition of
Afro-Cuban poetry, symphonic sonority, bongos and claves, and
chant for double male chorus found in Caturla's *Liturgia* produces
an incredible mélange of sounds. The magic, ritual, imagery, and
folklore (including "Papa Montero," the holy rooster "Enkiko,"
"Luna," "diablitos") found in Carpentier's poetry justify such
sounds. Caturla enriched Carpentier's poetry by setting the Afro-
Cuban elements of *Liturgia* with exotic and surrealistic sounds
that, at times, seem to symbolize the mixture of colors found on
African masks. To evoke the ritual aspects of Carpentier's *Liturgia*, two male choruses chant back and forth in a declamatory call
and response fashion against the orchestra (see figure 4.1 below).
Carpentier suggested the use of megaphones for the choruses to
facilitate piercing the orchestral textures, an idea that was eventually abandoned for practical reasons. For the magical-ceremonial
aspects of the text, in which Carpentier exploited the colorful idiom of *jitanjáfora* (rhythmic use of words that have no meaning,
"tra-la-la," for example), Caturla added Afro-Cuban instruments
to the percussion section (bongos and claves), marking his first attempt to integrate Afro-Cuban folk instruments with the symphony orchestra.[7]

Figure 4.1. *Liturgia,* mm. 25–31 (selected parts from unpublished score).

Other examples of Caturla's unorthodox use of instruments in his free setting of Carpentier's text (to which he added the phrase "Oh mi Cuba" several times against strings and bongos) include the following instrumentations: altered tuning of timpani, extended trills on cymbals and timpani, bass glissandi, juxtaposition of harp and bongos (to introduce the holy rooster "Enkiko"), and combining harp, xylophone, piano, and flute (to introduce Papa Montero).

Although *Liturgia* was never performed in its original version, it formed the basis for a revised orchestral version, *Yamba-O,* which Caturla later referred to as "my most Cuban composition." Caturla saw *Liturgia* as his most progressive composition to date, intended to shock the conservative Cuban audiences in Havana by asserting the aesthetic of Afro-Cuban culture in the context of a new symphonic-vocal genre. Caturla's *Liturgia* is music of the times, music he later considered sending out of Cuba to the American composer Henry Cowell.

Shortly after returning to Cuba Caturla wrote to Carpentier "I have told Dr. Ortiz—I will premiere *Liturgia.*" He also pressed the Quevedos to influence Sanjuán to perform *Liturgia,* while trying to have the score published by Maurice Senart's publishing house in

Paris. Subsequently, he told Carpentier that he wanted to publish an arrangement of *Liturgia* for two pianos and timbales.

Caturla's efforts to express Carpentier's Afro-Cuban poem *Liturgia* in a new symphonic language that included Afro-Cuban folk instruments became a cornerstone for his article "Posibilidades sinfónicas de la música afrocubana" (dedicated to Alejo Carpentier) written one year later.

NEWS FROM HAVANA

As Caturla's busy life in Paris progressed, so did his correspondence with the Quevedos in Havana. They wrote of their admiration for Mlle. Boulanger, urging Caturla to influence Carpentier to solicit an article by her for their new journal *Musicalia*.[8] The Quevedos also encouraged Caturla to submit an article on the music of Argentina (then popular in Paris); neither project materialized. More exciting news from the Quevedos, however, was the great success in Havana of Roldán's ballet *La rebambaramba* (text by Carpentier) and María Muñoz's enthusiastic plans for the future of *Musicalia*, expressed in a letter to Caturla:

> Today Roldán's Rebambaramba was premiered. A tremendous success for a splendid work, prodigiously rich in rhythms, full of life, mag-ni-fi-cent. We think Roldán has fully revealed himself with this work. The Interludio is a beautiful piece, originally modern, of strong and sturdy symphonic character. We are planning to go all the way out in Musicalia. No more washed out folklore, no more sentimental little ballads, no more light opera lyricism. You'll have a chance to hear how great it is.[9]

Surely such news spurred Caturla's ambitions, but perhaps not as much as news from the Quevedos that Henry Cowell had written them, seeking names of "Cuban composers of modern music" for his *New Music Quarterly* in San Francisco. The Quevedos advised Caturla to write him directly, and to mention their publication *Musicalia*. Caturla's initial letter to Cowell was quite different from the letter he previously wrote to Carlos Chávez, now one of the vice presidents of PAAC, and whose music was published in Cowell's *New Music Quarterly* later the same year (*Sonatina for violin and piano*,

October 1928). Dated 9 September 1928 from Paris, Caturla's letter to Cowell stressed the fact that he was a student of Pedro Sanjuán, who very successfully conducted his own music at the Hollywood Bowl concerts in California the previous year. Concerning his own compositional style, Caturla simply asserted in his "bad the English": "I am very prod [*sic*] of that my works can be issued in NEW MUSIC because I write upon Cuban typic ritms [*sic*] and want that in U.S.A. known its [*sic*]. Nothing better than your review."[10]

With this letter Caturla established a lifelong friendship with Cowell, placing himself in a position to network the complete international roster of PAAC composers to his advantage. Eventually this enabled Caturla to spread his music internationally through broadcasts, concerts, and publications by members and associates of Cowell's PAAC.

PLANS, PROJECTS, AND HOPES FOR THE FUTURE

Before leaving Paris, Caturla negotiated publication of *Tres Danzas Cubanas* with Maurice Senart's firm. Printing of the full orchestral score was not completed until the following summer, at which time it was sent to him by his friend, Mexican composer Manuel María Ponce.[11] However, he did succeed in bringing home a published conductor's score of his *Tres Danzas Cubanas*. Caturla also provided copies of his *Liturgia* to Alfred Cortot for possible performances in Paris and made contact with Carpentier's friend Marius-François Gaillard, conductor, composer, impresario, and proponent of contemporary music in Paris at that time.[12]

It would be difficult to evaluate the full impact Caturla's trip to Paris had upon his creative process. He did not study or learn a method but rather studied and analyzed his own music through the eyes and ears of an exceptional teacher. Caturla did not conform to the patterns followed by young composers in Paris at that time; instead, he resisted European influence with "furious independence" (Carpentier's words) focusing on his immediate needs. The text of Carpentier's *Liturgia* provided him freedom and independence from tradition and historical position, conditions that enabled him to incite a musical revolution of his own making, one determined to place Afro-Cuban musical elements into the mainstream of international contemporary symphonic music.

NOTES

1. Modesto Gutiérrez Heredia was a wealthy landowner in Remedios and good friend of Alejandro's father, Silvino. Caturla looked upon Modesto as a kind of uncle.

2. Gómez, *Alejo Carpentier,* Vol. I 19–20.

3. Muñoz de Quevedo, "Alejandro García Caturla," 10–11.

4. Gómez, *Alejo Carpentier,* 21.

5. Muñoz de Quevedo, "Alejandro García Caturla," 10–11.

6. Ñáñigos were members of the Secret Society of Abakuá, a particular magical-religious sect that was formed in Cuba by the slaves brought from the region of the Calabar river in Africa. Carpentier's *Liturgia* appeared in the Paris journal *Genesis* that summer (1928). Language related to the initiation rites of the Ñáñigo found in Carpentier's *Liturgia* had already been documented in his first novel, *Écue-Yamba-O.*

7. For the complete orchestration of *Liturgia* see chapter 11 of this book. Cuban musicologist Hilario González suggested that the idea of using megaphones for the declamatory male chorus passages was inspired by the use of megaphones in the popular Rudy Vallee movies, known in Havana.

8. Shortly before Caturla's departure for Paris, Antonio and María Muñoz de Quevedo launched the premiere issue of their publication *Musicalia,* which was a musical equivalent of the progressive *Revista de Avance* in Havana. Writers such as Francisco Ichaso, Antonio Quevedo, Alejo Carpentier, and others related to the Minoristas contributed to both journals. *Musicalia* became a milestone for Caturla, who not only became its youngest staff member, essayist, and music critic—voicing his and other composers' polemics—but one of its most enthusiastic supporters. As you will see, Caturla's connection with the PAAC through *Musicalia* that summer (1928) set the stage for an international exchange that influenced the rest of his creative life.

9. Henríquez, *Correspondencia,* 11 de agosto 1928, 318–19. Undoubtedly Alejandro was proud of Roldán's success, but with it came the obvious disappointment that it was Roldán and not himself that gave birth to Carpentier's first literary interludes for the stage. Caturla had been pressing Carpentier for ballet interludes as early as 25 January 1927. Subsequent to that, he wrote to Carpentier: "I'm impressed by your project on the Cuban ballet" (29 March 1927). Later: "I'm begging you for the last time for a ballet text that I can put to music" (8 March 1928). Eventually Carpentier did send him the opera libretto *Manita en el suelo* that he later set as a one-act opera. He also sent two scenes, *Circo* and *Embó,* which Caturla did not set to music. But the issue of Carpentier's preference of Roldán's talent prior to that caused Caturla to pout and complain.

10. Caturla to Cowell, 9 September 1928, from García Caturla, "Correspondencia inédita."

11. Manuel María Ponce, Mexican composer, was born in 1882 in Fresnillo, Mexico, and died in 1948 in Mexico City. Prior to meeting Caturla and studying composition with Paul Dukas in Paris, Ponce lived in Havana for a short time during World War I. When Caturla met Ponce in Paris, he was editor of *Gaceta Musicale*. He also edited music for Maurice Senart's publishing house. Ponce became one of Caturla's most important foreign agents. He negotiated the shipping of Caturla's scores, published by Senart, to Cuba. Ponce also wrote about Caturla in the *Gaceta Musicale*, which published the piano score of Caturla's *Danza del Tambor*. They later met in Barcelona where Ponce introduced him to a host of Latin composers.

12. That same year the French composer Marius-François Gaillard produced his *Yamba-O: Tragedia Burlesca* (based on Carpentier's *Liturgia*) at the Théâtre Beriza in Paris. Gaillard also composed music to a number of Carpentier's other Afro-Cuban poems and sponsored Cuban composers and performers in his famous concert series at Salle Gaveau in Paris. Gaillard became an important figure in the future success of Caturla's music.

Chapter Five

From Paris to Remedios and Beyond

Caturla's return trip to Cuba via New York was uneventful, landing him in Havana on 25 October 1928. He was met at the harbor by María Muñoz de Quevedo, who drove him to her apartment in the city. María later wrote about this occasion:

> He returned with a Russian coat and a bundle of scores under his arm. He had not lost his good humor and traditional appetite. On the trip from the harbor to my house, several times he seemed as if he were going to jump out of the car, especially when a willowy "muchacha" would go by. I well remember the joy with which he tasted his first Cuban coffee after his lunch.[1]

Although Caturla was pressed to return directly to Remedios, he was eager to take advantage of the opportunity to see Sanjuán while in Havana. Caturla called on Sanjuán with the idea of arranging for a performance of his music by the Filarmónica as soon as possible. Based on Sanjuán's positive reception, Caturla wrote to the Quevedos that "at last people in Havana will know what my work is really worth."[2]

While in Havana Caturla also managed to fit in a short visit with Amadeo Roldán. They discussed the possibility of launching a concert of their own compositions the following February, based on Carpentier's latest Afro-Cuban texts including *El milagro de Anaquillé* (a ballet) and Caturla's own *Liturgia*. Brimming with confidence, Caturla wrote to Carpentier of these plans saying that he expected this concert would be "the scandal of the century . . . a true dynamic orgy."[3]

Among other last-minute details Caturla took care of prior to departing for Remedios was delivering a message to Carpentier's mother, then living in Havana. The closeness of his relationship with Carpentier is reflected in the following lines Caturla wrote to him shortly thereafter: "You know as you told me that mothers are always grateful for visits which are made in regards to their children, especially if they are away. . . ."[4] Caturla also intended to visit the Quevedos, but time ran out; instead, he left a letter for them in which he hurled some biting criticism at the conservative musicians in Havana, referring to them as "pestilence" and citing "Sanchesfuentism" (a reference to Sánchez de Fuentes's rejection of Afro-Cuban musical elements) as an example. He further blasted Sánchez de Fuentez (in reference to his latest project *Anacaona*), saying: "The poor man; fixed on the heights when he doesn't even see the beginning of the rise."[5]

With Sanjuán's commitment to perform two of his *Tres Danzas Cubanas* (*Danza del Tambor* and *Danza Lucumí*) Caturla realized some of the success in Havana he hoped for. However, *Liturgia*—his most progressive composition, the one that reflected the real cutting edge of his talent, the one he wanted most to have performed in Havana—was simply too large a project to launch at that time. Caturla's aim to purposely cause a scandal in Havana with a concert featuring *Liturgia* and Roldan's new Afro-Cuban symphonic music (something he hoped would parallel the famous premiere of Stravinsky's *The Rite of Spring*) did not materialize. However, while preparing the way for the premiere of *Liturgia*, Caturla published his controversial article "Posibilidades sinfónicas de la música afrocubana" in *Musicalia*, dedicating it to Alejo Carpentier. Caturla's article set forth his creed concerning the integration of Afro-Cuban musical sources and the symphony orchestra.

Caturla's article "Posibilidades sinfónicas de la música afrocubana" is daring, definitive, and critical of the musical status quo in Cuba. In this article, Caturla confirmed his belief that

> Afrocuban music has everything needed to definitely triumph in the symphonic genre which in turn would profit greatly by incorporating this rich and fluid vein. . . . Afrocuban music is the largest, strongest and most balanced inspiration in the new music of Cuba . . . the potency of its elements give it an undeniable aesthetic supremacy for the music of Cuba.

Continuing in the same article, Caturla criticized popular Cuban songs of the *guajirada* ("hicks") type that represented tastes of the white *bohío* (peasant hut). He stated that this music was influenced by the Italian mellifluous style of Puccini and Leoncavallo and was "cut out from within a colorless frame of a tearful Tosti aria and the morbid native bolero [a brand of Donizetti]." Before closing this article, Caturla was unable to resist a blow at Sánchez de Fuentes's *Anacaona* referring to its "sporadic outbreaks of Indian music of very arguable originality and origin." Addressing the professional musicians who denied the intrinsic value of Afro-Cuban music, Caturla had this to say in his article:

> To mobilize a drum battery in a symphony or to play maracas or bongos in a symphonic poem, or use the "tres" and the claves as well as other rhythmic and melodic elements of the typical Cuban orchestra, to make small orchestral music, constitutes for the musicians, musicologists and critics afore mentioned, the greatest blasphemy, the worst affront that can be inflicted on the music of the fatherland.[6]

As a consequence of this article, Caturla was, in his own words, "tagged as an opportunist," a view held by his adversaries in Havana. Because his article expressed his musical creed, Caturla referred to it several times later in his life in different contexts. The most notable example is in his short essay "Realidad de la utilización sinfónica del instrumental cubano," which was later published in *Atalaya*, the journal he published with his brother Othón in Remedios. Caturla considered *Musicalia* heroic for publishing his article "Posibilidades sinfónicas" and told the Quevedos they represented a "living torch of confidence and idealism" when it came to the new aesthetics of music.

Caturla's homecoming in Remedios was filled with excitement and celebration. He brought gifts from Paris for his family (especially Manuela, for whom he brought French plumed hats and dresses), and proudly shared his new success as a composer of international rank with all. Adding to the exuberance of his homecoming was greeting his baby daughter Diana (named after his mother), born shortly before his departure for Paris. Caturla's spirits were heightened even further when he received a letter from Henry Cowell that was awaiting him in Remedios. In his letter, Cowell (then president of PAAC) invited Caturla to submit his compositions to him for performances in California.

After less than a month at home, Caturla returned to Havana where he met with Sanjuán to go over the orchestral parts of two of his *Tres Danzas Cubanas* in preparation for the concert that was to take place on 9 December 1928 at the Teatro Nacional, with Sanjuán conducting and Alberto Roldán (Amadeo's brother) as solo cellist. Compared to his *Preludio,* performed less than two years before, Caturla's *Danzas Cubanas* demonstrated a significant leap in style and development in orchestration.

Reviews of Caturla's music in the Havana press were mixed. *Musicalia* issued a positive review, describing Caturla as an *"apóstol de arte moderno"* (apostle of modern art) who expressed himself with a musical *"lenguaje complicado y barroco"* (complicated and baroque language) of *"diáfana claridad"* (diaphanous clarity). The same review also mentioned the brilliant color Caturla achieved in *Danza Lucumí,* which roused the audience to applaud for it to be repeated.[7] However, Antonio Quevedo wrote a review for *Revista de Avance* that did not seem to grasp the real significance of Caturla's music. Apparently confused by Caturla's unorthodox orchestrations, Antonio Quevedo found the overall expression of Caturla's *Danzas Cubanas* "obscured" by the "predominance of technical resources." Quevedo did, however, point out in his review that Caturla was filled with healthy and youthful optimism, and "has yet much to tell us."[8]

Despite the overall success of Caturla's *Danzas Cubanas,* performances of his compositions were not frequent in Havana during the ensuing years, while his music was constantly gaining acceptance abroad.

Following the success of having his music performed by Sanjuán in Havana, Caturla resumed life in Remedios as district judge while pursuing an independent career as a composer and managing his domestic life with Manuela and his children. It was a time of great fulfillment for Caturla. He realized he had reached a higher level as a composer, describing his accomplishments in terms of "glorious beauty . . . filled with satisfaction"[9] to his brother, Othón. Caturla also told Othón that he had confirmed the positive opinions of his talent held by Carpentier and Nadia Boulanger with his *Tres Danzas Cubanas.*

THE SPANISH CONNECTION

In March of 1929, the renowned Spanish composer Joaquín Turina conducted his own music with the Filarmónica in Havana, sharing the podium with Pedro Sanjuán. Turina was also sponsored by the Instituto Hispano Cubano de Cultura to deliver a lecture on modern music at Caibarién, where Caturla worked as a lawyer. According to Caturla, Turina's lecture in Caibarién focused more on Romanticism than contemporary music, which, in Caturla's opinion, was treated superficially by Turina. However, with his published orchestral scores from Paris soon to be available throughout Europe, Caturla took advantage of the possibility of having this music performed in Spain through Turina's influence. Caturla wrote soon thereafter to Othón: "With Turina, I have managed to arrange that my *Danzas* [*Tres Danzas Cubanas*] will be played in Madrid by the orchestra of Pérez Casas."[10]

Following his meeting with Turina in Caibarién, Caturla sent his *Tres Danzas Cubanas* to the Spanish conductor Mario Mateo for acceptance as a delegate to the Festivales Sinfónicos Ibero-Americanos scheduled for the following October. The Festivales Sinfónicos were to be part of the 1929 Barcelona Exposition, a massive industrial world trade fair that also sponsored a wealth of music, including symphonic concerts. Subsequently the Diputación Provincial de Barcelona announced that Caturla's *Tres Danzas Cubanas* and *Anacaona* by Eduardo Sánchez de Fuentes had been selected for the Festivales Sinfónicos. Both composers were invited as delegates to the Exposición Internacional de Barcelona with all expenses to be paid by the Spanish government.

News of the award spread quickly; it was announced in the Havana journals *El Excelsior* and *El País* in their June 1929 issues. On the one hand, Caturla was exuberant and proud, immediately writing to Antonio and María Muñoz de Quevedo expressing his joy at becoming a delegate to the Exposición and honored guest of the "City of Nobles." On the other hand, he was dismayed and disappointed by the selection of *Anacaona* by Sánchez de Fuentez. Caturla explained his attitude about this in a letter to Alejo Carpentier expressing "irony and surprise" at having his music juxtaposed to that of Sánchez de Fuentes. He also stated in the same letter that he could not understand why the jury in Barcelona (which included Pablo Casals and Mario Mateo among others) chose, in his opinion, such "musical nonsense" and "artistic pretense" as *Anacaona* when there existed such Cuban music as *La rebambaramba* by Roldán and *Guajira Suite* by Valdés Costa. Caturla ended this letter with the suggestion that *Anacaona* was chosen because of "official pressure" and cited the fact that Sánchez de

Fuentez had recently been criticized in the current issue of *Musicalia*, something he felt Carpentier would applaud.[11]

Whether Sánchez de Fuentes's award was given out of "official pressure" or not is a moot point, since he had by then established an international reputation and was well known in the leading musical circles of Barcelona.[12] More interesting is the fact that he represented the opposite end of Cuba's musical spectrum from that of Caturla. As previously mentioned, Sánchez de Fuentes disputed the existence of African elements in the folk music of Cuba, placing him constantly at odds with Caturla. Thus the older, more conservative school of Cuban composers represented by Sánchez de Fuentes (twenty-two years older than García Caturla) collided head-on with the youngest composer to participate in the Festivales Sinfónicos Ibero-Americanos, the twenty-three-year-old delegate from Remedios, Alejandro García Caturla.

CATURLA BECOMES AN EXECUTIVE IN COWELL'S PAAC

Responding to Caturla's initial letter from Paris, Henry Cowell (as previously mentioned) invited Caturla to submit his compositions for publication in the *New Music Quarterly* of San Francisco, California, which he owned and edited. At the same time Cowell responded to María Muñoz de Quevedo's request to write something for *Musicalia* by submitting an article entitled "Compositores Modernos de los Estados Unidos." In addition, Cowell invited Roldán and Caturla to become executive members of the PAAC as soon as he became president of that organization in 1929. In response, *Musicalia* published a feature article on Cowell, complete with a portrait photo and reprint of his *Exultation,* a composition that later became a centerpiece for Caturla's concerts and lectures on contemporary music in Remedios. The interaction between Cowell and Cuban composers resulted in the most significant exchange of international contemporary music Cuba had ever seen. On a more personal level, the relationship developed by Caturla and Cowell proved to be most fruitful for both. Not only did they derive inspiration from one another's music and share their professional connections by sponsoring performances of one another's music, but each expressed their conviction about the other's music in various journals. Caturla and Cowell were geniuses of similar spirit; each a pioneer of new music driven by unsurpassable passion and energy to further their cause.

One of the first signals that Cowell would become a major influence upon Caturla was Cowell's letter from Berlin stating that Caturla's music had been "extraordinarily well received" abroad at the concert of 12 March 1929. Caturla shared this news with the Quevedos and his brother, Othón, to whom he wrote of Cowell:

My dear Godowsky; [Caturla's jocular salutation for Othón]
    You cannot imagine what a good person and friend this Mr. Cowell is. An advanced agent. Standard bearer of the new music, he is very enthused with the young Hispanic-American music and is looking for ways to develop it everywhere—because he is one of the young Yankee composers he has great influence—and he especially likes my music. I am already a member of the Pan American Association . . . and now he has asked if I would like to be an honorary member of the magazine New Music that he edits in California and has a magnificent board of directors.[13]

As Caturla's exchange of music with Henry Cowell developed, his ambition surged. Caturla lost no time taking advantage of his executive position in Cowell's PAAC to have his music performed abroad. After informing the Quevedos that he regularly received letters "from our faithful friend Cowell . . . twice from Berlin and now from London,"[14] Caturla declared that he was a ratified member of PAAC and that requests by them to submit more of his music for performance abroad had been made. It would only be a matter of months after this letter was written (1 May 1929) that performances of Caturla's music would once again come under the auspices of PAAC and he would arrange for an invitation for Cowell to come to Havana.

In the meantime, Caturla persisted in trying to find ways to have *Liturgia* published and performed. He sent the score to Sanjuán in Havana and then wrote to Manuel Ponce in Paris, asking him to thank Mlle. Boulanger for bringing this music to the attention of Alfred Cortot.[15] Caturla also tried to negotiate the publication of *Liturgia* with Maurice Senart in an arrangement for two pianos and timbales. However, all this was to no avail.

With his participation as a Cuban delegate to the Barcelona Festivales Sinfónicos now confirmed and steps already taken to also have his music performed in Madrid, Caturla worked feverishly that summer (1929) toward advancing himself to a higher status as an avant-garde composer. The recent performance of his music by Sanjuán and the Filarmónica and now an invitation from Cowell and the League of Composers of New York to submit his latest compositions for performance also fueled Caturla's ambitions. On this point, Caturla notified the Quevedos in Havana that he was planning to submit to the League of Composers in New York his latest work for piano and small orchestra—*Bembé*.[16]

Bembé is Caturla's most highly stylized Afro-Cuban composition, one that represented his concept of a new aesthetic of contemporary Cuban classical music. As to be expected, *Bembé* was among the compositions Caturla took to Barcelona, with hopes of having it performed abroad. Anxious to play a piano reduction of *Bembé* for the Quevedos, Caturla spent his last evening in Havana, prior to his departure for Barcelona, at their apartment. Their enthusiastic reception of *Bembé* strengthened his conviction that he had created a masterpiece. Little did he know that *Bembé* would become his most famous and frequently performed orchestral composition. It is not surprising that Caturla dedicated *Bembé* to "María Muñoz et Monsieur Antonio Quevedo" when it was published in Paris the following year by Maurice Senart. Following Caturla's departure, the Quevedos anxiously awaited Caturla's reviews of the Barcelona concerts and other music news from abroad for publication in *Musicalia*.

NOTES

1. Muñoz de Quevedo, Alejandro García Caturla, 10. (See also Muñoz de Quevedo, "Alejandro García Caturla," 8–14.)
2. Henríquez, *Correspondencia*, 3 de noviembre 1929, 44.
3. Henríquez, *Correspondencia*, 3 de noviembre 1928, 41.
4. Henríquez, *Correspondencia*, 1 de mayo 1929.
5. Henríquez, *Correspondencia*, 2 de noviembre 1928, 39.
6. García Caturla, "Posibilidades sinfónicas de la música afrocubana."
7. Muñoz de Quevedo, "Crítica a Alejandro García Caturla," 144.
8. Quevedo, "Orquesta Filarmónica—*Dos Danzas Cubanas*, de Alejandro García Caturla," 364.
9. Henríquez, *Correspondencia*, 3 de noviembre 1929, 44.
10. Henríquez, *Correspondencia*, 1 de mayo 1929, 45.
11. Henríquez, *Correspondencia*, 7 de noviembre 1929, 53.
12. Sánchez de Fuentes representó Cuba in 1911 at the Congreso Internacional de Música celebration in Rome; he became involved with the

Cuban National Theater in 1922 and traveled to Mexico, Italy, France, and the United States. Sánchez de Fuentes met Pablo Casals, the Catalan musician from Barcelona, in 1924, when Casals visited Havana as guest conductor of the newly established Sinfónica de La Habana.

13. Henríquez, *Correspondencia,* 1 de mayo 1929, 47.

14. Henríquez, *Correspondencia*, 29 de junio 1929, 53.

15. Caturla's connection with Cortot (Alfred Cortot became internationally famous as a pianist, specializing in the music of Chopin) was through Nadia Boulanger. Cortot and Boulanger were associated with the École Normale de Musique at that time. Caturla submitted his score *Liturgia* to Cortot (through Nadia Boulanger) before leaving Paris in the summer of 1928.

16. Apparently, Caturla did not submit this music to the League of Composers in New York after all. The original version of *Bembé* is for five instruments and piano; later Caturla expanded the instrumentation to more than double the original version.

Chapter Six

Barcelona: Festivales Sinfónicos Ibero-Americanos

García Caturla set out for Spain aboard the SS *Orduna* on 4 September 1929. While at sea the passengers were treated to a "Program de la Velada Literario-Musical" on 12 September, in which Caturla participated by playing several of his *Danzas Cubanas* at the piano. Upon arriving in the port city of Santander, where his music was scheduled to be performed, he stayed over a few days. Before leaving for Madrid, "the enchanting capital of the motherland" as he referred to it, Caturla also visited the neighboring town of Santillana del Mar.[1]

Caturla was relatively well known among music circles in Madrid prior to his arrival, thanks mainly to Alejo Carpentier and Turina.[2] As a result, Caturla was hosted by Madrid's leading musicians, including Joaquín Turina, Ernesto Halffter (Manuel de Falla's prodigy), Adolfo Salazar (musicologist and critic), Pérez Casas, Hernández Catá (conductor of the Madrid Philharmonic Orchestra), and others. The most promising aspect of Caturla's visit in Madrid was an invitation by Ernesto Halffter to conduct his *Tres Danzas Cubanas* in Seville with de Falla's Bética Chamber Orchestra.[3] Excited by the possibility of launching himself as a conductor, "one of my most immediate ambitions" (as he wrote home to his father), Caturla accepted Halffter's invitation. Caturla was quick to notify María and Antonio Quevedo of this news, stating, "I am letting you know that I am starting my career as a conductor."[4] Caturla also wrote to Sanjuán from Madrid, expressing his hopes that some day he would be entrusted to conduct the Havana Filarmónica, an engagement that never took place.

During his short stay in Madrid, Caturla discussed with his hosts various possibilities of having his music performed there and other cities in Spain. Having accepted Halffter's invitation to conduct in Seville, Caturla made arrangements to leave copies of his *Tres Danzas Cubanas* in Madrid for Hernández Catá and Adolfo Salazar, who had recently written about him in the Madrid newspaper *El Sol.*

Caturla's last days in Madrid were filled with a variety of activities, including a visit to the Cuban consulate, some last-minute sightseeing (including a visit to Goya's tomb), and a reception at which he met a number of journalists. Among them were editors from *Cosmopolis* and *Revista de Occidente* of Madrid and the editor of Cuba's magazine *Social,* Conrado W. Massaguer. Caturla also met a number of Cuban musicians who were in Madrid at the time; later, he dispatched news reports of his experiences in Madrid to Havana for publication in *Musicalia.*[5]

Upon his arrival in Barcelona on 30 September, Caturla realized what was in store for him at the Festivales Sinfónicos concerts. Unlike his arrival in Madrid, there were no welcoming parties to greet him, and he was soon lost in a crowd of foreign delegates and tourists. To make matters worse, after a long and fatiguing journey by train, the damp chilling weather that awaited him in Barcelona brought on a feverish cold.

There were many disappointments Caturla was to face after his arrival in Barcelona. First, there were changes in the concert programs, schedules, and locations for the Festivales Sinfónicos concerts that resulted in a shortening of rehearsal time. Second, Mario Mateo, the conductor chosen to direct his music, was not, in Caturla's opinion, musically qualified to do so. Third, programming for his concert was particularly disadvantageous. The program included a total of seven composers (including Sánchez de Fuentes), and required the participation of over two hundred performers. Finally, the time, place, and atmosphere for Caturla's concert could not have been worse. The concert took place on Sunday, 13 October 1929, at 5:00 P.M. at the enormous Palacio Nacional amidst multitudes of visitors roaming about viewing the Spanish art that was on exhibit in the same building. Indeed, the atmosphere of Caturla's concert must have been one of an exhibition.

The review of Caturla's music that appeared two days after the performance simply stated "the *Tres Danzas Cubanas* of García Caturla are very modern in sonority and lend themselves particularly well to the flavor of the themes."[6]

CATURLA AS MUSIC CRITIC

While Caturla was disappointed by the poor performance of his music and the general standard of the music he heard at the Festivales Sinfónicos concerts, there were many positive consequences as a result of his being there as a Cuban delegate. For one thing, publicity about his music was far-reaching, placing him in a higher status as a composer of international rank than before. One of the preconcert press notices, for example, stated: "He [Caturla] is the youngest of the Ibero-American composers and his music has awakened a lively interest in the world of new music"[7]—a profile that certainly would have pleased Caturla. Another positive outcome was his role as music critic for *Musicalia*; Caturla reviewed the first three concerts, covering eighteen of the twenty-one Iberian composers on the Festivales Sinfónicos programs. Caturla's reviews boldly rejected music that he found stylistically dated and thus musically redundant. He blasted the flow of Latin music tinged with nineteenth-century romantic nationalism and musical references to ethnic music dressed in cosmopolitan harmonies. For example, in his review of *Suite Incaica* by Teodoro Valcárcel of Peru, Caturla wrote:

> It's a pity that the Inca melodies and rhythms are so mistreated by Valcárcel. The four movements of his *Suite Incaica*, without their strictly folkloric attraction, are in construction and orchestration, a series of colorless and unresounding musical moments that remind one successively of the syrupy final chorus of the second act of *Madame Butterfly* and the dense manner and orchestration of Brahm's *Hungarian Dances*.[8]

Caturla also expressed a sense of charm, wit, and sophistication of musical literacy in his reviews. For example, he described *Argentine Scenes* by Carlos Buchardo as "overflowing with a lyricism that admirably translated the warm and spontaneous accents of the Argentinean pampa, with its jealousies, loves and sadness."[9]

Judging by the standards that Caturla set forth in his reviews, he apparently found the score of Manuel María Ponce's symphonic triptych *Chapultepec* conservative but praiseworthy. After stating that Ponce brought about a "restoration of prestige of symphonic music to the festival," Caturla went on to say, "The Triptych of Ponce is truly praiseworthy: the symphonic interweaving of counterpoint produced sensuous effects which reached at some moments of warm exaltation a peak of incredible beauty. He was acclaimed by the public with their prolonged applause."[10]

The third and final concert Caturla reviewed included his own music and that of Eduardo Sánchez de Fuentes. He alluded to this concert in his reviews by saying only: "To be scrupulous I will not comment on the aboriginal poem *Anacaona* of Sánchez de Fuentes or naturally my *Tres Danzas Cubanas*." With the exception of the Chilean composer Humberto Allende's *La Voz las Calles*, which he simply described as *"un bello poema"* (a beautiful poem), Caturla was dissatisfied with the rest of the music he reviewed at the final concert. For example, he found the Mexican composers Estanislao Mejía and Rafael Tello stale and monotonous, and the *Gran Concierto en re mayor* by Enrique Soro of Chile saturated with romanticism. From the same concert, Caturla also rejected Carlos Lavin's (Chile) *Tres Cantos Araucanos*, which were supposedly sung in an Indian dialect, saying they sounded as if they were sung in three or four languages at once and were of no interest at all.[11]

Of all composers Caturla reviewed for *Musicalia*, the one he most admired and to whom he gave special attention (including a personal interview) was Monserrat Campmany. Originally from Barcelona, Monserrat Campmany was the only woman composer on the Festivales Sinfónicos programs. Caturla described her composition *Visión Sinfónica* as "an exquisite, well constructed poem full of character." He reported in his review for *Musicalia* that "Monserrat Campmany has told me she works specially with Argentine themes, adjusting them to the pentatonic scales of the Incas which gives her work originality and unusual exoticism." After citing her *"virilidad orquestal"* (virile orchestration), which reminded him of Stravinsky, Caturla closed his review by saying her composition *Visión Sinfónica* was "a lullaby of immense sublimity reflecting clearly a sensitive femininity."[12]

CALL FROM PARIS

Amidst the pressures of supervising rehearsals of his *Tres Danzas Cubanas* for the Festivales, fulfilling formal obligations as an official Cuban delegate in Barcelona by attending banquets, conferences, and receptions, and writing reviews for *Musicalia*, Caturla's circumstances suddenly changed. He received an urgent message from Alejo Carpentier in Paris to immediately start work on two songs for Cuba's leading prima donna, Lydia de Rivera. De Rivera was to sing Caturla's new songs (proposed by Carpentier) in Paris at a special concert of Latin music in a matter of weeks. Carpentier explained to Caturla that de Rivera "begged me to ask on her behalf that you compose something for her."[13] He further explained that the texts of these songs were his own *Dos poemas afrocubanos* (*Mari-Sabel* and *Juego Santo*), adding that Caturla's name had already been announced as the composer. Ironically, since arriving in Barcelona, Caturla had already undertaken his own song on an anonymous text about "Mari-Sabel" (a popular Afro-Cuban folklore subject), and erroneously assumed Lydia de Rivera would include it on her forthcoming concert program in Paris.[14] In any case, *Mari-Sabel* marked the beginning of Caturla's new type of Cuban art song based on Afro-Cuban poetry (see figure 6.1 below) and the end of composing popular songs.[15]

Figure 6.1. *Mari-Sabel*, mm. 1–7.

The circumstances Caturla faced during his last days in Barcelona were extremely pressing. He had to be in Paris as soon as possible to complete the two new songs on Carpentier's texts, and also to complete the instrumentation of his *Bembé,* which was to be premiered at the same concert in Paris by Marius-François Gaillard.

Caturla's decision to leave Barcelona earlier than originally planned created several problems. For one thing, it meant canceling his reviews of the final Festivales Sinfónicos concert (a tribute to Villa-Lobos) for *Musicalia.* Also, he had to cancel his previous commitment to conduct his *Tres Danzas Cubanas* with Manuel de Falla's Bética Chamber Orchestra (for which he had made a special arrangement for chamber orchestra) in Seville—a circumstance that brought stinging criticisms from Ernesto Halffter and Adolfo Salazar.[16]

Somehow, Caturla managed to find time to meet Manuel Ponce and Marius-François Gaillard in Barcelona just before he left for Paris. He was anxious to discuss the instrumentation of *Bembé* with Gaillard, and discuss with Ponce some details of having his music published in Paris with Maurice Senart's firm (as previously mentioned, Ponce was one of Senart's editors). As you will see, Gaillard and Ponce were instrumental in the future success of having Caturla's music published and performed in Paris.

Caturla's hasty departure from Barcelona took place on 17 October 1929. There is no record of farewell parties this time, as was the case when he left Madrid, and he headed for Paris without his traveling companion, Manuel Ponce, as originally planned.

BEYOND BARCELONA

Following his departure from Barcelona, Ernesto Halffter conducted Caturla's arrangement of *Tres Danzas Cubanas* (a reduction from full symphony orchestra to piano and chamber orchestra) in Seville on 30 October 1929. The press in Seville responded to Caturla's music in more detail than the critics in Barcelona:

[I]n our opinion, Alejandro García Caturla unites in his *Tres Danzas Cubanas* the most contradictory qualities in such a mixture that makes it difficult, after listening to it just once, to separate the good from the bad, although the work abounds in both. It is to be said on his behalf, that these dances, the first and third in particular, offer a rhythmical power and energy which, if combined with beautiful themes, could produce good compositions. However, in this case, the weakness of the themes, particularly their harmonic progression which deliberately and aggressively search out unresolved harmonic dissonance, create such tension that one anxiously desires the end. Possibly, as years go by, this young Maestro, with otherwise excellent qualities, will rectify his procedures.[17]

The reviewer's observation about Caturla's "unresolved harmonic dissonance" is of particular interest because such procedures were already a permanent characteristic of Caturla's music.

In retrospect, Caturla wrote off the Festivales Sinfónicos as a failure. In his review for *Musicalia*, Caturla rebuked the participants of the Festivales for composing symphonic music that was "decadent and obsolete." He wrote to the Quevedos that "the major portion of the composers were worse than our Sánchez de Fuentes and Mario Mateo was totally unknown in his own Spain and is not a good conductor." On a more positive note, Caturla also wrote home to family and friends about the banquet he was to attend in Barcelona at which "kings and ministers . . . ambassadors and consulates of the Latin American Republics" would be present.[18]

Caturla's participation in the Barcelona Festivales Sinfónicos afforded him a rare opportunity to make connections with important composers and publishers and to propagate his own music and speak out as music critic against European influences in contemporary Latin American music. As a result, he was regarded in Barcelona as the younger generation Cuban composer whose highly original and dissonant musical style was undeniably Afro-Cuban in essence.

Caturla's new song *Mari-Sabel*, composed during his short stay in Barcelona, may be seen as his reaction to the type of music he criticized at the Festivales Sinfónicos. *Mari-Sabel* also established Caturla's extension of his Afro-Cuban style to a new genre: the art song. Free in form, yet held together by drumlike rhythmic motives (in this case dissonant repetitious chords for piano that function as a drum—see mm. 1–3 in figure 6.1), *Mari-Sabel* effectively exploits Afro-Cuban musical sources in the context of Caturla's daring harmonic progressions. African musical elements such as call and response (between voice and piano), complex syncopations (including absence of downbeats), and chantlike declamations for the voice are part of the changing textures. Unlike Roldán's *Danza Negra* (text by Luis Pales Matos) for voice and instruments (premiered at Gaillard's concerts in Paris the previous year), Caturla's *Mari-Sabel* captures the *aesthetics* of Afro-Caribbean culture vividly by colorful word painting, use of a wider vocal range, rhythmic textures that are more complex, and an extravagance of imagination.

NOTES

1. From Spain he wrote a card to his brother Othón saying, "Yesterday I fulfilled one of my fondest dreams. I visited Santillana del Mar, where the action in my favorite novel *Casta de Hidalgos* by Ricardo de León takes place. The old medieval town is just like the author described it, with its old homes of stone facades with the coat of arms crafted on the huge front doors." (Olga Caturla de la Maza, Caturla's first cousin, related this information to me at in an interview at her home on 3 August 1993.)

2. It was through Ernesto Halffter, codirector of the Bética Chamber Orchestra in Seville, that Carpentier made important contacts for Caturla.

3. Based on this invitation, Caturla apparently tried to negotiate a recording of his *Tres Danzas Cubanas* in Seville with Odeon Records, a project that did not materialize. He wrote home, saying: "I am hoping that soon my fellow citizens will be able to listen to my music quietly sitting in their houses in Remedios" (Henríquez, *Correspondencia*, Caturla to Juan Morenza Abreu, 23 de septiembre 1929, 59).

4. To his father: Henríquez, *Correspondencia*, 23 de septiembre 1929, 63. To the Quevedos: Henríquez, *Correspondencia*, 23 de septiembre 1929, 60–61.

5. Among the Cuban musicians Caturla met in Madrid was the Cuban pianist José Echaniz, who was also mentioned in Salazar's column for *El Sol*. Other musicians Caturla met while in Madrid included members of the Prague String Quartet, whom he heard in concert at the Teatro de la Comedia performing the recent music of Bohuslav Martinu and Fernando Ember (Hungarian pianist) and who took great interest in his music. He also met José Cubiles, Spanish pianist and head of the Madrid Conservatory. Cubiles's wife, also a pianist, was a close personal friend of María Muñoz de Quevedo.

6. *Diario de Barcelona*, 15 de octubre 1929, 9.

7. *Diario de Barcelona*, 11 de octubre 1929, 15.

8. García Caturla, "Festivales Sinfónicos Ibero-Americanos," 105.

9. García Caturla, "Festivales Sinfónicos Ibero-Americanos," 104.

10. García Caturla, "Festivales Sinfónicos Ibero-Americanos," 105.

11. García Caturla, "Festivales Sinfónicos Ibero-Americanos," 103.

12. García Caturla, "Festivales Sinfónicos Ibero-Americanos," 104. The music of Caturla and Monserrat Campmany was broadcast by WEVD, New York, Henry Cowell, director, on 19 November 1933.

13. See Henríquez, *Correspondencia*, 13 de octurbre 1929, 400–401. In the same letter Carpentier assured Caturla: "I believe this would interest you,

and be good for you. It is necessary for your name to be heard as much as possible in Paris. And as the publicity that Lydia is going to get this time is formidable, it is imperative that your name appear on the program and posters."

14. Caturla wrote to the Quevedos that he was working on *"Tres poemas"* for voice and piano "that will be sung by Lydia de Rivera at her concert on November 17 in Paris." As it turned out, that was not the case, as Caturla's third "poema" (that is, the *Mari-Sabel* composed prior to the one on Carpentier's text) was replaced on Lydia de Rivera's program by Eduardo Sánchez de Fuentes's *Canto Esclavo* (1870). See Henríquez, *Correspondencia,* 21 de octubre 1929, 79–80. Lydia de Rivera's concert actually took place on 19 November 1929 at the Salle Gaveau in Paris.

"Mari-Sabel" is an Afro-Cuban colloquialism for the name Maria Isabel or Maria Elizabeth. Several Cuban musicologists, including Hilario González and Edgardo Martín, suggested that Caturla may have written the text for *Mari-Sabel* himself. Documentation to that effect has not yet been established.

15. Caturla's last popular song was *Ingratitud* (1928), a typical Cuban criollo-bolero. He dedicated *Ingratitud* to his cousin Martica, daughter of his uncle Marcelo Caturla in Havana. Caturla wrote the words to this song, a rather sentimental love song text in a popular style.

16. Adolfo Salazar rebuked Caturla for his abrupt cancellation of the invitation to conduct his music in Seville with de Falla's Bética Chamber Orchestra. Later, when Caturla returned to Cuba, he wrote to Salazar: "I find it unfair that you write me off as an ingrate" and then apologized for missing the opportunity to meet Manuel de Falla. He also informed Salazar that he sent the recently published full orchestral score of *Tres Danzas Cubanas* to de Falla and Ernesto Halffter. For more details see Henríquez, *Correspondencia,* 23 de diciembre 1929. Caturla's acquaintance with Salazar ripened into an important friendship for both, after Salazar's visit to Cuba the following year.

17. "Alejandro García Caturla, y sus *Tres Danzas Cubanas.*" Edición Andalucía, 31 de octubre 1929, 29.

18. For "decadent and obsolete": García Caturla, "Notes From Abroad," 104. For "the major portion of the composers": Henríquez, *Correspondencia,* 21 de octubre 1929, 80. For " kings and ministers": Henríquez, *Correspondencia,* 30 de septiembre 1929, 70–71.

Chapter Seven

Return to Paris

Upon arriving in Paris, "a city unique in its class . . . unsurpassable" (in his own words), Caturla saw his name in the press and on advertisements for Lydia de Rivera's recital on the picturesque kiosks along the boulevards. Although he wrote to the Quevedos that he was "a bit more calm since the turbulent days in Barcelona," Caturla was faced with completing the music for Carpentier's *Dos poemas afrocubanos* in time for de Rivera's recital in a matter of days.[1]

Lydia de Rivera's recital might very well have been labeled "Festivales Canciones Iberoamericanas," inasmuch as the program included fifteen composers representing Spain, Argentina, Peru, Brazil, Mexico, and Cuba. And for Caturla, it may have been ironic that a number of these composers were also heard in Barcelona at the Festivales Sinfónicos, including Manuel Ponce, Villa-Lobos, Alberto Williams, and Sánchez de Fuentes. Joaquín Turina's *Soneto*, dedicated to Lydia de Rivera for its premiere, was also on the program. Cuban composers (other than Sánchez de Fuentes and Caturla) included Moisés Simons, Jorge Ankermann, and Ernesto Lecuona, who closed the program by accompanying Lydia de Rivera in two of his songs: *Andar* and *Por Allá se ha Ido*. Caturla also accompanied his own songs at Lydia de Rivera's recital, which took place at Salle Gaveau on 19 November 1929. Following the recital, Caturla wrote the following lines to his father:

> Lydia [de] Rivera's concert was a great success—there was a good turn out so she made some good money. As far as I am concerned she sang my

poems very well and for this reason people have come to congratulate me, particularly eminent critics. All my good friends were there including Carpentier who was beside himself with happiness.[2]

While in Paris, Caturla was beleaguered by his own ambition to do everything possible to further his career. Meeting musicians who could perform or influence the performance of his music, negotiating for the publication of his scores, keeping up with his dispatches as a correspondent for *Musicalia,* and corresponding with musicians in Cuba, Spain, and Italy were just some of his priorities. Added to this was keeping up with the social rounds that Carpentier had arranged, including a meeting with "the great Yankee composer" (Caturla's words) Edgard Varèse who had recently returned to Paris from New York.

Shortly after Lydia de Rivera's concert, Caturla wrote to his former teacher in Paris, Nadia Boulanger, asking if she would show his music to composers Paul Dukas and Maurice Jaubert. Caturla was also eager to invite Mlle. Boulanger to contribute an article to *Musicalia* (as he had promised the Quevedos he would do); because of conflicting schedules Caturla did not meet with Mlle. Boulanger, and neither project materialized.

Because of such an array of activities at hand, Caturla was unable to complete the new instrumentation of *Bembé* in time for Gaillard's concert at Salle Gaveau scheduled for 15 December 1929.[3] Although Caturla did finish the orchestration in time for a postponement date (21 December 1929), he decided to leave for Cuba prior to the premiere of *Bembé* so he could be home in time for Christmas. Pleas by Carpentier and others for him to stay in Paris were ignored.

The premiere of Caturla's *Bembé* in Paris was a great success. However, the enigmatic title and mixture of Afro-Cuban and diverse contemporary musical sources, including his own inventions, found in *Bembé* confused the music critics. For example, the Paris journal *Le Menestrel* reported that *Bembé* juxtaposed references to black magic, literature, music, expeditions, dances, hunts, and city luxuries:

> *Bembé* by M. G. Caturla [*sic*] is, according to the program, an Afro-Cuban movement. It is a work of Black Magic, to borrow the title of one of Paul Moraud's books. The instruments give the impression of a vi-

bration which is at the same time exasperating and monotonous. The multi-colored harmonies keep the listener's attention and according to his readings, travels and the integrity of his imagination, evoke in turn tom-tom scenes, war-like festivities, sorcerer's dances, locust hunts and the shop windows of the rue la Boëtie [address of Salle Gaveau]. Moreover, all this is by no means tedious. In order to better appreciate *Bembé*, I wish I could hear it once more.[4]

Other reviews were equally confused in coming to terms with Caturla's music, including an allusion of *Bembé* to Langston Hughes's *Weary Blues* by the Paris critic George Guy (*La Griffe*) and ambiguous references to the music of *Bembé* found in the *Courrier Musical et Théatral*.

BEMBÉ: THE APOTHEOSIS OF CATURLA'S NEW AESTHETICS OF MUSIC

No other music by Caturla, up to 1930, exemplifies his new aesthetics of music so boldly as *Bembé*.[5] Caturla's *Bembé* is a noncollaborative work that captures the spirit of Santería, a spirit that was part of his immediate environment in Remedios.[6] The musical language Caturla developed in *Bembé* is clearly influenced by aspects of primitivism, the avant-garde, contemporary composers such as Stravinsky, Gershwin, and Ives, and musical inventions of his own that evoke frenetic aspects of Santería ritual. Based on a main theme that symbolizes African music by its pentatonic structure (see figure 7.1 below), the final (Paris) orchestration of *Bembé* consists of flute, oboe, clarinet, bass clarinet, bassoon, two horns, trumpet, trombone, percussion, and piano.

Filled with shrill dissonance, complex syncopation, surprising and frequent changes of timbre—all rising and falling in coordinated polytonal sequences—*Bembé* is built upon a series of short uninterrupted instrumental episodes. Each episode develops its own rhythmic matrix that in most cases generate a "motor rhythm,"

Figure 7.1. *Bembé*, mm. 1–4.

which drives the accumulating dissonant textures to an extremely
abrasive climax (see figure 7.2 below). Caturla rationalized this procedure by pointing out his technique of using "dissonance as sys-
tems." Short variations of the main theme bring about a filigree of
passages that are stylistically inconsistent. For example, the dry
counterpoint of the woodwinds (see figure 7.3 below), clashes of
tonality in the reed and brass sections (see figure 7.4 below), and an
extraordinary moment of "jazzy" syncopation against sounds of the
clarinet (see figure 7.5 below) reflect the music of Stravinsky, Ives,
and Gershwin. The musical process and structural profile of *Bembé*
reflect Caturla's most radical transformation of musical thought.
The exigency surrounding completion of *Bembé* may account for
this; also, Caturla's obsession with Afro-Cuban culture intensified
following his return to Cuba in the fall of 1928. Such circumstances
moved Caturla to a different world, one that relates to the future
Cuban paintings of Wilfred Lam, described in part by Carpentier as
a world of "symbiotics, metamorphosis, confusions." Parallel to
Lam's great synthesis as a Surrealist, Caturla demonstrates in *Bembé*
"a close contact between tribal ritual and the cultural and artistic sophistication of the Western intellectual."[7]

PLANS FROM ABROAD

Prior to his departure from Paris, Caturla faced the issue of what was
ahead for him upon his return to Cuba. To dedicate himself solely to
music was out of the question; his growing family relied upon his
support—a circumstance that meant resuming his career as a lawyer
and judge was inevitable. When his father notified him in Paris of the
new position that awaited him as a judge in Caibarién, Caturla responded with a sense of resignation and frustration: "This will bring
about a great contrast from my life in Paris . . . the happiness of certain lives like mine depend on these contrasts *since I am still single*"
[italics mine].[8] With the reality of having to return to a career in law
on his mind, Caturla intensified his struggle for recognition abroad
with hopes of establishing a place for himself in the musical life of
Havana upon his return. A major step in that direction was having
his *Tres Danzas Cubanas* for orchestra published by Maurice Senart's
firm. Soon after Senart published *Tres Danzas Cubanas,* Caturla wrote
to his father that his music would now "go all over the world." He

Figure 7.2. *Bembé*, mm. 168–71.

Figure 7.3. *Bembé*, mm. 183–86.

Figure 7.4. *Bembé,* mm. 295–97.

Figure 7.5. *Bembé,* mm. 250–54.

also wrote to Ernesto Halffter, Pérez Casas, and Renzo Massarani from Paris, soliciting their assistance in having *Tres Danzas Cubanas* performed in Spain and Italy.

Caturla's *Tres Danzas Cubanas* became his "entrance piece" into the musical life of Havana following his return to Cuba. To prepare for this, Caturla wrote directly to Roldán, suggesting he perform the complete orchestral version of *Tres Danzas Cubanas* or his latest composition *El velorio* (The Wake).[9] Although Roldán was well disposed toward such a plan, Caturla's freshly printed orchestral score of *Tres Danzas Cubanas* (which he sent to Roldán from Paris) was not performed by the Filarmónica until the following February under the baton of Pedro Sanjuán.

As to his homecoming in Remedios, Caturla was anxious to spread the good news of his recent success while still abroad. From Paris he wrote to his brother Othón that he sent postcards to everybody, including his closest cousin in Remedios, Olga, and other members of the family. He also wrote letters to his two closest friends in Remedios, Lorenzo "Lordi" Martín y Garatea and Juan Morenza Abreu, a local journalist who kept him abreast of what was going on at home during his travels abroad.[10] In an effort to impress upon the Remedians that all went well abroad, he wrote to Morenza Abreu that "Barcelona was really as pleasant as possible" (quite a different impression from the one that he had written to the Quevedos). Knowing that Morenza Abreu planned to publish his critic reviews in the local Remedios press, Caturla wrote to him: "you can shout them like a Carpentier poem from the very popular columns of *El Rebelde* or *La Tribuna*."[11]

In coming to terms with what lay ahead at home, Caturla turned once again to the idea of improving the musical life of Remedios. With his success abroad behind him, and the possibility of conducting still fresh in mind, he made a proposal to Augustín Crespo (director of the Banda Municipal de Remedios) to that end. In his proposal, Caturla made the following points in a manner that was diplomatic, enthusiastic, and promising:

Mi buen amigo:
  I never stop thinking about ways in which to elevate the cultural level of this city [Remedios] and I would like to bring our city into the mainstream of art of contemporary music.
  As a first step I have already decided and planned conferences to be given to the girls and boys at the municipal academy . . . that you administer with so much love and confidence. . . .

As you can see by looking at the programs I am going to get them interested in the different schools until we arrive at a synthesis like Stravinsky, Schoenberg, de Falla. . . .

When I arrive I will have to talk to you, my main collaborator in Remedios, about a very beautiful project which I would like to have take place in our city. It is a very big and serious thing . . . I am telling you now so that you will be saving your energy to be my right hand with this project.[12]

The "very big and serious thing" Caturla alluded to in the above letter was the development of a concert orchestra in Remedios; one in which he envisioned himself conducting programs of contemporary music, including his own. Eventually, Caturla succeeded in carrying out his plans, but much to his bitter disappointment, not in Remedios, as he originally intended.

Caturla's departure from Europe aboard the British steamer SS *Orduna* was hurried and uneventful. In retrospect, the success of his music at Gaillard's concerts was far-reaching, for his *Dos poemas afrocubanos* and *Bembé* were eventually published by Maurice Senart in Paris; also, this music was soon heard in Havana and at concerts abroad sponsored by Henry Cowell's PAAC. As for Alejo Carpentier, his goal to advance the cause of Cuban contemporary music abroad was accomplished. His sponsorship of Lydia de Rivera to sing at Marius Gaillard's concerts at the Salle Gaveau in Paris brought forth the music of Amadeo Roldán and García Caturla, bringing both composers wide acclaim among international musicians and critics.

NOTES

1. "A city unique": Henríquez, *Correspondencia,* 26 de octubre 1929, 81. To the Quevedos: Henríquez, *Correspondencia,* 21 de octubre 1929, 79.

2. Henríquez, *Correspondencia,* 25 de noviembre 1929, 91–92. Caturla also informed his father in the same letter of his business arrangements with Maurice Senart, who had agreed to publish his recent music and future editions.

3. Rescheduling this concert was an immeasurable loss for Caturla because the original program included such important composers as Darius Milaud, Jacques Ibert, and Edgard Varèse. The program at which Caturla's music was later performed on 21 December 1929 consisted of the following: Mozart, *Serenade in C minor;* M. P. Petridis, *Concerto grosso;* A. G. Caturla,

Bembé; M. Pipkoff, *Concerto*; Marius F. Gaillard, *Images d'Epinal*; and M. Passani, *Sinfonietta*.

4. Belvaines, "*Bembé* de Caturla."

5. The term *bembé* has been defined by Fernando Ortiz as follows: "An African dance well known for quite a long time in Cuba. . . . *Bembem* is the royal jubilee or sensational festival of the Yoruba and Lucumí kings." During Caturla's time, the *bembé* was widely known, as it is today, as a public music ceremony.

6. Although Caturla himself was deeply interested in Santería ceremonies such as the *bembé*, he never became a "Santero" himself.

7. Mosquera, "Modernidad y Africanía," 44.

8. Henríquez, *Correspondencia*, 25 de noviembre 1929, 92.

9. *El velorio* was originally intended as music to be choreographed as part of *Olilé*, a ballet that Caturla never finished. It may have been inspired by the success of Roldán's ballet *La rebambaramba*. The initial pages of *El velorio* were composed during his stay in Madrid.

10. Lorenzo Martín y Garatea was trained as a paralegal (in today's language) by Caturla. Younger than Caturla, they shared a very close camaraderie, as if they were natural brothers. Of pure Spanish background, "Lordi" traveled with Caturla when he was later assigned to out of town posts as a judge. Juan Morenza Abreu, an Afro-Cuban born in Remedios, was an active journalist there. Both Lordi and Morenza Abreu later lived in exile in Miami where they died.

11. Henríquez, *Correspondencia*, 31 de octubre 1929, 84. Apparently, after receiving the Bética Chamber Orchestra program from Seville, Caturla was counting on a review in *El Sol* by Adolfo Salazar that he could forward to Morenza Abreu. However, Salazar did not review the concert. Before leaving Paris Caturla sent (as promised) the full orchestral score of *Tres Danzas Cubanas* to Salazar with a dedication. Having learned of Salazar's invitation to visit Cuba in the near future under the sponsorship of Pro-Arte Musicale, Caturla took the opportunity of soliciting his help in his and the Quevedos' campaign for new music.

12. Henríquez, *Correspondencia*, 2 de diciembre 1929, 96–97.

Chapter Eight

Eminent and Distinguished Son of Remedios

I'm from Remedios, I come from a couple from Remedios. . . . And Remedians I want to give my all to you.

Caturla, Christmas Eve, 1929

Caturla arrived in Havana from the coast of Spain on 16 December 1929. Anxious to make a full report of his recent experiences abroad to the Quevedos, he remained in the capital for a few days. During that short time he was treated as a celebrity by the editors of *Diario de la Marina* and *Carteles*, who sought him for interviews.

Because of the advance publicity of his success abroad and his role as an official delegate to the Barcelona Festivales Sinfónicos, Caturla's local homecoming was more lavish this time than it had been the previous year. The Banda Municipal de Remedios greeted him with a fanfare at the train station as an official welcoming party looked on and applauded. Family, friends, and townspeople arranged parties and other activities to celebrate the event.

In less than one week at home, Caturla was to realize the full impact of his success abroad. In a special ceremony at City Hall of Remedios, Caturla was awarded a citation on Christmas Eve, 1929, officially designating him as "Eminent and Distinguished Son of the City of Remedios." Caturla gave a speech at the ceremony that included the following passages:

For me this act, this honor is greater, more beautiful, more promising and significant than any other I have received in my artistic life. Because this piece of red earth, this old house [City Hall in Remedios] are

85

more sacred, more dear to me than the National Palace of Barcelona, the Havana National Palace, Birchard Hall of New York, the Theater of Seville, the Teatro de la Comedia of Madrid, the Salle Gaveau in Paris, the Staton Theater of Berlin, the Hollywood Bowl of California and other splendid places . . . because, oh, gentlemen, brothers who hear me, in those artistic places I could not find the essence of the village where I was born. I'm from Remedios, I come from a couple from Remedios, and my first teacher and visions of art are from here. And Remedians I want to give my all to you because there is no ungratefulness such as that toward the generous and loving land that gave us life. A thousand heartfelt thanks from the bottom of my soul, of my life and my gratitude to my people, so legendary, so traditional, so generous and great and so dear.[1]

Following this occasion Caturla was also honored with a banquet in Havana on 11 January 1929 at the Hotel Plaza by Remedians then living in the capital. He described the banquet in a letter to his closest friend and confidant in Remedios, Lordi Martín y Garatea: "Most select people. Remedians. Artists. All friends. Not one stranger. . . . Good menu. Dancing. Happiness everywhere." Caturla also mentioned in the same letter that during the banquet, Fernando Ortiz gave a speech in support of Afro-Cuban music: "Dr. Ortiz gave a marvelous speech; profound and full of truths. He talked about useful concepts for defending Afro-Cuban music and by extension, my own. Dr. Ortiz laid Sánchez de Fuentes out flat with his affirmations."[2]

While in Havana for the banquet in his honor, Caturla participated in the high society of Havana by attending a wide variety of concerts, plays, and dinners; he also enjoyed some of the latest movies in Havana (including a viewing of Lon Chaney in *The Train*). Caturla reported these activities in a letter home to his father, mentioning that he mingled with such important figures as Fernando Ortiz and the music critic from *Revista de Avance*, Francisco Ichaso. Caturla also explored various ways to arrange for performances of his music in Eastern Europe by Maestro Fitelberg, and in Cuba and Latin America by the Argentine pianist Ruiz Díaz.[3] Caturla met these musicians through Antonio and María Muñoz de Quevedo, whose apartment was by then a steady gathering place for famous musicians visiting Havana.

Despite the honors recently bestowed upon him at home, Caturla realized what was ahead, should he return to Remedios permanently. Havana was where he wanted to be, and to that end he appealed to his father, saying: "I feel like another person here in Havana which, like Paris and New York is exciting in every sense."[4] However, there was business to tend to in Remedios and domestic responsibilities concerning his own children, circumstances that compromised his freedom. Caturla expressed his frustrations with these circumstances by confiding to Lordi that Remedios engendered a state of mental anguish that drained his energies and made him feel neurotic. Such negative attitudes were not new, but the frustrations associated with them were growing in intensity and becoming an obsession.

Following his homecoming celebrations in Remedios, Caturla took action to have his music performed in Havana. He began by reminding Roldán that he relied upon him to have a complete rendition of his *Tres Danzas Cubanas* performed by the Filarmónica, a project that was eventually undertaken by Sanjuán. In the meantime, Caturla pressed Carpentier for more publicity in Havana about his success abroad, urging him to write articles for *Musicalia* and *Carteles*.[5]

With Sanjuán's commitment to perform the complete *Tres Danzas Cubanas* on 23 February 1930 confirmed, Caturla prepared for his return to Remedios. He wrote to Augustín Crespo outlining plans for a concert in Remedios, an event that included a performance of George Gershwin's *Rhapsody in Blue*, in a special arrangement by Caturla for the Banda Municipal de Remedios. However, these plans were postponed until after the performance of his *Tres Danzas Cubanas* in Havana.

Caturla returned to Remedios for less than a month, arriving on 31 January 1930. Apparently one of the first things on his agenda was to follow up on the appeal he made to his father to give up law and settle in Havana permanently as a musician. After convincing his father to agree to this plan, including partial support from him in Havana, Caturla, filled with confidence and hope, shared the good news with Carpentier. Caturla's youthful optimism filled him with enthusiasm; he wrote to Carpentier: "I'm already an editor for *Musicalia* in Havana, and when the economy improves, you'll see me over there."[6]

But Cuba's economy gradually worsened, and Caturla's workload as a judge was increased to match the demand on Cuba's judicial system, postponing his plans to move. Caturla pursued his judicial duties with great concern for problems related to juvenile delinquency. Eventually, he wrote progressive legal briefs on this problem, including one called "Medidas de seguridad para menores delincuentes," advocating training and education for troubled youths, rather than imprisonment.

After temporarily freeing himself from his judicial duties, Caturla returned to Havana hastily on 23 February 1930 in time for the performance of his *Tres Danzas Cubanas* by Sanjuán and the Filarmónica. He remained in Havana until 1 April 1930.[7]

Caturla's *Tres Danzas Cubanas* was well received at Sanjuán's concert and reviewed by Francisco Ichaso, among others. Ichaso found the new second movement of Caturla's *Tres Danzas Cubanas* (*Motivos de Danza*) "did not possess the raw emotion nor the rich folkloric qualities of the first and third [movements]." But then, he closed his review as follows:

> These three Danzas—which would have been a success anywhere because development of the daring folkloric element in them was well conceived—reveal a musician who already knows how to use popular sources for transformation into a mature work with certainty.[8]

Ichaso's ambiguous review, particularly his comments about *Motivos de Danza,* are typical of the misunderstandings Caturla's music engendered in the critics of his time—including those abroad. Caturla's use of unusual harmony, texture, and rhythmical permutations of typical Cuban musical motives left Ichaso and other critics confused. The following observations of passages from *Motivos de Danza* may reveal, to some extent, the complexity of Caturla's style and explain the basis of such confusion.

The main "motivo" at the very beginning of *Motivos de Danza* serves as a basis for the entire movement. The rhythmic and melodic fragments found therein relate to many types of Cuban folk music (see figure 8.1 below) and were later extended by Caturla as a recurring leitmotiv in *Primera suite cubana* and *Manita en el suelo.* Separated by rhythmic motives derived from the *danza* (see figure 8.2 below), the variations are short in length and narrow in range (see figures 8.3 and 8.4 below). Eventually a more lyrical "motivo" follows, played by the string section (see figure 8.5 below). Caturla brings back the opening "motivo" in yet another variation of rhythm and instrumentation as *Motivos de Danza* comes to an end (see figure 8.6 below). Caturla's skillful mixture of woodwinds and viola in unison found in this variation is but one example of his imaginative and colorful use of orchestration.

Figure 8.1. Motivos de Danza, mm. 1–5.

Figure 8.2. Motivos de Danzas, mm. 69–71.

Figure 8.3. Motivos de Danzas, mm. 85–88.

Figure 8.4. Motivos de Danzas, mm. 156–159.

Figure 8.5.   Motivos de Danza, mm. 171–181.

Figure 8.6.   Motivos de Danza, mm. 191–194.

Motivos de Danza is the longest movement of *Tres Danzas Cubanas*, reflecting Caturla's art of developing short motives into longer variation forms of his own invention; in this case, one related to a type of rondo-variation form. Caturla's creative use of form, combined with his mastery of exploiting impressionistic orchestral tone colors, results in one of Caturla's most sophisticated scores. For some reason, Caturla was never to repeat the rich and elegant sonorities to be found in *Motivos de Danza*.

Listening to Sanjuán's performance of his complete *Tres Danzas Cubanas* in Havana was an historic moment for Caturla, for it was the last time Sanjuán conducted his music; this concert was also Caturla's final audition of *Tres Danzas Cubanas* during his short lifetime. The disappointing premiere of this music at the Festivales Sinfónicos in Barcelona the previous year was now replaced by a performance that fulfilled promises of success made to his father and supporters of his music in Havana, particularly María Muñoz and Antonio Quevedo.

With the success of Sanjuán's performance behind him, Caturla worked feverishly to realize the plan, recently approved by his father, to move to Havana. To strengthen chances of being able to do that and in conjunction with his quest to become known outside of Cuba, Caturla asserted his image as an internationally recognized composer in *Musicalia,* for he was now one of their chief editors. This entailed a campaign of acquiring his published scores from Senart, distributing them internationally, and then assembling as many reviews for publication in *Musicalia* (and other Cuban journals) as possible.

Caturla started this campaign by gathering reviews of the premiere of *Bembé* in Paris the previous year and had them published in *Musicalia*.[9] The next step in his campaign was to seek possibilities of having *Tres Danzas Cubanas* performed abroad. To this end, Caturla wrote to Carlos Chávez (who had recently become director of the National Conservatory of Music in Mexico City), Henry Cowell, and Edgard Varèse, mentioning that Sanjuán had recently performed this music with the Filarmónica (he included a program in his letter to Chávez).[10]

Concerning the distribution of his music, Caturla sent multiple copies of his recently published *Dos poemas afrocubanos* to Cowell for PAAC, making available to him additional arrangements of *Tres Danzas Cubanas* (arrangements for piano solo, piano and violin, and piano and cello for the first and third *danzas*: *Danza del Tambor* and *Danza Lucumí*), and ordered copies of *Bembé* from his publisher Senart in Paris. He also placed advertisements of his music in *Musicalia*.

In addition to overseeing publicity about himself and his music, Caturla also became known as a local music critic for *Musicalia*. His reviews of orchestral concerts in Havana for *Musicalia* were consistent in style and content with his previous reviews for the Festivales Sinfónicos in Barcelona—candid and uncompromising. The only difference now was that he was challenging his own peers from the city in which he wanted above all others to be accepted. He simply dismissed

Sanjuán's *Babaluyé* on the grounds that is was not authentic Afro-Cuban music. And then, in the same review, he conceded that his former teacher demonstrated "a progressive comprehension of the spirit of this [Afro-Cuban] music." On another occasion, Caturla reviewed Havana's Orquesta Falcón. After referring to director Alberto Falcón's orchestra as "completely disoriented," Caturla issued the edict that any suggestions for improvement would be like "preaching in the desert." Before ending the review he reminded the readers of the injury Falcón was incurring upon himself, his musicians, and his audience because of his obstinate position to resist change. It is just this kind of painfully accurate candor that characterizes Caturla's reviews and explains to some degree the disenchantment of many musicians in Havana concerning his presence there.[11]

Submerged in editing for *Musicalia* while tending to judicial and family responsibilities left little time for Caturla to compose; thus, the ballet music *El velorio*, a project he wanted so much to complete, was once again sidetracked. By 1929, Caturla's professional life was divided into two worlds: one off the island, via Henry Cowell and the PAAC to propagate his music internationally, and one deep in the interior of Cuba where, as a local judge, he confronted some of the island's worst social crimes and racial prejudice. Between these two worlds there was an oasis of hope—the newly formed Sociedad de Música Contemporánea in Havana.

NOTES

1. Initially, Caturla's speech was printed in the local Remedios newspaper, *El Faro*, in 1929. Later, in 1977, Carmen Valdéz included excerpts of Caturla's 1929 speech in her article, "Alejandro García Caturla."

2. Henríquez, *Correspondencia*, 12 de enero 1930, 106–7. Another honored guest at Caturla's banquet was the president of Pro-Arte Musical, María Teresa García Montes de Giberga; she excused herself from the banquet after Ortiz's speech. In the same letter to Lordi, Caturla quipped: "Pro-Arte does not relate to my ideals or my music." It may be worth mentioning that the banquet in Caturla's honor was reported in the Havana newspapers *El Mundo* and *El País*.

3. Maestro Fitelberg was in Havana to conduct the Russian Opera. Caturla also met the young Russian tenor Michel Benois to whom he wanted to give a copy of his *Dos poemas afrocubanos*. However, the published score did not arrive from Paris before Benois's departure.

Ruiz Díaz settled in Cuba and became a leading pianist in Havana. Known for his support of avant-garde music, he performed Caturla's music in Santiago de Cuba. He became a faculty member at the Bach Conservatory of Music in Havana, established by María Muñoz de Quevedo. He was given an impressive profile in the Jan.–Feb. 1929 issue of *Musicalia.*

4. Henríquez, *Correspondencia,* 23 de enero 1930, 114.

5. Carpentier did not respond as Caturla had hoped. Instead of a "big article about me," as Caturla put it, Carpentier wrote a glowing two-and-a-half-page essay about Lydia de Rivera's success with the Orquesta Lamoureux in Paris. In it he alluded to her previous success at Salle Gaveau, mentioning Caturla's *Dos poemas afrocubanos* as *"trepidantes y sabrosos"* (deliciously exciting).

6. Henríquez, *Correspondencia,* 11 de febrero 1930, 122.

7. The complete program consisted of the following music: Glinka, *Kamarinskaia;* Caturla, *Tres Danzas Cubanas;* Mozart, *Symphony No. 40;* Wagner, *Die Meistersinger Overture.*

8. Ichaso, "Caturla: *Tres Danzas Cubanas,"* 95. "Estas tres danzas—de éxito en cualquier parte porque lo típico está tratado en ellas con audacia bien orientada—revelan al músico que ya sabe elegir lo folklórico para hacer interesantes ensayos. Etapa previa para trabajar ya decididamente sobre la materia popular y realizar con ella obra madura."

9. For the *Bembé* reviews, see *Musicalia,* January–March 1930, 60–61. It was mainly through Justo Pastor Gutiérrez Heredia and Manuel Ponce that Caturla acquired the Paris reviews of *Bembé,* which were translated into Spanish with the following introductory note: "Sobre el *'Bembé'* de Caturla—La última obra de Caturla: *Bembé,* estrenada en los conciertos Gaillard, en Paris, ha sido objeto de diversos comentarios críticos que reproducimos a continuación, por considerar de gran interés para la música afrocubana las reaciones que ésta provoca en auditores no familiarizados con ella "About the Bembé by Caturla—Caturla's latest work: Bembé, which premiered at the Gaillard concerts in Paris, has been the object of diverse critical commentaries, which we reproduce in the following, considering of interest for afrocuban music the reaction the latter produces in listeners unfamiliar with it."

10. Caturla's letter to Varèse is of particular interest, as it became an important link in the chain that led to one of his most formidable successes. After a warm greeting and an assurance that "our friendship will not cool off on account of the distance," Caturla wrote: "Did you show Mr. Poulet the score of my *Tres Danzas Cubanas*? Don't forget, my dear friend Varèse, that I also need you to show them to Mr. Stokowski and other 'ace' conductors from North America" (Henríquez, *Correspondencia,* 16 de marzo 1930, 128). One must not assume that Varèse personally contacted Stokowski on Caturla's behalf; it was through Cowell's PAAC that the connection actually

took place. Eventually, Leopold Stokowski conducted two performances of Caturla's music; one at Carnegie Hall, New York, on 30 December 1930, and another on 2 January 1931 in Philadelphia. Both concerts were performed by the Philadelphia Symphony Orchestra. The pieces performed at these concerts were *Danza del Tambor* and *Danza Lucumí* from *Tres Danzas Cubanas*.

11. García Caturla, "Filarmónica," and "Orquesta Falcon," *Musicalia* (January–March 1930): 34.

Chapter Nine

Interlude: Transition from Apprentice to Local Celebrity

The sociopolitical climate in which Caturla lived following his restless years at the University of Havana was volatile and finally led to the revolution of 1933 and overthrow of Cuba's president, Gerardo Machado. Leading up to that point, the University of Havana was closed for a period in 1930, outbreaks of violence protesting Machado became more frequent, and the sinking economy caused unemployment and poverty throughout Cuba.[1] Such were the conditions Caturla faced in Cuba as he struggled to establish himself in Havana as a professional resident musician. Although Caturla was recognized internationally as one of Cuba's leading composers of a new Afro-Cuban style of concert music by 1929, he was doomed to the life of a rural judge in his own country. He complained bitterly about his fate, but accepted his duties with pride, uncompromising justice, and commitment to the cause of social equality for the lower working class. Eventually, Caturla's determination to challenge the corruption he found in his district courts cost him his life.

CATURLA'S NEW IMAGE IN REMEDIOS

Publicity covering Caturla's success at the Sociedad de Música Contemporánea concerts and subsequent sponsoring of Cowell's music spread quickly from Havana to Remedios. Much to the chagrin of the local musicians in Remedios, Caturla was now recognized at home as an authority on contemporary music.[2] The pursuit of his ideals to raise cultural standards in Remedios, expressed so poignantly to Augustín Crespo, intensified. At the same time, however, he faced the predicament of pursuing his own goals as a composer while enforcing his duties as a judge, maintaining a growing family of his own, and keeping up with the musical life in Havana. In addition, Caturla's quest to be at the cutting edge of contemporary music abroad enlarged his already demanding correspondence with Cowell and members of the PAAC.

Caturla's personal life in Remedios remained divided between the household he shared with Manuela and their children, and that of his parents. His professional life in Remedios also remained divided between law and music. However, Caturla's image in the community changed. By the time of his twenty-fourth birthday, Caturla was the father of three children with the fourth due to arrive in a matter of weeks.[3] His reputation as a composer of Afro-Cuban music combined with his fierce defense of the lower working class (many of whom were descendents of African slaves in Cuba) as a lawyer placed him at odds with the establishment. As a result, many in his community identified Caturla as a zealot committed to social reform and an intimidating progressive idealist. His recent status as "Eminent Son of Remedios" was also part of his new image, one that was envied by his adversaries in Remedios, who eventually forced Caturla to go elsewhere to develop his progressive ideals.

INFLUENCES—INNOVATIONS—TENACITY

The musical influences upon Caturla's creative process during the period 1928–30 are manifold, coming from regional, national, and international sources. Joining the staff of *Musicalia* and becoming a board member of Cowell's PAAC and subsequently the Sociedad de Música Contemporánea in such quick succession placed Caturla in a unique position—one that influenced his vision of the future of Cuban music.

One of the most significant ways in which Caturla changed the direction of contemporary Cuban concert music was his use of musical form. Traditional song and dance forms were replaced with forms of his own invention. For example, Caturla's *Liturgia (Yamba-O)*, *Mari-Sabel* (Barcelona version), *Dos poemas afrocubanos,* and *Bembé* stretched the use of musical form to accommodate his free style of composition. There are no rules in Caturla's concept of composition, yet there is a logic that preserves the Afro-Cuban essence of his music.

Keeping in touch with the pulse of contemporary music in Havana meant, for Caturla, knowing the details of every serious concert, particularly the Filarmónica, under the direction of Pedro Sanjuán and Amadeo Roldán. Caturla was keenly aware of Roldán's success at home and abroad and vied to keep up with him on his own terms; for each step Roldán took in the development of his own Afro-Cuban music, Caturla matched it by taking one step further. However, the fact that Roldán was first to be commissioned by Carpentier (*La rebambaramba*) and first to be sponsored by Gaillard in Paris (*Danza Negra*, 1928) placed Caturla in a secondary position to Roldán. A similar situation developed when Henry Cowell had Roldán's orchestral music performed in San Francisco by Sanjuán and later Silvestre Revueltas in Mexico City (through PAAC). Such circumstances contributed to Caturla's self-consciousness as a composer; however, they also intensified his determination to gain international and national recognition as a leading composer of Afro-Cuban concert music.

MUSIC AS A CAUSE

Extremely sensitive of his public image as a composer, Caturla worked relentlessly during this short period (1928–30) to further his own cause. His cause, musically and as a judge, was imbued with a new kind of patriotism that demanded sociopolitical change in favor of lower working class Cubans.

Keeping himself well informed on racial issues in Cuba meant that Caturla read "Ideales de una Raza," the so-called black page published regularly in Havana's leading newspaper *Diario de la Marina*. "Ideales de una Raza" was edited by one of Havana's most forceful spokesmen for racial equality, Gustavo E. Urrutia.[4] Urrutia's "black page" featured polemics on racial issues, poetry and essays by Afro-Cubans, and notices about outstanding figures in Afro-Cuban pop and sports culture, such as the famous boxer Eligio Sardiñas, better known as "Kid Chocolate."

Caturla identified with the cause and ideals expressed in Urrutia's "Ideale de una Raza" editions and soon became a familiar name in his columns. As you will see, Caturla was the composer whom the editors of *Diario de la Marina* sought to introduce to the Afro-American poet Langston Hughes when he visited Cuba in 1930. The pages of "Ideales de una Raza" were filled with details of Hughes's notorious departure from New York and the ensuing confrontation with racial issues he experienced in Havana.

THE LANGSTON HUGHES CONNECTION

Caturla celebrated his twenty-fourth birthday on 6 March 1930 in Havana with his brother, Othón. It was just at this time that the main editor of *Diario de la Marina*, José Antonio Fernández de Castro,[5] and Nicolás Guillén (who was to become Cuba's national poet) were hosting the African-American poet Langston Hughes. It was Hughes's second visit to Cuba and this time he was on a mission seeking an Afro-Cuban composer with whom he could collaborate on a "black-oriented opera."[6] Wishing to assist Hughes, Fernández de Castro suggested a meeting with Roldán and Caturla for this purpose. Although Caturla was in Havana at the time, Fernández de Castro was (for reasons unknown) unable to locate him. He did, however, make arrangements for Hughes to meet Roldán, but they did not develop a collaborative relationship.[7]

Upon returning home to the United States, Hughes found a letter from Caturla waiting for him. In it, after declaring Fernández de Castro as their mutual friend, Caturla went straight to the point of identifying himself as follows:

> Fernández de Castro must have told you that I am a Cuban composer of the new generation, that I work principally in the rhythms and melodies of the black folklore of my country and thus *all the serious, mature works I have done and published until now, belong to Afrocubanismo.* [italics mine][8]

Caturla closed the letter by notifying Hughes he was sending samples of his music because he understood that Hughes was going to write something about modern Cuban composers (a piece on this topic never came to pass). After hearing Caturla's music played to him by the PAAC composer Colin McFee, Hughes was impressed. He wrote to Caturla shortly thereafter, describing his compositions as "modern and extremely interesting. . . . They have a fascinating rhythm." Hughes was particularly fond of "the one on Carpentier's poem about the *'camisa ñáñiga'*" (a reference to "Mari-Sabel" from Caturla's *Dos poemas afrocubanos*). In closing the letter, Hughes left little doubt that Caturla was just the composer he was looking for in Havana:

> I am very sorry that I didn't find you in Havana, since I heard about you there and I would have liked very much to meet you. I am asking John Alden Carpenter to send you, in Remedios, at your other address, his four *Negro Poems* and also Grant Still to send you *Breath of a Rose*, all on my texts.
>
> If some of my poems should strike your imagination, I assure you that I would be very happy to have them in your music.[9]

In the meantime, Hughes sent copies of his two books *Weary Blues* and *Fine Clothes To The Jew* to Caturla who, after thanking him, added (in English): "I am delighted with them. . . . Waiting that I could put music of mine to your very good works, I'm your truly [*sic*] friend."[10]

As it turned out, Caturla did not compose any songs to the texts of Langston Hughes. Unlike the poetry of Guillén that spawned a corpus of songs by Cuban and other Latin composers, including Caturla, Eliseo and Emilio Grenet, Amadeo Roldán, and others, the poetry of Langston Hughes was destined to remain poetry to be read and not sung throughout Latin America.[11] However, Caturla later dedicated *Sabás* (1937), the last of his four songs on texts by Nicolás Guillén, to Langston Hughes. As a result, *Sabás*, the most African of all Caturla's songs and one of Guillén's strongest protest poems, joined together the spirit of three creative artists in their fight against the social injustices of their times.

NOTES

1. For more details, see Thomas, *Cuba*, 586–602.

2. By then, his article on the fourth movement of Charles Ives's *Symphony No. 4* was published in Cowell's *New Music Quarterly* and also appeared in *Musicalia* ("Charles E. Ives 4a Sinfonia," 190–91).

3. Following the birth of his first child, Alejandro, born on 29 December 1923, were Silvino (named after his father), born on 12 February 1927, and Diana (named after his mother), born on 15 April 1928. The fourth child, Dolores, was born on 31 March 1930.

4. Urrutia, "Ideales de una Raza: Espiritu de Raza."

5. José Antonio Fernández de Castro y Abeille was born in Havana in 1897. A graduate of law from the University of Havana, he later taught courses there on the history of Cuba, specializing in Colonialism of 1823–79. He distinguished himself as a literary critic, historian, and essayist. In addition to editing for *Diario de la Marina,* he wrote for a number of "anti-imperialistic" journals including his own *Orbe.* Fernández de Castro was one of Caturla's strongest and most influential supporters in Havana.

6. Originally, Hughes had in mind a "singing play" called *Emperor of Haiti* featuring Paul Robeson; the project was abandoned. Over a decade later and after the trip to Cuba and Haiti in 1931, his play *Troubled Island* was set as an opera by the Afro-American composer William Grant Still. For details, see Ramperstad, *The Life of Langston Hughes,* 165–66, 336–37. Langston Hughes's *Weary Blues* and *Fine Clothes to the Jew* were well known by the literati of Havana, and a review of each appeared in *Revista de Avance,* 15 June 1930, 187.

7. Hughes and Roldán met at a tourist night club (*Infierno*) where Roldán played the violin and led "a rather bad ordinary orchestra playing popular hits for dancing." Roldán could not accept Hughes's invitation to sit down at his table, so he only shook hands and agreed to a luncheon the following day. In his diary Hughes described Roldán: "Roldán is what we would call a 'rhiney' negro—very light but with bad reddish hair. He is tall and beginning to be fat. Looks rather bored and heavy." (Both quotes are from Hughes, *Journals 1920–1937.*)

8. Henríquez, *Correspondencia,* 1 de abril 1930, 132. "Fernández de Castro debe haberle dicho que yo soy compositor cubano de la nueva hornada, que trabajo principalmente en los ritmos y melodías del folklore negro de mi país y que por lo tanto todas las obras serias, maduras, que llevo hechas y publicadas hasta ahora, pertenecen todas al afrocubanismo."

9. Henríquez, *Correspondencia,* 19 de junio 1930, 333. Caturla makes no reference to the receipt of the music mentioned in Hughes's letter. However, the Cuban journal *Social* published Grant Still's *Breath of a Rose* in the October 1930 issue.

10. Hughes, *Journals, 1920–1937.*

11. The sole and significant exception is the song *Canto de una muchacha negra* ("Song for a dark girl" from *Fine Clothes to the Jew*) composed in 1938 by Silvestre Revueltas of Mexico. Hughes was disappointed in the Afro-American composer Grant Still's setting of *Breath of a Rose.* He considered it "so complex that almost nobody could sing it." For details see Arnold Ramperstad, *The Life of Langston Hughes,* 175–76.

Chapter Ten

Sociedad de Música Contemporánea: Cowell and Slonimsky in Havana

In truth all of us Latin Americans are very indebted to Cowell.

Caturla to Pedro Sanjuán

Concert programs of classical music in Havana leading up to 1929 were decidedly conservative in taste. Except for the few performances of music by Roldán, Sanjuán, and Caturla, the Orquesta Filarmónica programs remained within the limits of conservative concert music, mainly of the eighteenth and nineteenth centuries. The same was true with Pro-Arte Musical Sociedad, an organization that sponsored (among other events) leading international solo celebrities of the day, such as Arthur Rubenstein and Jascha Heifitz. However, at the same time, younger musicians and intellectuals in Havana were yearning for the performance of new music. The time was ripe in 1929 to launch a project in Havana dedicated to that purpose. Realizing the urgency of such a project, María Muñoz de Quevedo and members of *Musicalia*'s staff, including Caturla, established the Sociedad de Música Contemporánea to sponsor concerts of new music in Havana. Their first step had already been taken on 5 April 1929 when *Musicalia* sponsored *una sesión de música moderna* (a session of modern music) to coincide with the visit of Joaquín Turina, who participated in the program.

Later, when the Sociedad de Música Contemporánea was officially announced in *Musicalia*, a "Profesión de fe" (profession of faith) was included, making clear their opposition to concerts of standard classical repertoire "consecrated by virtuosity," which the Sociedad considered to be nothing but recreation. The "Profesión de fe" also pointed out that the Sociedad de Música Contemporánea was not a concert society, but rather "one of cultural activities with an educational purpose," whose cultural goals could be reached only if "the artist will be at the service of art and not art to him."[1] The position taken by the Sociedad was clearly a reaction to the flow of international concerts for the upper class in Havana sponsored by Pro-Arte Musical—an organization that Caturla referred to with contempt as "pompiers."

PREMIERE OF CATURLA'S DOS POEMAS AFROCUBANOS IN HAVANA

The first of Caturla's music to be heard at the Sociedad de Música Contemporánea concerts was *Dos poemas afrocubanos*. These songs were included in the second of two *"Lieder modernos"* (modern songs) recitals presented by Lydia de Rivera on 28 October 1930, with Caturla accompanying at the piano.

The premiere of *Dos poemas afrocubanos* in Havana was an over-whelming success. Caturla wrote to Manuel Ponce (then in Paris) that the recitals were "something extraordinary," adding, "They were given in front of the 'elite' public of Havana. . . . She [Lydia de Rivera] obtained two great triumphs. . . . They [*Dos poemas afrocubanos*] were much applauded, and she had to repeat the last one [*Juego Santo*]."[2]

Musicalia published generous reviews of Lydia de Rivera's recitals, including one written by María Muñoz de Quevedo. In her review, María Muñoz explained the relationship Caturla made to Cuban folklore in *Dos poemas afrocubanos*, praising his original and refined blending of forms (*son, danza, comparsa,* rumba), sonority, imitation of the *tres*—a rustic string instrument—in certain keyboard figurations of the accompaniment, and relationship of melody and rhythm to the text (see figure 10.1 below).

More important, however, is Caturla's own perception of his *Dos poemas afrocubanos*. Writing to Cowell (in English), Caturla explained that *Dos poemas afrocubanos* represented "a new form of mine of Cuban Song," pointing out that he integrated a "fantastic negro-monodia" in the second song of the set, *Juego Santo* (see figure 10.2 below).[3] Caturla's innovative use of form, assimilation of Afro-Cuban dance rhythms, and use of dissonance as rhythm found in these songs remain unsurpassed in twentieth-century Cuban music.

Figure 10.1. *Mari-Sabel.* mm. 5–8.

Figure 10.2. *Juego Santo*, mm. 39–46.

CATURLA'S ROLE IN THE
SOCIEDAD DE MÚSICA CONTEMPORÁNEA

Following the success of his *Dos poemas afrocubanos* in Havana, Caturla resumed working as a lawyer in Remedios; he kept pace with the Sociedad by frequent visits to Havana and an extensive, continuing correspondence with all the affiliates, including Cowell and the PAAC. By then, Caturla's music was known to Cowell, who planned to publish and perform Caturla's scores (already sent to him by Caturla) in the United States. Realizing the potential of an exchange program between PAAC and the Sociedad, Caturla negotiated invitations by the Sociedad to have Cowell, and later Nicolas Slonimsky, director of Cowell's New Music concerts abroad, come to Havana.

Cowell's debut in Havana consisted of two piano recitals of his own music at the Salón del Hotel Ambassador (23 and 26 December 1930); later, Cowell performed his *Concerto for Piano and Orchestra* with the Orquesta Filarmónica under Pedro Sanjuán. Clearly, Cowell was now an influential figure in the development of Cuba's contemporary music. Members of the Sociedad hosted him with genuine Cuban hospitality, including visits to local clubs to hear "Negros Typical Orchestras" (in Caturla's words) play, sing, and dance. Cowell experienced, firsthand, the type of music that he later described in his article "The 'Sones' of Cuba." He also heard Caturla play his new *Son in E♭* for piano solo at the home of the Quevedos, a composition that Caturla later distributed to Cowell and members of the PAAC.

Less than three months after Cowell's debut in Havana, the flamboyant Nicolas Slonimsky appeared in Havana, thanks to Caturla's arduous efforts. A special chamber orchestra was assembled by the Sociedad to accommodate Slonimsky's extraordinary concerts of new music—including the premiere in Cuba of Caturla's *Bembé*.

The success of Caturla's *Bembé* at Slonimsky's second concert (21 March 1931 at the Salón del Hotel Ambassador) was formidable. In the spirit of warm friendship and camaraderie, Caturla shared the success of this occasion with Cowell in a letter written in his English:

Slonimsky two concerts: WONDERFUL, SPLENDID. The public enthusiastic. The musician very very well. . . . Excellent the Slonimsky conducting. He is a very good friend of mine, and also of you, and the Quevedos. He amused very much here. . . . Do you remember? And he saw to play to sing and to dance the Negros Typical Orchestras, the same that you.[4]

Caturla's meeting Slonimsky in Havana established the beginning of a long and important artistic relationship; while this relationship was at times troublesome for both, the results were most rewarding for Caturla. For example, not only did Slonimsky conduct the first performance of *Bembé* on Cuban soil, but he also introduced Caturla's music to audiences in the United States, Europe, Mexico, and Latin America.

NEW FRONTIERS

As a result of negotiating the visits of Cowell and Slonimsky, combined with the success of his music abroad and at the Sociedad de Música Contemporánea concerts, Caturla was catapulted into a challenging new role. He was now an acclaimed "Cuban modernist" (*Boston Globe*) whose "electrifying" Afro-Cuban music advanced his "cultural mission" (*Musicalia*). At the same time, Caturla established himself as an effective entrepreneur intent on sustaining his success abroad through the international channels of Cowell's PAAC and connections he made through Alejo Carpentier in Paris.

Implementing his executive role in Cowell's PAAC, Caturla initiated a barrage of publicity to promote performances and publication of his music abroad. A variety of his scores (including *Tres Danzas Cubanas, Dos poemas afrocubanos, Bembé, Bito Manué* and *Son in E♭*) had already been sent to Cowell, Slonimsky, and others, resulting in performances of his music in Berlin, New York City, Stanford, Boston, San Francisco, and Los Angeles.

Eager to utilize the success of these performances, Caturla also sent his scores to Carlos Chávez (through the League of Composers), Edgard Varèse, Adolfo Salazar, Nadia Boulanger, Manuel Ponce, Manuel de Falla, Charles Ives, Colin McFee, and others. Caturla solicited these musicians for opinions of his music; he also sought connections through them for future performances of his music.

CATURLA'S CHANGING DISPOSITION

While Caturla's music was gaining recognition abroad, his reputation as a progressive composer of Afro-Cuban music spread throughout Cuba. He praised the people of Santiago de Cuba for taking interest in his type of music: "It is necessary that we all contribute to the well-being and growth of the fatherland; some making politics, others music, others journalism, others athletics, in all, the growth of the 'parts' for the enlargement of the whole."[5]

Such postulations were to be expected because Caturla's perception of himself as a composer related directly to his patriotic cause. He also perceived himself as superior to his peers in Havana, bragging of his success abroad while criticizing their music:

> At the age of only twenty-four I already have my main work published, due largely to the two trips I have made to Europe, which gives me an advantage over him [Roldán]. . . . It seems to me that Peter [Sanjuán] has *denaturalized* himself. A case analogous to that of Joaquín Nín who is not recognized as genuine in Cuba nor in Spain either. The first [Sanjuán] in treating our "Afrocuban music" has introduced into his stock such a hybrid that it will spoil somewhat his fame as a Spanish composer and count him out among the Spaniards and criollos here.[6]

Such rhetoric reveals Caturla's defensive disposition at a time when he passionately yearned to be in Havana. As previously noted, his main musical lifelines in Havana were María Muñoz and Antonio Quevedo; through them, and their publication *Musicalia*, Caturla reached out to a wide circle of Cuban supporters as his music gained recognition abroad.

At home, Caturla took on the role of music educator, bringing Cowell's innovative music to Remedios and Caibarién. Shortly after Cowell's departure from Havana, Caturla presented a series of lectures on his music at the Municipal Academy of Music in Remedios and Caibarién. In his lectures Caturla explained specific technical aspects of Cowell's piano music by analyzing and playing such compositions as *Exultation, The Banshee, The Harp of Life, Fabric,* and others. He also spoke of Cowell's unique place in the world of modern music from the perspective of Cowell's creative process.[7]

Among the many musicians to whom Caturla sent printed announcements of his lectures in Remedios on Cowell was Sanjuán. He included a note saying: "In truth all of us Latin Americans are very indebted to Cowell and I—for my part—am doing everything possible to reciprocate to whatever degree in my power."[8]

NOTES

1. Muñoz de Quevedo, "Sociedad de Música Contemporánea," 19–21.

2. Henríquez, *Correspondencia*, 1 de noviembre 1930, 155.

3. Caturla to Cowell, 2 February 1930, from García Caturla, "Correspondencia inédita."

4. Caturla to Cowell, 24 March 1931, from García Caturla, "Correspondencia inédita." He also wrote to his father in Remedios: "Yesterday I had a great triumph with the debut of *Bembé*. My work was much applauded, and brilliantly performed by the professors of the Sinfónica. . . . Slonimsky is very cordial and an excellent musician. I have very good relations with him" (Henríquez, *Correspondencia*, 22 de marzo 1931, 189).

5. Henríquez, *Correspondencia*, Caturla to Ramírez Brunet, 3 de febrero 1930. The Argentine pianist Ruiz Díaz performed Caturla's music in Santiago de Cuba.

6. Henríquez, *Correspondencia*, Caturla to Antonio Quevedo, 29 de agosto 1930, 144. Caturla later wrote to Antonio: "At last Cowell has decided to express himself in public that he finds more talent in me than in Roldán and that my work is more sincere" (see Henríquez, *Correspondencia*, 12 de febrero 1931, 179).

7. Caturla's lectures on Cowell's piano music concentrated on background and influence—specifically the sonorities of Chopin and textural possibilities in the keyboard music of J. S. Bach—polyrhythmic content, vertical and horizontal aspects of harmonic progression, and Cowell's innovations, such as tone clusters by use of the arm and forearm for key presses, exploiting the harp sonorities of the piano with and without melodic piano figures, chromaticism combined with harplike glissandos, percussive use of the piano, and devices used for *grandiosa explosión sonora* (magnificent sonorous explosion). (For details, see "Crítica Musical," *El Faro*, 15 January 1931, 3. Also lectures given on 22 January 1931, 3–6; and 2 February 1931, 3.)

8. "Crítica Musical," *El Faro*, 15 January 1931, 3.

Chapter Eleven

Bound to the Interior

CATURLA'S HOPES FOR A FULL-TIME MUSICAL CAREER IN HAVANA: A LOST CAUSE

Following a previous discussion with his father (mentioned earlier) about moving to Havana, Caturla appealed to a close friend and confidant of the Caturla family, Juan Pérez Abreu de la Torre, for support before confronting his parents with a proposition that he would drop his career in law and move to Havana permanently to pursue a career in music.[1] In the meantime, Caturla applied to Antonio Quevedo for a teaching position at his and María's newly established Bach Conservatory in Havana. Caturla appealed to the Quevedos, saying, "you will be helping me . . . so that my musical star won't be lost in the obscurity of a third class judicial post and the dullness of correctional sentencing."[2]

Quevedo responded to Caturla by advising him to study abroad (possibly with Ravel), warning Caturla that, by staying in Cuba, even Havana, he would ruin his artistic life. Quevedo cited the case of Roldán, who, in his opinion, was doomed to failure for that very reason. In the same letter, Quevedo also pointed out that Caturla's parents "should not spoil forever a temperament of unequivocal musical force" by denying him their support.[3] In addition to applying to Antonio Quevedo for a position in Havana, Caturla considered returning to Paris for two years, counting on legal fees owed him by the government to cover living expenses. However, the declining condition of the Cuban economy forced him to abandon such plans.

Concerning the disposition of Caturla's parents, they stood firm by their original agreement to help him and Othón settle in Havana. In a long letter to his sons, Silvino García expressed understanding and compassion, concluding with the following sentiment: "It burdens me to see you vegetating in this old city [Remedios] without horizons or stimulation for youth. . . . Struggle, both of you, to remain there [Havana] and make your way."[4]

Silvino García's willingness to support his sons was sincere, but the ever-worsening political and economic climate that pervaded Cuba at that time rendered such plans impossible. Upon completion of his studies at the University of Havana, Othón, like his older brother, was assigned judicial duties in the interior of the island. In the meantime, Alejandro's ultimatum to his parents about settling in Havana disintegrated. Although he was destined to remain bound to the interior of Cuba, Caturla continued to export his music beyond the island, enhancing his international reputation as one of Cuba's most progressive young composers. While he was unable to settle in the capital, Caturla traveled to Havana as frequently as possible in quest of his musical cause.

THE PEOPLE'S POETRY MEETS THE PEOPLE'S VOICE: *MOTIVOS DE SON* AND *BITO MANUÉ*

By 1930 Caturla's entourage of progressive intellectuals in Havana was formidable; among them was José Antonio Fernández de Castro. In addition to supporting Caturla through *Diario de la Marina*, *Revista de La Habana*, and in his own publication *Orbe*, Fernández de Castro prompted the initial correspondence between the Cuban poet Nicolás Guillén (then on the staff of *Diario de la Marina*) and Caturla.

Among the many Cuban poets and writers Caturla met, none—with the exception of Alejo Carpentier—would have such an enduring influence upon his creative life as Nicolás Guillén. While Carpentier expressed the exotic qualities of *Ñáñigo* and *Lucumí* Afro-Cuban culture in his poems (such as *Dos poemas afrocubanos*) in a highly sophisticated style, Guillén wrote directly about the lower working class in his negrista poetry that emphasized the use of *jitanjáfora* (an extrasemantic phenomenon exploiting sound and rhythm in language). Aesthetically, Guillén's poetry related directly to the world in which Caturla lived and worked; but more important, it was protest poetry that cried out for social change. And in that respect, it exemplified Caturla's concept of Afro-Cubanismo.

The creative spirits of Caturla and Guillén were immediately bound together by the publication of Guillén's folk poetry *Motivos de Son*, which first appeared in Gustavo Urrutia's "Ideales de una Raza" section of the *Diario de la Marina* on 6 April 1930. Writing to Langston Hughes about *Motivos de Son*, Guillén stated emphatically: "they caused a real scandal, since they are a completely new genre in our society."[5] Later, Guillén stated in an interview: "No hay poesía negra, ni mucho menos el llamado Afrocubanismo [There is no such thing as a negro poetry, much less one called Afrocubanismo]."[6] Unlike the Minorista poets (Carpentier and José Tallet) Guillén was a mulatto, and the source and inner meaning of his *Motivos de Son* sprang directly from the black sector of Cuban society, real-life experiences, and family history (his father was shot to death in 1912 because of his affiliation with a political party of color). As a result, Guillén expressed a true picture of racial prejudice in his poems and not a caricature based on the novelty and exoticism of black culture, as found in the poetry of the Minoristas.

Once Guillén was notified by Fernández de Castro of Caturla's enthusiasm about his *Motivos de Son*, Guillén sent Caturla a special edition of these poems. Caturla responded to Guillén: "In our country few are the poets devoted to the new movement, especially Afro-Cubanismo, which in music as well as in art in general, I will always consider to be the most powerful and rich of artistic sources."[7] Continuing in the same letter, Caturla acknowledged their mutual disposition as artists, but with the difference that he needed Guillén and not the other way around—a reference to his isolation in Remedios. After explaining in a letter to Guillén his desire to set *Motivos de Son* to music, Caturla laid the grounds for collaborating with Guillén on a larger work, possibly an ethnic poem with six or eight cantos for choir and soloists—a project that never developed.

Besides *Motivos de Son*, Caturla took an interest in two earlier poems of Guillén's—*Mujer negra* (Black woman) and *Pequeña Oda a Kid Chocolate* (Small ode for Kid Chocolate)[8]—asking Guillén to send copies of them to him in Remedios, which he did. Excited by the news of Caturla's enthusiasm over his poetry, Guillén, believing that Caturla had already started setting *Motivos de Son* to music, wrote to him: "I am truly desperate to know the work, which must be as magnificent as is everything else of yours."[9]

Caturla answered enthusiastically, announcing that he had already finished one of the *Motivos* that could be used for publicity in the Havana journals such as *Social* or *Musicalia* or even abroad in Cowell's *New Music Quarterly*. Such publicity could be used to advertise the remaining poems as a suite for voice and orchestra. Ironically, Caturla chose "Tú No Sabe Inglé," from *Motivos de Son*, the very one he considered excluding at first, changing the title to *Bito Manué*.[10] Upon completion of *Bito Manué*, Caturla sent a copy to Henry Cowell with the idea of having it performed abroad at a PAAC concert. Shortly thereafter he sent another copy of *Bito Manué* to Manuel Ponce in Paris where it was published by Maurice Senart the following year with a dedication to the American soprano Radiana Pazmor.[11]

During a lull in correspondence over the following four months, Guillén wrote a new *Canto Negro* [*Yambambó*] and published it, in the *Diario de la Marina* "Ideales de una Raza" section (as before) with a dedication to Caturla; subsequently, Guillén sent a copy of his new *Canto Negro* to Caturla's address in Remedios. Perplexed by Caturla's silence, Guillén inquired among his friends in Havana as to his situation. Realizing Caturla's unhappy circumstances, Guillén wrote to him as follows:

> What's with your life, brother? . . . I see that you are a Judge over there, and I feel sorry for you. I suppose that you must feel more of a prisoner than many of those you sentence, since I don't believe that a man such as you avails himself well in the exercise of so small a discipline.[12]

In concluding the letter, Guillén made clear how eager he was to know more of Caturla's music (citing his admiration of *Danza del Tambor* in particular) and expressed hopes they would soon meet in Havana. Caturla answered immediately announcing the possibility of having *Bito Manué* performed abroad through Cowell's PAAC connections and plans to have a complete edition of his settings of *Motivos de Son* published in Paris by Maurice Senart. Undoubtedly, Caturla was sincere about such plans, but the fact is, by then, he had completed only one of Guillén's *Motivos de Son*—"Tú No Sabe Inglé" (*Bito Manué*).

Following the publication of *Bito Manué* by Senart in Paris, Fernández de Castro published a glowing tribute to Guillén and Caturla in his publication *Orbe*, which included a reprint of the first page of the *Bito Manué* (see figure 11.1 below).

Figure 11.1. *Bito Manué*, mm. 1–15.

Unlike his previous songs on Carpentier's texts (*Dos poemas afrocubanos*), *Bito Manué* is not based on Afro-Cuban rhythms such as the *Son*, rumba, or *comparsa.* Instead, Caturla expressed the social issue characterized in Guillén's poem with freely invented rhythms that provided him a way to superimpose the melodic line over an extended rhythmic ostinato, building tension throughout.

Short and dynamic, *Bito Manué* is filled with piercing dissonance, rhythmic cross currents in 3/2 meter (hemiola), assertive syncopation, and exciting, sudden upward shifts of tonality that bring this miniature to a startling conclusion. Caturla's musical delineation of character in *Bito Manué* is vivid; while his syllabic setting of Guillén's stinging words brilliantly emphasize the poet's call for social change, Caturla made no attempt to follow the rhythm of Guillén's poem.[13]

CONFLICT OF INTERESTS: ROLDAN'S *MOTIVOS DE SON*

The intensity of Caturla's commitment to Guillén (and himself) that he would set the complete *Motivos* to music surfaced in April 1931. By then it developed that Roldán finished the complete set of Guillén's *Motivos de Son* ahead of Caturla in an arrangement for chamber orchestra and voice. Stunned by this, Caturla wrote to Guillén:

> Yesterday I had the unpleasant news that Roldán has finished his musical adaptation of your 8 Motivos de Son which I had also started to set to music. In effect, these are already in the hands of our handsome compatriot Lydia de Rivera who plans to perform them shortly.
>
> As I told you, I have only finished Bito Manué, which is being edited by my publisher in Paris; in view of this news (confirmed, naturally), I have decided to stop the composition of the rest. . . . Bito Manué will remain published as an Afrocuban poem for voice and piano and we will work together on any other poems of yours that are still unpublished and written for this express purpose, so that this won't happen again.[14]

Little is know about the genesis of Roldán's *Motivos de Son*. Guillén was not aware that Roldán was working on a musical setting of his *Motivos* at the same time as Caturla. Much later (1962), Guillén left the following details about this issue:

> The interesting thing about this case is that I never received a line from Amadeo Roldán. Unfortunately, we had very little contact and he always seemed to me a withdrawn and difficult man. Roldán worked on the Motivos as a "Res Nullius," which, of course, didn't bother me at all. I told as much to Caturla, from whom I could never know if he thought I had asked the composer of La Rebambaramba to undertake an effort parallel to his. Something else; where is the work begun by the talented musician from las Villas [Remedios]? That he accomplished his objective is, at least technically, a fact to be assumed if we take into account what he himself says, as we have seen in one of his letters. "The rest I am revising to have it published later on in a special edition. . . ." Has this work been lost? Was it perhaps destroyed by Caturla himself when he realized the futility of a task already accomplished by his formidable rival?[15]

Although Guillén's questions remain unanswered, it is unlikely that Caturla destroyed what work beyond *Bito Manué* he may have done on the *Motivos;* he did produce *Mulata* (number three in *Motivos*) in 1932.

Prior to the completion of *Mulata,* Caturla wrote to Carpentier, saying, "I don't want to leave off without finishing all the *Motivos de Son.*"[16] Although Caturla did not finish composing the entire set of Guillén's *Motivos de Son,* he did go on to set one more poem of Guillén's, as previously mentioned: *Sabás* (from the collection *West Indies Ltd.* of 1934), dedicated to Langston Hughes. Caturla and Guillén remained close friends, and Caturla's wish that Guillén provide him texts for a large work did not diminish. Guillén captured a glimpse of their rare relationship in his reminiscences, written after Caturla's death:

> I have a kind and gentle memory of Caturla. Although we were not friends who had daily contact, we saw each other every time he could shake off the judicial yoke and escape to Havana. He was nervous, restless, a talker, persuasive. His mind shone, full of projects related to music, his obsession. His blue eyes, a little crossed, swam in a sweet, childish, innocent pool. Sometime we had dinner together and afterward took long walks around old Havana, which he loved so much. He constantly encouraged me to write a work "of great breath," about which we were always planning to sit down and talk as soon as he could free himself from his oppressive provincial post.[17]

Caturla's collaboration with Guillén strengthened his musical cause, a cause (as already mentioned) committed to social justice and cultural liberation from stagnant traditions. No other poet evoked such forceful, passionate music from Caturla as Guillén.

SLONIMSKY CONDUCTS *BEMBÉ* IN PARIS

Less than a year after Caturla's involvement with Guillén's *Motivos de Son,* Slonimsky achieved great success in Paris with a repeat performance of Caturla's *Bembé*—"Movement Afro-Cubain," at Salle Gaveau on 11 June 1931. The performance was part of a PAAC festival that was announced in Paris:

UNDER THE AUSPICES OF THE PAN AMERICAN
ASSOCIATION OF COMPOSERS

Thanks to Alejo Carpentier, a full account of this event was published in the Cuban journal *Carteles*. Entitled "Dos Festivales de Música Cubana y Americana," Carpentier's article emphasized the fact that such musical celebrities as Henri Prunières (musicologist), Arthur Honegger, Alexandre Tansman, Sergey Prokofiev (who had recently visited Cuba), Marius-François Gaillard, Arthur Hoeré, Edgard Varèse, and others were in the audience. And after praising the "unsurpassed instrumentalists" of the Straram Orchestra who performed the concert under Slonimsky's baton, Carpentier offered his own perspective of Caturla's *Bembé*:

A few moments later, in the same program, one could hear the first bars of Alejandro García Caturla's *Bembé*, whose promoter I am in a certain way since it was written at my request to be performed at the Gaillard Concerts two years ago. What good fortune that *Bembé* has! It must be believed that its title, which refers to an Afro-Cuban dance banned by the police, has brought magical luck to it. The critics in Boston, New York, Havana and Paris have saluted it as the biblical waves opening before the holy hordes. Despite the fact that its construction presents some imperfections, and its orchestration is occasionally somewhat excessive, this work surprises every audience because of its freshness, its rhythmic movement and the striking irony of some of its central motifs. I can state that during its performance at the Slonimsky concerts, the great Arthur Honegger after hearing it was visibly surprised. The critic and composer Arthur Hoeré declared it simply *épatante* [Paris slang that means "way out," fenómeno].[19]

Apparently Carpentier's concept of a *bembé* was not the same as Caturla's, who observed and understood the significance of this ceremony since childhood from a completely different perspective. In any case, having his music performed at a PAAC Festival in Paris and the resulting publicity could not have come at a better time for Caturla. Shortly thereafter, he intensified his efforts to settle in Havana; at the same time, Caturla strove for his greatest success by committing himself to the reorchestration and debut in Havana of his earlier *Liturgia*, now renamed *Yambo-O*.

NOTES

1. Juan Pérez Abreu de la Torre was president of the Caibarién branch of Havana's Instituto Hispano Cubano de Cultura. A wealthy Mexican lawyer, he lived in Remedios in a grand house by the Parque José Martí close to the Caturla residence. Juan Peréz Abreu was an important patron of the arts in the district and influenced Caturla's father to finance his son's first trip to Paris in 1928. Among the many artists Juan Peréz Abreu hosted at his house was García Lorca, whom he sponsored at the Instituto Hispano Cubano de Cultura at Caibarién in 1930.

2. Henríquez, *Correspondencia,* 19 de augusto 1930, 142.

3. Henríquez, *Correspondencia,* 23 de augusto 1930, 337.

4. Henríquez, *Correspondencia,* 24 de marzo 1931, 349–50.

5. See Hughes, *Journals 1920–1937,* letter from Guillén, 21 April 1930. Guillén's Cuban biographer, Angel Augier, had this to say about the first publication of *Motivos de Son:* "It is possible that neither before nor after has a collection of poems provoked a greater journalistic stir in Cuba" (see Ellis, *Cuba's Nicolás Guillén,* 64).

6. Guillén went on to say in the same interview: "Mi poesía no ha hecho más que incorporar la sensibilidad del negro a las formas Hispánicas de la cultura aportadas por el blanco [My poetry has done nothing but to incorporate the negro sensibility to the Hispanic forms of culture brought by the white man]" (see Guillén, Nicolas."No Hay Poesía Negra," Vanguardia 1).

7. Guillén, *Prosa de Prisa,* 41.

8. "Kid Chocolate" was the "ring name" of Eligio Sardiñas, born in Havana, 1910. He won 100 amateur fights (86 by knockout) before his eighteenth birthday. Sardiñas left Cuba for New York and fought his first fight in Madison Square Garden late in 1928. He became quite popular in New York and was something of a national hero at home. When Sardiñas retired (around 1938), he held both the Featherweight and Junior Lightweight championships. . . . 'Small Ode to a Black Cuban Boxer' was written for Sardiñas and originally entitled 'Small Ode for Kid Chocolate.' Guillén himself referred to 'Small Ode for Kid Chocolate' as 'my first *black* poem'" (see Márquez and McMurray, trans., *Guillén: Man Making Words,* 200).

9. Henríquez, *Correspondencia,* 10 de mayo 1930, 328.

10. "Bito Manué" is a nickname for "Victor Manuel," who represents the typical flirtatious Afro-Cuban whose image Guillén ridicules in "Tú No Sabe Inglé" for boisterous behavior and the pretentious use of a few words in English to attract American female tourists.

11. Radiana Pazmor was a close friend of Henry Cowell's and an affiliate of PAAC.

12. Henríquez, *Correspondencia,* 8 de octobre 1930.

13. Later in an interview, Guillén was asked to comment on the musical settings of his *Motivos de Son* by Eliseo Grenet, Roldán, and Caturla. Guillén

responded: "¡Uy, eso sí es serio! ¡Qué sé yo! No sé nada de música. A lo mejor, estoy equivocado, pero pienso que Eliseo y Neno se dejan llevar por el ritmo del poema. En cambio, Caturla y Roldán resisten un poco más. Digo, no sé. [Say, that is serious! What do I know? I know nothing about music. I may be mistaken, but I think that Eliseo and Nene allow themselves to be carried away by the rhythm of the poem. On the other hand, Caturla and Roldán resist a little more. But say, What do I know.] ("See "Roldán, Caturla, Yo. . . .")

14. Henríquez, *Correspondencia,* 5 de abril 1931, 320.

15. Guillén, *Prosa de Prisa,* 45.

16. Henríquez, *Correspondencia*, 27 de octubre 1931, 237.

17. Nicolás Guillén, *Prosa de Prisa*, 45.

18. "Sous les auspices de la Pan American Association of Composers, deux concerts de musique, americaine, cubaine, & mexicaine, sous la direction de nicolas slonimsky, directeur du Chamber Orchestra of Boston." The first concert included music by Adolph Weiss, Charles Ives (*Three Places in New England*), Carl Ruggles, Henry Cowell (*Symphony*) and Roldán (*La rebambaramba*). The second concert included music by Pedro Sanjuán (*Sones de Castilla*), Carlos Chávez, Carlos Salzedo, Alejandro García Caturla (*Bembé*), Wallingford Riegger, and Edgard Varèse (*Integrales*).

19. Carpentier, "Dos Festivales de Música Cubana y Americana."

Chapter Twelve

Rebirth of *Liturgia: Yamba-O*

YAMBA-O—THE ZENITH OF CATURLA'S AFRO-CUBAN ORCHESTRAL MUSIC

Caturla's unbridled drive to establish himself in Havana as a professional musician remained unabated, despite family circumstances that bound him to live in Remedios. He was still possessed by the idea of creating a musical "hit" that would shock the conservative Havana concert audiences and cause a scandal. The music initially intended for such purpose—*Obertura Cubana* and *Liturgia*—had already been composed but remained unknown in Havana.

Anxious to have Pedro Sanjuán conduct *Liturgia* in Havana, Caturla met with the maestro just prior to his departure to conduct abroad. Although Sanjuán promised Caturla he would conduct *Liturgia* (suggesting that Caturla change the title), he left Havana for Spain (August 1931) and remained out of Cuba for over three months.[1]

Aware that Sanjuán's departure might be final, Caturla saw this as an opportunity to negotiate the premiere of *Liturgia*, now retitled *Yamba-O*, with Roldán and the Filarmónica; he also hoped for a steady position in the Filarmónica as violist.[2] Writing home to his father, Caturla summarized his plans: "If the idea of Sanjuán becomes definite, I will be in place to aspire to assistant conductor of the orchestra with Roldán as the main conductor."[3] As it turned out, Sanjuán did indeed return, and Caturla's position as violist with the Filarmónica was temporary.

In the meantime, a steady means of income had to be established if indeed Caturla were to remain in Havana. Caturla took action by applying for a position as music critic at *Carteles* (with the support of the editor, Conrado Massaguer) and another position as piano accompanist of classical music on the Majestic radio program, neither of which materialized.[4] However, Caturla assured his father that if he could only remain in Havana for three or four months this time (beginning September 1931) he could secure a permanent position.

Surrounded by such circumstances, Caturla began the formidable task of reorchestrating *Liturgia*. Although Caturla adhered to his original idea of having Carpentier's poetry recited or chanted as part of the performance as late as May 1931, for practical reasons, he finally abandoned that idea. In essence, he transformed *Liturgia* from a theatrical dramatization of Carpentier's poem (with two male choruses projecting the text over the orchestra with megaphones—as already mentioned) to *Yamba-O,* a purely instrumental symphonic poem. Caturla completed the reorchestration of *Yamba-O* in just over one month—a remarkable pace.

As rehearsals of *Yamba-O* began, Caturla informed Alejo Carpentier in Paris of his final version of *Liturgia*. Caturla mentioned the new "innovative" orchestration and his decision to abandon use of the chorus altogether, even with megaphones. Finally, Caturla assured Carpentier that his poem, *Liturgia,* upon which the music is based, would be printed in the program.

Caturla's reference above to changes in orchestration is clearly reflected in his expansion of ethnic percussion, *instrumentos típicos cubanos* (typical Cuban instruments), in *Yamba-O*. The absence of vocal parts in *Yamba-O* gave Caturla the possibility to manipulate the musical themes taken from *Liturgia* with more freedom. An explanation of this rationale may be found in the following program notes, which also express an opinion of this composition:

> *Yamba-O* does not follow the poem literally nor is it a musical weaving constructed around the poem, but rather his [Caturla's] ideological reaction to the ceremony of the Ñáñigo religious ceremony. . . .
>
> The themes of *Yamba-O* are completely original and have an uncharacteristic popular flavor. They consciously avoid the cheap which is easily confused with the popular, but diametrically opposed thereby maintaining an artistic solidity. These themes represent three principles— following, with some variations, the free sonata form, maintaining during the course of the work, despite the great variations in rhythm and changes of sonorities through which it travels, a great unity and depth.[5]

Prior to the premiere, a fragment of *Yamba-O* was published in the Havana magazine *Social*. Although presented in a piano reduction of the full orchestral score, this fragment illustrates the complex rhythms and extremely dissonant harmonies (including tone clusters) that were now established characteristics of Caturla's style (see figure 12.1 below).

While the elements of melody, harmony, and rhythm are stretched to the limit in the above example, the real impact of *Yamba-O* lay in its orchestration. From that point of view *Yamba-O* is a true tour de force, reflecting Caturla's mastery of using timbre and texture for endless changes of sonority. In this respect, *Yamba-O* exemplifies Caturla's thesis found in his essay "Posibilidades sinfónicas de la musica afrocubana" of 1929.

Caturla's integration of *instrumentos típicos cubanos* (claves, *güiro*, maracas, and *cencerro*) in *Yamba-O* required special preparation. With the help of Miguel A. Matamoros, timpanist for the Filarmónica, Caturla engaged a team of extra percussionists (out of his own and his father's pocket) to manage the elaborate mix of traditional and Afro-Cuban percussion parts in the score. In language reminiscent of his earlier enthusiasm for *Obertura Cubana*, he shared the intended effect of *Yamba-O* with Lorenzo ("Lordi") Martín y Garatea:

> *You can imagine the scandal the performance will produce* if I tell you only that there are 11 percussionists, since every instrument has material all the time. . . . *The work is going to be the "clou"* [hit] *of the concert* and it will be conveniently announced that it is dedicated to the Orchestra. [italics mine][6]

Having depleted the stipend afforded him by his father in just a little over one month, Caturla left Havana for home. He returned to Havana on the eve of the premiere of *Yamba-O*, but without the large entourage of family and friends from Remedios he hoped would be there. The program Roldán announced for the premiere of Caturla's *Yamba-O* on 2 December 1930 consisted of the following compositions:

Haydn: *Sinfonia no. 104*
García Caturla: *Yamba-O*
Borodin: *Danza no. 17 (Prince Igor)*
Pergolesi: *Salve Regina*
Carpenter: *Water Colors*
(Mina Hager, contralto soloist)

Figure 12.1. *Yamba-O* (piano arrangement by Caturla), mm. 1–8.

Following the concert, Havana's leading music critics confirmed Caturla's belief that *Yamba-O* would be a "hit." Caturla shared the success of *Yamba-O* with Carpentier (whose mother attended the concert):

You cannot imagine . . . how good the orchestra sounded to me. I am completely satisfied with my orchestration and Roldán conducted it with real interest. The effects of typical [Afro-Cuban] percussion, well conceived for the ensemble, are marvelous. Nena Benítez and Juan Bonich [music critics for *Diario de la Marina* and *El Mundo*, respectively] have published beautiful articles . . . and both were as full of praise as they were capable of [expressing]. . . .

With the debut of *Yamba-O* Fernández de Castro "threw the house out the window" [pulled out all the stops] at Orbe including my picture, a great deal of information about me . . . and photographs of the typical instruments I use in it."[7]

Unfortunately, Fernández de Castro's feature article in *Orbe* cited Caturla instead of Roldán as the first to use "typical instruments" (Afro-Cuban) with the symphony orchestra—a blunder that would cost Caturla some embarrassment. After thanking Roldán for his performance of *Yamba-O*, Caturla found it necessary to appease him in this matter, saying he would have this misinformation rectified.[8] Eager for a second performance of *Yamba-O*, Caturla also notified Roldán that many people from the press expected him to repeat *Yamba-O*, and called upon Antonio and María Muñoz de Quevedo to influence Roldán in that direction.

In the meantime, realizing that Sanjuán would in fact return to Cuba, Caturla took yet another step toward ensuring that *Yamba-O* would be heard in Havana again. He wrote to Sanjuán in Madrid as follows:

My good friend;
I write to you about the premiere of *Yamba-O*, dedicated to you and the Filarmónica. It was a beautiful concert . . . I was very satisfied with Amadeo's [Roldán] conducting . . . the reviews have been abundant. *I am counting on you to conduct it again* upon your return, if Roldán doesn't repeat it before. [italics mine][9]

Subsequent to the premiere of *Yamba-O*, Roldán conducted three concerts with the Filarmónica prior to Sanjuán's return, none of which included Caturla's music.[10] When Sanjuán returned to Havana, he conducted his own *Liturgia negra*, but not Caturla's *Yamba-O*. In the meantime, another opportunity to have his music performed developed: the visit to Havana of Leopold Stokowski, then conductor of the illustrious Philadelphia Symphony Orchestra.

RUMBA

While *Yamba-O* would not be his last symphonic score, it belongs to a set of two compositions that represent Caturla's most advanced skill in orchestration, both reworkings of previous compositions. The other composition in this set is *Rumba,* a revised version of his earlier *Obertura Cubana* of 1927. Later, when copies of *Yamba-O* and *Rumba* were finally made, Caturla sent these scores to Cowell, with hopes for possible publication, and Slonimsky, whom he hoped would perform *Rumba* in Havana on a proposed return engagement. Filled with enthusiasm at such prospects, Caturla wrote to Carpentier:

> Maria, Antonio, Amadeo [Roldán] and I are making titanic efforts to make it possible for Slonimsky to return to Havana to conduct three concerts of modern music. One with a large orchestra where for the first time in Latin America Stravinsky's *Sacre [Rite of Spring]* would be played, and two with a small orchestra, all three with musicians from the Filarmónica, premiering my *Rumba* in the large concert and Roldán's new work for 22 instruments entitled *Tres Toques,* with *Integrales* or *Octandre* by Varèse and some very interesting things, such as, for example, *Histoire du Soldat* by Stravinsky.[11]

Programming such as this indicates just how advanced in his thinking Caturla was for his time. Ultimately, Caturla's plans for the above concerts came to naught. Slonimsky's invitation to return to Havana was preempted temporarily to accommodate the engagement of Leopold Stokowki. Unfortunately, there were no performances of *Rumba* during Caturla's lifetime; he simply shelved the score and went on to other projects. Ironically, *Rumba* was revived with its original title *Obertura Cubana* and submitted by Caturla to a Cuban national competition for new orchestral music in 1938. The revised *Obertura Cubana (Rumba)* was selected for first prize, but there was no performance of the music.

THE STOKOWSKI INVITATION TO HAVANA

One of the more bittersweet experiences of Caturla's musical career was the Stokowski connection, which placed Caturla's music in the top ranks of world-class symphonic concerts and at the same time placed him in conflict with plans already under way to host Slonimski's return to Havana. Leopold Stokowski's ties with the League of Composers in New York led to his performance of Caturla's music in Philadelphia and New York with the Philadelphia Orchestra in January 1932. Prior to these concerts, the League notified Caturla of

Stokowki's interest in his music, asking him to send his music and the names of other Cuban composers. The League also informed him of Stokowski's desire to visit Havana, possibly meeting Caturla in Remedios. Caturla's reaction was enthusiastic: "I cannot feel other than happy, optimistic and delighted when I read and re-read the letter from the League of Composers, a copy of which I enclose,"[12] he wrote to Antonio Quevedo.

Realizing the significance of Caturla's letter from the League of Composers, Quevedo responded arrogantly to the young composer. After congratulating himself on the success of his (and María's) publication *Musicalia*, Quevedo took credit for Caturla's success by pointing out that *"Musicalia* has had a good part in disseminating your work, and without this publication it would have taken you a lot longer to become known in Europe and America."[13] Quevedo then advised Caturla to first write the League of Composers to thank them and to inform them that he (Caturla) would be at Stokowski's disposal upon his arrival in Havana. Quevedo also advised Caturla against sending *Yamba-O*, explaining: "[*Yamba-O*] cannot be understood outside of the Antilles." Peeved by Quevedo's remark, Caturla's responded to his advice about *Yamba-O*:

> Pardon me if I disagree with your opinion about the Antillian quality of *Yamba-O*. I don't believe that works such as this one of mine are to be confined to Latin American audiences only, as that would suppose that the European public is lacking in comprehending such music, which it isn't, and that the work has little power of its own.[14]

Prior to contacting Roldán about his letter from the League of Composers, and after taking steps to form a welcoming committee for Stokowski upon his arrival in Havana, Caturla learned that the famous maestro had already been in direct contact with Roldán, expressing his desire to conduct the Orquesta Filarmónica de La Habana. Realizing the possibility of another misunderstanding with Roldán, Caturla informed him that "at no time did I think of doing anything with him [Stokowski] without your consideration . . . you can count on me in whatever you prepare for Stokowski."[15] Regarding the possibility of Stokowski's arrival causing a conflict with Slonimsky's pending visit, Caturla wrote to Antonio Quevedo saying he wished he had been better informed and that he would "try to solve this difficulty as best as possible."[16]

Finally, after the return of Sanjuán, arrangements were made to host Leopold Stokowski to appear with the Orquesta Filarmónica, and plans to bring Slonimsky to Havana again were cancelled for the time being. In the meantime, as already mentioned, Stokowski performed Caturla's music with the Philadelphia Orchestra in New York and Philadelphia prior to his arrival in Havana.

For reasons unknown, Stokowski performed "Two Cuban Dances," a shortened version of Caturla's *Tres Danzas Cubanas,* at his Philadelphia and New York concerts. The longer, more interesting, *Motivos de Danza* (the second of the set) was dropped. Thus the American public heard but fleeting examples of Caturla's music. The reviews were mixed, and in Philadelphia, *Danza Lucumí* was translated on the printed program as "Dance of Vegetation"! Of the two reviews that appeared, that of Olin Downes of the *New York Times* captured the reality of audience response with great precision:

> Before anyone knew what had happened, Leopold Stokowski had leapt upon the conductor's stand last night in Carnegie Hall and launched the orchestra into a shrill Cuban dance by one A. G. Caturla.
>
> There were two dances by this Caturla, who was born at Remedios, Cuba, in 1906, and who lives there today. Furious, tonally bifurcated music was this, projected by the blond one with the racket of a thunderbolt.
>
> The first piece was over almost before it began. The audience had barely time to quiver before the second dance was on. It came to an end, in turn, with an abruptness that positively stunned the audience. They, stupefied, to a silent moment to gather their wits and applaud. No one had had time to find out what they thought of this music.[17]

Leopold Stokowski's performances of Caturla's music—despite the reviews—increased Caturla's hopes of also having *Rumba* and *Yamba-O* performed abroad.[18] There was also the possibility that Stokowski might perform Caturla's music when he came to Havana. But such was not the case. Upon his return to Havana, Sanjuán intervened and shared the podium in front of the Orquesta Filarmónica with Leopold Stokowski on 24 January 1932. As previously mentioned, it was Sanjuán's music, not Caturla's, that appeared on the program:

Glinka: *Kamarinskaia*
Sanjuán: "Iniciación" and "Babaluayé" (*Liturgia negra*)
Cassadó: *Hispania* (George Copland, piano soloist)
Wagner: *Overture to Die Meistersinger* (Stokowski conducting)

With the postponement of Slonimsky's visit, Caturla's hopes of having him conduct *Rumba* in Havana were for the time being dashed. And with the return of Sanjuán, all hopes of having Stokowski conduct *Yamba-O* were also dashed. While Slonimsky did return to Havana in 1933, it would be George Gershwin's *Rumba* that he would conduct, and not the music of Caturla. Thus Caturla's two most prized large symphonic compositions, *Rumba* and *Yamba-O*, met similar fates: scarcely performed during his lifetime and never to be published.

NOTES

1. Sanjuán was trying desperately to find a better post abroad, as economic conditions in Cuba were worsening. Because Sanjuán had plans to conduct his own suite *Liturgia negra* with the Havana Filarmónica upon his return, he suggested Caturla change the title of his composition. Turning to Carpentier's text, Caturla considered changing the title from *Liturgia* to *En casa de Acué*; he later decided upon *Yamba-O*.

2. Musicians ("professors") in the Filarmónica were not paid a living wage. Many taught in schools or privately, played in theaters, or found other means of income. Roldán himself, for example, played in the cafés of Havana.

3. Henríquez, *Correspondencia,* 22 de septiembre 1931, 226.

4. Caturla later reported to "Lordi": "For now I won't have any more performances on the radio at the best station, better said, one of the best programs which was the Majestic, has informed me that in view of the difficult economy at the moment, they will cancel their broadcasts" (Henríquez, *Correspondencia,* 10 de mayo 1931, 234).

5. Notes taken from autographed copy of *Yamba-O* in the Fleisher Collection of Orchestral Music at the Free Library of Philadelphia.

6. Henríquez, *Correspondencia,* 7 de septiembre 1931, 228.

7. Henríquez, *Correspondencia,* 27 de octubre 1931, 236.

8. Roldán had already used Afro-Cuban instruments in his *Obertura sobre temas cubanos* in 1925. Caturla's attempt to have *Musicalia* publish a clarification of Fernández de Castro's article did not materialize.

9. Henríquez, *Correspondencia,* 3 de noviembre 1931, 240.

10. Although Roldán looked favorably upon an additional performance of *Yamba-O* he was not at liberty to do so without Sanjuán's approval. Also, the matter of paying the extra Afro-Cuban percussionists could not be undertaken by the Filarmónica as Caturla had suggested.

11. Henríquez, *Correspondencia,* 17 de octubre 1931, 237.

12. Henríquez, *Correspondencia,* 7 de diciembre 1931, 249.

13. Henríquez, *Correspondencia,* 11 de diciembre 1931, 369.

14. Henríques, *Correspondencia,* 14 de deciembre 1931, 254.

15. Henríquez, *Correspondencia,* 18 de diciembre 1931, 255.

16. Henríquez, *Correspondencia,* 18 de diciembre 1931, 256.

17. Olin Downes, "Stokowski Offers Novel Items Here," 25. (Slonimsky later referred to Olin Downes's review as a "humorously benevolent write up.") The *Philadelphia Inquirer* music critic Linton Martin was not so sophisticated ("Stokowski Offers New Year's Concert"). After erroneously translating Caturla's *Danza Lucumí* as "Dance of Vegetation" on the program, he had the following to say in his review: "The 'Two Cuban Dances' of A. G. Caturla that came first were exceedingly short, each being about a minute or less in length, and, while robustly rhythmic and lavish in the use of drums, both were frankly inconsequential, with no mystical musical meanings."

18. Eager to share the importance Stokowski's interest in his music, Caturla wrote to Modesto Gutiérrez Heredia (now returned to Remedios from abroad), saying, "I want you to know that Stokowsky, the present conductor of the Philadelphia Symphony Orchestra has incorporated my *Danzas* and *Bembé* in his repertory of modern works and that he will conduct the premiere of *Yamba-O* in New York during the coming season of 1932." As it turned out, Caturla was mistaken about the pieces that would be performed.

Chapter Thirteen

New Standards for Old Forms

While much of Caturla's energy during 1931 was spent revising and finishing *Yamba-O* and *Rumba*, two new compositions soon came to light: *El caballo blanco* (described by Caturla as "armonización de una tema popular para voces mixtas" [harmonization of a popular theme for mixed voices]), for six-voice a cappella chorus, and *Primera suite cubana,* for winds and piano. In each of these compositions, Caturla strives to redefine the use of form in music, a process that dates back to his *Piezas para cuarteto de Cuerdas* (string quartet) of 1927. Subsequently, with the realization of a new Cuban song form (*Dos poemas afrocubanos*) and his freely invented use of sonata form (*Yamba-O*) behind him, Caturla stepped further into the future with *El caballo blanco* and *Primera suite cubana.* Caturla reached new heights as a composer in each of these compositions, mainly in respect to his "specially invented" forms, free counterpoint, polyrhythmic development, and—in the case of *Primera suite cubana*—a stunning use of timbre as rhythm, coloration, and effect.

EL CABALLO BLANCO (SON)

El caballo blanco was initially intended for the inaugural concert of María Muñoz de Quevedo's newly formed Sociedad Coral de La Habana; the music is dedicated to her. Sponsored by the Instituto Hispano Cubano de Cultura, the inaugural concert of María's Sociedad Coral de La Habana was private and took place at the Instituto Hispano on 25 November 1931. Unable to attend, Caturla asked Antonio Quevedo about reviews and later registered a complaint when he found out that *El caballo blanco* was dropped from the first public concert of the Sociedad Coral, scheduled for 21 January 1932 at the Teatro Nacional. He wrote to Antonio Quevedo:

> I am a bit sad because of the exclusion of *Caballo blanco* from the public concert the Chorale is preparing for January. Why is it almost the only one removed from the program? Wasn't it liked? Did the singers protest because of technical difficulties? Tell me frankly.[1]

Antonio Quevedo responded by explaining to Caturla that in programming, the Sociedad Coral sought to present a variety of Cuban composers in succession. Therefore Roldán, Sanjuán, and others were taken into consideration. Realizing that Caturla was disappointed, Quevedo told him, "The first presentation [of the Sociedad Coral] was one of the greatest successes in Cuba (and I say this without exaggeration)," adding that there were no real reviews of the inaugural concert.[2]

The fact is, Caturla's *El caballo blanco* is written in an abstract harmonic language that, in combination with its rhythmic complexities, tests the musicianship and skill of the conductor and singers to the utmost. It was based on a popular song, but Caturla's arrangement of *El caballo blanco* was not addressed to popular taste. For one thing, the basic rhythmic pattern of the *Son* is hidden in a myriad of complex rhythmic permutations. Also, Caturla expressed the inherent motion of the text in a unique way by rapidly shifting short cell-like motives throughout the parts (from bass to soprano); the resulting counterpoint is dissonant and necessitates a freely invented form to accommodate the flow of text among the vocal parts.

Aesthetically, *El caballo blanco* may be looked upon as an extension of Caturla's *Son in E♭* for solo piano (distributed internationally in a special edition of *Musicalia*) the previous year. In each case, Caturla transforms the essence of music that is essentially Afro-Cuban to music that transcends social classification.

PRIMERA SUITE CUBANA

Sometime during the summer of 1932 Caturla completed his new suite for winds and piano, *Primera suite cubana*. The genesis of Caturla's *Primera suite cubana* extends back to the aftermath of Slonimsky's premiere performance of *Bembé* in January 1931 with the Chamber Orchestra of Boston. Caturla then first mentioned to

Slonimsky that he would, out of gratitude, compose a "work for small orchestra . . . naturally, on folkloric themes of my country" for him. Once the composition began to take shape, he informed Slonimsky that he was working on a "suite for seven instruments and piano. . . . It is composed on Cuban themes from Colonial times."[3]

Primera suite cubana consists of the following movements:

I—Sonera: Allegro scherzando
II—Comparsa: Adagio con moto
III—Danza: Allegro vivace

A bass clarinet was added to the original plan, resulting in the following final instrumentation: flute, oboe, English horn, clarinet, bass clarinet, bassoon, French horn, trumpet, and piano. Upon completion of the score, Caturla wrote to Alejo Carpentier mentioning that his new suite was dedicated to Nicolas Slonimsky, the "generous Yankee-Russian." After mentioning in the same letter that he planned to have this music performed abroad at one of the Cowell PAAC concerts, Caturla continued: "My Suite is based on Colonial Afrocuban themes and I think I have done something really new and authentic."[4] Eventually the premiere of *Primera suite cubana* took place at the New School for Social Research in New York on 4 November 1932 under the direction of Nicolas Slonimsky. Unfortunately, Slonimsky took the liberty of cutting parts of Caturla's music. Eventually, when Caturla's score of *Primera suite cubana* was returned, with indications of Slonimsky's cuts, Caturla was furious and wrote to Cowell:

> I see in the parts of my "Suite" that I have received from Mr. Riegger, that Slonimsky has introduced to it such suppressions of such vital importance to the merit of the entire musical work that changes it or alters it as a whole. The first part has been cut down almost entirely and realli [*sic*] I cannot explain myself the real cause of it. On account of this I wish to let it know [*sic*] to all Conductors that may play my Suite, that I most earnestly object to have it played by them in such a way without my expressed consent. I am most surely [*sic*] that New Music will have my Suite printed just exactly as it appear in my original copy at your disposal. Please be sure not to forget to send me the printed copies of the edition before finished as I wish to correct them personally.[5]

The music of Caturla's *Primera suite cubana* is based on three Afro-Cuban musical forms, *Son, comparsa,* and *danza,* unified by rhythmic and melodic motives common, not only to these, but other forms of Afro-Cuban music as well. Assimilating raw musical material in such a way became an essential part of Caturla's creative process from 1927 onwards, a process he explained as follows:

> The living folklore . . . should be polished until the crudities and exterior influences fall away; sane theoretical disciplines should be applied, and the music should be condensed into musical forms which shall be specially invented to be suitable.[6]

Catuarla's *Primera suite cubana* exemplifies this statement. Each movement of *Primera suite cubana* has its own "specially invented" form, designed to accommodate condensed themes—four to five measures in length—that migrate from one instrument to another against polyrhythmic and polytonal textures. The forms in each movement of *Primera suite cubana* are designed to yield to the internal development of Caturla's counterpoint; as a result they remain asymmetrical throughout. The first movement, *Sonera,* for example, exploits rhythm and timbre by migrating thematic fragments in a stream of polytonal texture from one instrument to another against a running obbligato of sixteenth notes. Once the sixteenth-note obbligato is initiated by the clarinet, it quickly falls into the hands of the pianist, creating a timbral rhythm that pervades the whole piece. Such is the texture set up by Caturla for the entrance of the main theme (based on rhythmic aspects of the *Son*), which falls quickly and smoothly into place, first with the oboe, then alternately with each instrument in the ensemble.

Unlike Roldán's *Comparsa* (from his ballet suite *La rebambaramba*), which celebrates the joy and festive spirit of carnival music, Caturla transformed the *comparsa* from a lively street dance into a dirge in the second movement. Using the piano as a percussion instrument that throbs constantly in dissonance, like a drum, the ghostly sounds of a muted French horn announce the main theme (see figure 13.1 below). And when a short burst of exuberance breaks out toward the end, it is not joy, rather anxiety, that Caturla seems to express before the piece ends as it began, creating an atmosphere of despair. In this respect, Caturla's *Comparsa* may be seen as a protest piece against the harsh times (recent closing of the University of Havana, political bankruptcy, unemployment, and a dire state of poverty in the interior) and social injustice that pervaded the island at that time.

Figure 13.1. *Comparsa*, mm. 1–7.

Danza, the final movement of *Primera suite cubana,* is a tour de force of instrumental virtuosity (for all instruments), intended to exploit rhythmic aspects of the *danza* in the context of constantly changing timbre, texture, and dynamics. Like the previous movements in *Primera suite cubana,* the form of *Danza* is unique—in this case a monothematic free variation form. Caturla's juxtaposition of various combinations of wind instruments at their highest range together with loud, thick, repetitious chords at the lower range of the piano (a technique Caturla perfected in *Bembé*) is but one of the many unique instrumental colors to be found in *Danza.* Caturla ends *Danza* with the piano frenetically poundings chords at the top range of the piano, against the entire wind ensemble blasting repetitions of severe dissonance, before the piano splits into a double glissando in opposite directions—music that may aptly be described as "wild."

Because of the many compositional elements Caturla was able to assimilate in *Primera suite cubana,* it transcends any one classification of style. Although Caturla used Afro-Cuban musical elements of rhythm and melody as a basis for this music, the compositional *process* involving timbre, texture, harmony, and counterpoint relate to the aesthetics of European and contemporary North American music. *Comparsa,* for example, reflects sonorities found in the music of Charles Ives, whose scores were well known by Caturla. Also, the instrumentation of *Primera suite cubana* itself is similar to Colin McFee's *Concerto for Piano with Wind Octette Accompaniment,* a composition

Caturla knew from Cowell's *New Music Quarterly*. However, this is not to say that Caturla was imitating European or North American composers. McFee's *Concerto for Piano with Wind Octette Accompaniment*, for example, stands pale against Caturla's fiery *Danza* and his highly imaginative use of timbre and assimilation of thematic sources throughout the rest of this music. *El caballo blanco* and *Primera suite cubana* reflect Caturla's *intentions* to identify himself as a composer whose music is built upon his own unique forms—a topic he wrote about that year (1931), which was later published in Cowell's *American Composers on American Music*. Caturla perceived himself as an inventor of new forms, a concept Antonio Quevedo warned him about, only to witness the young Remediano continuing to expand his concepts in later compositions.

NOTES

1. Henríquez, *Correspondencia,* 14 de diciembre 1931, 254. "Estoy un poco triste por la exclusión del *Caballo blanco* de concierto público que para enero prepara la Coral. ¿Porqué lo han quitado casi a él solo del programa? ¿No gustó? ¿Lo protestaron por dificultades técnicas los cantantes? Háblame francamente."

2. The Cuban periodical *Carteles* did publish a glowing commentary about the value of the Sociedad Coral de La Habana in their 13 December 1931 issue. The commentary concluded:

"La Habana cuenta ya con una Sociedad Coral gracias a los esfuerzos generosos de María Muñoz de Quevedo, cuyas iniciativas musicales denotan no sólo su elevada cultura y moderna orientación, sino un selecto espíritu organizador, capaz de intentar y conseguir empresas de arte que hasta ahora parecían inabordables. . . . Cuenta esta Coral con magníficos elementos que han secundado con entusiasmo la ardua labor de dotar a La Habana de un conjunto tan notable, digno por su exquisita presentación, disciplina y calidades vocales de cualquier gran ciudad tradicionalmente culta.

[Havana now has a choral society thanks to the generous efforts of María Muñoz de Quevedo, whose musical initiatives do not only denote her elevation of culture and modern orientation, but an exceptionally spirited organizer capable of trying to bring about enterprises of art that are now viewed as unapproachable. . . . This chorale possesses excellent assets that have enthusiastically supported the ensemble's difficult task of playing in Havana, a chorale as remarkable and noteworthy as any from an important city of longstanding cultural tradition for its exquisite presentation, discipline and vocal qualities.]

For details, see *María Muñoz de Quevedo centenario de su nacimiento (1886–1986) y cincuenta y cinco aniversario de la fundación de la Sociedad Coral de La Habana.* It is worth noting that Roldán's *Curujey: Son para voces mixtas, dos pianos, clave, y güiro,* based on a text by Nicolás Guillén, was on the first public concert of the Sociedad Coral (21 January 1932). Miguel Matamoros played the clave and *güiro* parts.

3. Henríquez, *Correspondencia,* 31 de enero 1931, 167; 4 de octubre 1931, 232.

4. Henríquez, *Correspondencia,* 6 de augusto 1932, 264.

5. Caturla to Cowell, 4 March 1933, from García Caturla, "Correspondencia inédita." Cowell did publish a correct edition of Caturla's *Primera suite cubana* in his *New Music Quarterly* of 1937.

6. Alejandro García Caturla, "The Development of Cuban Music," 174.

Chapter Fourteen

Reality of Life in Remedios

By the end of 1930, it was apparent to Caturla that finding means to support himself in Havana as a musician was impossible—despite the recent success of *Dos poemas afrocubanos*, *Yamba-O*, and press reviews of his success abroad. As a result, Caturla's efforts to build a musical environment in Remedios in which he could thrive became increasingly exigent. Lectures, performances (including his role as piano soloist in George Gershwin's *Rhapsody in Blue*), musical reviews and essays in local newspapers (such as *El Faro*), memberships in social societies (such as La Tertulia), and collaboration with Othón in establishing a new library in Remedios (Biblioteca Pública José Martí) were his main fields of action in Remedios.

Caturla was looked upon as a celebrity in Remedios by then; particularly since he was awarded the title "Eminent and Distinguished Son of Remedios," following his success in Barcelona and Paris. At the same time, however, he was also looked upon as an eccentric, because of his lifestyle, relentless determination to modernize musical tastes in Remedios, and overall dissatisfaction with the town's environment. Inevitably, Caturla's attempts to organize concerts of contemporary music (among other endeavors) in Remedios were met with resentment and hostility by most of the local musicians.

Eventually, a rift developed among the musicians in Remedios as a result of Caturla's sponsorship of a small group of exceptional music students who took an interest in his music and ideals. Headed by Abelardo Cuevas, Caturla's student followers formed a saxophone septet, making their debut at the Teatro Miguel Bru on 10 November

1931. In a review for *El Faro*, Caturla described the Septimino Cuevas thereafter as "a new musical institution of Remedios, born from the heat of the ideal of intellectual betterment, from the bosom of the Municipal Band and sponsored by Maestro Augustín Crespo and a few music lovers."[1] Continuing his review, Caturla blasted negative criticisms of the Septimino by other members of the Banda Municipal, whom he simply wrote off as being ignorant of the elementary rules of music and narrow in their tastes.

Caturla continued his support of the Septimino Cuevas by inviting them to join him in a benefit concert at Teatro Bru the following month (29 December), at which time he was to conduct the Banda Municipal de Remedios. The Septimino Cuevas participated in the concert with a rendition of Caturla's *Berceuse* (arranged specially by the composer) in a program that included poetry readings and popular music performed by members of the Banda Municipal de Remedios.[2] Caturla's benefit concert turned out to be a disaster. Catcalls, boos, and razzing sounds aimed at Caturla and the Septimino Cuevas broke out from a group headed by Herberto Romero, one of Caturla's most aggressive antagonists in Remedios. Expressing his grievances to Cuevas the following day, Caturla wrote: "I am not ignorant of the fact that the artistic-cultural level of Remedios has descended noticeably for the past fifty years . . . torpid and immoral manifestations have taken root as the ruling norm . . . injurious ridicule and odious satire preside . . . thus pure musical manifestations must suffer." In closing Caturla compared the incident to a "wave of mud" plaguing the republic and Remedios and ended by complimenting Cuevas as a distinguished and affectionate friend.[3] Full consequences of the shocking behavior by Romero's group at this concert were yet to come. The scandalous and humiliating incident brought about a schism between Caturla and the Banda Municipal de Remedios, one that had been building for some time. Less than a year later Caturla summarized the situation by saying he was forced to leave his hometown for a better environment to develop his own musical activities. Caturla's decision to do so became one of the most important turning points in his musical career; a point at which he stood up against all odds to fight for his artistic convictions. The environment Caturla chose was the neighboring city of Caibarién, where he soon launched his own chamber orchestra, the Orquesta de Conciertos de Caibarién.

FORMATION AND IDEALS OF CATURLA'S
ORQUESTA DE CONCIERTOS DE CAIBARIÉN

As 1932 drew to a close, Caturla worked feverishly, assembling and preparing his innovative "symphony orchestra without strings" (as he described it) for the inaugural concert of his Orquesta de Conciertos de Caibarién. The orchestra consisted of twenty-five musicians of the Banda Municipal de Caibarién, including their conductor José María Montalván (who played clarinet). Caturla took great care to publicize the new orchestra, using his influence to manage press releases in local papers and Havana journals that were distributed throughout the district. For example, Conchita Gallardo, who previously wrote a favorable review of his *Bembé* for Havana's *El País*, released an announcement of the inaugural concert of the Orquesta de Conciertos de Caibarién, saying in part: "Alejandro García Caturla—one of the newest and most dedicated composers of the present time, whose works are known by the public here and abroad, has organized a concert orchestra in Caibarién which is now preparing its inaugural concert." After listing the compositions to be performed, Gallardo continued: "The young composer's latest composition 'Primera Suite Cubana' will have its first performance by the Pan American Chamber Orchestra in New York. . . . The young Caturla is one of the latest legitimate hopes for the art of music."[4]

The inaugural concert of the Orquesta de Conciertos de Caibarién may be seen as one of the most remarkable accomplishments in Caturla's life. Caturla single-handedly organized and implemented a concert orchestra in Caibarién composed of local musicians performing programs for the working class that integrated their own Afro-Cuban music with that of the classics and modernists (Cowell) from abroad. In effect, the inauguration of Caturla's Orquesta de Conciertos de Caibarién set off a cultural alarm that resounded throughout the island. Eventually, Caturla's Orquesta was hailed with great enthusiasm by Cowell and the PAAC and others in Europe and Latin America.

The printed program for the inaugural concert of the Orquesta de Conciertos de Caibarién included Caturla's "Profesión de fe" (profession of faith), modeled in part on the ideals of the Sociedad de Música Contemporánea de La Habana. The political overtones, ideals of socialism related to cultural enlightenment of the working class (particularly in the countryside), patriotism, and the concepts of betterment through hope and art (aimed at youth) that are found in Caturla's "Profesión de fe" classify it as a manifesto of his ideals. The goals of the Orquesta de Conciertos de Caibarién, as pointed out by Caturla, consist of the following objectives:

> To project ourselves on the rest of the Republic *and the world* in general in order mainly to raise the name of the Fatherland, with the most noble aspiration of obtaining honest fruits for the youth who study musical arts in its various forms with all integrity, through the means of work, example and discipline. [italics mine][5]

At the time Caturla expressed his "Profesión de fe," Cuba was on the brink of a major revolution that would bring down the Cuban dictator, Presidente Gerardo Machado. The atmosphere throughout the island was filled with tension and apprehension. Inevitably, the rhetoric of Caturla's "Profesión de fe" caught the attention of young Cuban intellectuals who shared his ideals, intellectuals who engendered the forthcoming revolution against Gerardo Machado with conviction and fervor. Among such intellectuals was José Antonio Portuondo of Santiago de Cuba, a brilliant young essayist, poet, and literary critic, one of Cuba's best.

Inspired by Caturla's success in forming a new orchestra for the working class of the interior, Portuondo wrote an article on the subject of economic slavery caused by the "North American masters" and hope for a "new Fatherland" by imbuing the country folk of the land with a new spirit. Entitled "Compases de redención" (Measures of redemption), Portuondo's article cites Caturla as one of the men who had "rolled up sleeves" and has "gone to awaken the country man's consciousness." After identifying Caturla as a composer who "knows along with [José] Martí how music elevates and takes man's spirit out of himself," Portuondo described Caturla as an "Apostle" who had "outlined the new spirit of the sons of the countryside. He [Caturla] has waved his baton over the unredeemed land with measures of redemption." After quoting at length from Caturla's "Profesión de fe," Portuondo designated him a patriot who by "[waving] his baton over the fields blooming with hope will mark the measures of a victorious hymn which will joyously nail itself into the dawning soul of the redeemed sons of the earth."[6]

Writing to express his gratitude to Portuondo for his article (which Caturla described to Othón as "a healing balm"), Caturla summed up his present situation:

Comrade:

I too—like yourself—was greatly discouraged and in profound despair because of everything that has been happening, . . . and thanks to the warmth I have found in my twenty-five hard working companions of Caibarién and a good part of this town, . . . I have regained my usual energies, and this *blessed rebelliousness* that fill my veins moves my spirit and points it toward the realization of my ideals even when the path is bristling with quills. [italics mine][7]

ORQUESTA DE CONCIERTOS DE CAIBARIÉN CONCERTS

The Inaugural Concert: 12 December 1932

In addition to Caturla's "Profesión de fe" mentioned above, the printed program notes for the inaugural concert of the Orquesta de Conciertos de Caibarién also addressed specific aspects of protocol at public concerts—aspects fresh in Caturla's mind after his negative experiences in Remedios—by requesting the public to come on time, avoid talking during the program, and not to enter during the performance (unheard of demands for a small town in Cuba at that time). In addition to the printed program, Caturla distributed a monograph on Bembé that contained international press reviews acclaiming the success of this composition, which was to be performed at the inaugural concert with Santos Ojeda (then fourteen years of age) of Caibarién as soloist.[8] Following is the original program:

PROGRAM
December 12, 1932 Teatro "Cervantes" Caibarién

Overture to *The Magic Flute*	Mozart
Oriental	Cui
La Vida Breve (Danza Española No. 1)	de Falla
Scherzino (from Pulcinella)	Stravinsky
Bembé	Caturla
Rhapsody in Blue (soloist: Santos Ojeda)	Gershwin

The successful debut of Caturla's Orquesta de Conciertos de Caibarién was well documented in the regional papers and journals. Taking note that the inaugural concert of the Orquesta de Conciertos de Caibarién was played to a full house, critics from the local newspapers of Caibarién and Remedios released glowing reviews. After describing Caturla as "a world renowned young, valiant Cuban composer" the music critic L. Sanchéz de Algibay in Caibarién went on to say that the collaboration of Caturla and José María Montalván brought about a "grand advance in culture." The Remedios press was equally positive. Caturla was described as a master of Afro-Cuban music, having achieved international success with his *Bembé*. After mentioning the opening address given by Pedro Brú Valenzuela on the theme of politics and music, the Remedios review ended by describing the last moments of the concert with "our dear friend Alejandro García Caturla who stood with outstretched arms and expressions of gratitude in response to the continuing applause." Both reviews also gave great recognition to the young performers in the new orchestra, particularly Santos Ojeda, who was featured as piano soloist in Caturla's *Bembé* and Gershwin's *Rhapsody in Blue*.[9]

The Second Concert: 30 January 1933

Initially, the second concert of the Orquesta de Conciertos de Caibarién was scheduled to take place in Remedios on 28 January 1933. However, when a notice appeared in the Remedios journal *El Clarín* that a group of young musicians headed by Herberto Romero was soliciting the Orquesta de Conciertos de Caibarién to include their new saxophone quartet on the program, the concert was cancelled.[10]

Announced as a "Concierto Extraordinario (Dedicado a Martí)," the second concert of the Orquesta de Conciertos de Caibarién took place on 30 January 1933, again at the Teatro Cervantes in Caibarién.

In the meantime, Caturla lost no time in spreading the good news of the success of his inaugural concert. Among the first he notified was Amadeo Roldán, extending an invitation for him to appear as guest conductor and submit his music for performance (neither of which came to pass). He also contacted Henry Cowell, who in return was pleased to learn that Caturla had arranged his *Exultation* for the Orquesta de Conciertos to play at their forthcoming concert.[11]

Writing to Othón of Cowell's delight that the Orquesta Conciertos de Caibarién would play his music at their next concert, Caturla mentioned that he had made a special arrangement of Cowell's *Exultation* (for piano obbligato and band), adding: "We receive encouragement from all around, like a signal that the orchestra and I are achieving the attention that keeps us going."[12]

The Concierto Extraordinario program was basically the same as that of the inaugural concert, except that Cui's *Oriental* was dropped, leaving room for the music of Ravel and Cowell:

PROGRAM

January 30, 1933 Teatro "Cervantes" Caibarién

Overture to *The Magic Flute*	Mozart
Ma Mère l'Oye Suite	Ravel
La Vida Breve (Danza Española No. 1)	de Falla
Scherzino (from *Pulcinella*)	Stravinsky
Exultation (Poema)	Cowell
Bembé (Movimiento sinfónico)	Caturla
Rhapsody in Blue (soloist: Santos Ojeda)	Gershwin

The printed program for this concert was more elaborate than the inaugural concert. This time, the program listed the names of the orchestra members and provided program notes for each composition. The "Profesión de fe" on the printed program of the inaugural concert was replaced with a special announcement written by Caturla. Caturla's announcement is an inspired statement in which he not only expressed his gratitude for support and recognition of the Orquesta de Conciertos de Caibarién, but also hope for the future at a time when Cuba was already sliding into depression and was only months away from a complete collapse of the Machado government:

TO OUR PUBLIC

The Concert Orchestra of Caibarién does not have the words to express its profound gratitude to the public in this town for its generous response granted on the occasion of its inaugural performance. It is comforting in the extreme to feel backing in this manner by an entire town, in this hour full of confusion, disintegration and distaste; and in exchange for such gentility, the Orchestra has the firm purpose of continuing on the path just begun, and to reaffirm more each time the postulates put forth in its profession of faith; especially when the vigorous adherence from neighboring towns and even distant ones, such as Santiago de Cuba, Santa Clara, Havana, Manzanillo, Yaguajay, Vueltas and Remedios, whose presses, like the one here, have cooperated notably to lift up our humble labors. We are then, on the footpath of work, which means having our sights set on the path that leads to the summit.

The directors.[13]

The printed program for the Concierto Extraordinario also included Caturla's notes in which he cited Cowell as one of the most distinguished composers of new music in the entire world. He then went on to credit Cowell's sponsorship of his and Roldán's music in New York, Paris, Berlin, Prague, and other major music capitals of the world.

The Third and Final Concert: 15 April 1933

With the success of his first two concerts behind him, Caturla stepped deeper into the interior for his third (and final) concert of the Orquesta de Conciertos de Caibarién in the town of Vueltas. Smaller and less culturally developed than Remedios or Caibarién, the rural atmosphere of Vueltas, a rugged agricultural and ranch farm district, offered new challenges. It was the first "out of town" concert (by-passing Remedios) and an opportunity for Caturla to reinforce his convictions for upgrading cultural tastes in the country by present-ing concerts of contemporary music in keeping with PAAC stan-dards. Once the date and program for the Vueltas concert had been established, Caturla wrote to Henry Cowell, notifying him that *Exul-tation* would be performed again and that he was already presenting conferences in Caibarién on his (Cowell's) use of "tone clusters."

While the previous Concierto Extraordinario at Caibarién was in-tended as a tribute to José Martí, it also served to clarify its purpose as a chamber orchestra that would function as a counterpart to the PAAC. Caturla made this clear in a letter to the American composer Wallingford Riegger, written on the eve of the Vueltas concert:

> I find myself at the moment in front of the Concert Orchestra of Caiba-rién, an institution that would be most pleased if you would send your works to perform them in our concerts. My interest lies in doing my part to help my fellow composers of the Pan American, among which you find yourself, and in addition, to correspond to your attention. About our concert of tomorrow, in the program of which is included Henry Cowell's EXULTATION I have the pleasure of including samples of the same. Awaiting your news, I reiterate myself, your most affection-ate friend and sincere servant.[14]

While preparing publicity for the Vueltas concert, Caturla took great care to emphasize the premiere of *Kid Chocolate (Poema Negro)* by his former student Abelardo Cuevas, referring to it as the "twin brother" of *Bembé*. Writing to Nena Benítez, critic for Havana's *Di-ario de la Marina*, Caturla praised Cuevas, citing him as a possible "pioneer." Later he wrote to Cuevas (who by then had moved to Ha-vana to become oboe soloist and English horn player under Roldán in the Orquesta Filarmónica de La Habana), mentioning that notices of the premiere of his *Kid Chocolate* appeared in *Diario de la Marina* and *El País*. He also mentioned that programs for the forthcoming Vueltas concert had been sent to five different parts of the world.

The third concert of the Orquesta de Conciertos de Caibarién was presented on 15 April 1933, in Vueltas at the Teatro "Niza." The program consisted of the following pieces:

PROGRAM

Overture to *The Magic Flute*	Mozart
Ma Mère l'Oye Suite	Ravel
La Fille Aux Cheveaux de Lin	Debussy
Exultation (Poema)	Cowell
La Vida Breve (Danza Española No. 1)	de Falla
Kid Chocolate (Poema Negro)	Cuevas
Bembé (Movimiento sinfónico)	Caturla
Rhapsody in Blue (soloist: Santos Ojeda)	Gershwin

Following the Vueltas concert, Juan Morenza Abreu published a short notice in *El Faro* entitled: "Kid Chocolate—The Free Negro; Bembé—The Black Slave." After citing Caturla as the "sublime captivator of our rhythms, heart, soul and life of the orchestral ensemble," Morenza Abreu continued his review by stating that the fatherland can expect "a halo of improvement and hope and art" as a result of the diffusion of music by Caturla's Orquesta de Conciertos de Caibarién. Referring to the "epoch of transition in which we live" from Portuondo's "vibrant and most Cuban article about the nationalist labor that produced the gigantic effort of García Caturla," Morenza Abreu hailed Caturla as a genius who raised himself above an "atmosphere in which personal egoism drowns and destroys the best of projects most of the time." After mentioning the solo performances of Santos Ojeda, "a prodigy on piano who deserved much applause," Morenza Abreu concluded his article by noting: "Vueltas lived a moment of indescribable emotions. It showed its respect before great artists. . . . Complimentary conclusion: He left eyes open for the conquest."[15]

Caturla left for Havana shortly after the Vueltas concert to greet Nicolas Slonimsky, who had arrived there to conduct two concerts of contemporary music. During his stay in Havana, Slonimsky informed Caturla of his intentions to publish news about the Orquesta de Conciertos in *Modern Music* and mentioned that Gershwin was very pleased to know that his *Rhapsody in Blue* had been performed three times in Cuba by Caturla's Orquesta de Conciertos.[16] While in Havana Caturla wrote to José María Montalván and "Lordi" Martín y Garatea that news of his Orquesta de Conciertos de Caibarién was spreading and his friends in Havana were inquiring about future concerts. He also informed them that the possibility of bringing his orchestra to Havana had been proposed by Cuevas, a plan that did not materialize because of economic limitations. Seeking further developments for his orchestra, Caturla wrote to Wilfred Colon in Sydney, Australia, and Henry Cowell, suggesting an exchange of new music between PAAC and Cuban composers.

However, as August approached, neither of these plans materialized. Writing to José Ardévol on 2 August 1933, Caturla mentioned that the Orquesta de Conciertos was presently "in recess." Later that month he expressed hopes to continue his work with the Orquesta de Conciertos in a letter to Fernando Ortiz:

> I founded—in 1932—a Concert Orchestra in Caibarién, and have been working toward promoting culture in the towns in this sector. With the renewal of national life—a hint of which will soon appear—*my musicians and I will continue with this much needed work*. Can you imagine— you who know Caibarién—the audience for my concerts listening to Stravinsky, Ravel, Cowell, and the other paladins of avant-garde music. [italics mine][17]

As summer 1933 in Cuba drew to a close the consequences of political upheaval and economic depression brought about extreme hardships for everyone; district judges such as Caturla, caught up in the reorganization of the judicial court system, were faced with enormous workloads. Caturla's plans for the Orquesta de Conciertos de Caibarién had to be postponed—a postponement that became permanent. In the span of less than one year Caturla single-handedly (and against the odds in his hometown of Remedios) established a chamber orchestra that could function as a branch of PAAC while gaining recognition throughout Cuba and abroad. However, unlike Cowell's PAAC, whose goals were not politically motivated, Caturla's goals for the Orquesta de Conciertos were motivated by political as well as artistic ideals. The success of the Orquesta de Conciertos validated Caturla's mission to present music of the avant-garde to the working class of the interior by their own musicians. In doing so, he broke down existing class barriers that normally reserved such music for the privileged, proving that the interior of Cuba was ready for change to new, progressive cultural standards. The hope and stimulation Caturla offered his audiences may be seen as a reaction against the existing state of the arts in

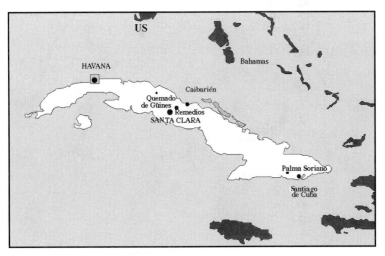

This map of Cuba indicates cities where García Caturla lived and worked.

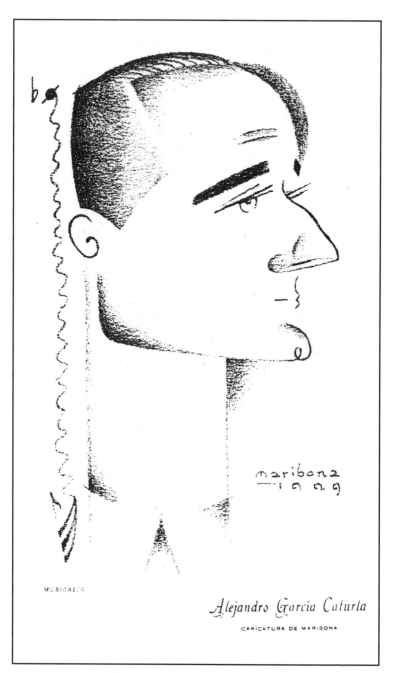

Caricature of García Caturla.

Caturla's maternal grandfather: Don José de Caturla Rojas (1837–1887).

Caturla's maternal grandmother, Laudelina García de Caturla (center), with her family circle, circa 1884. Caturla's mother, Diana, is in the top row, far right. His uncle Marcelo is seated in front of her (wearing the hat). The young man sitting front and center is Caturla's uncle Edgardo, one of his strong supporters in the family.

Caturla's father: Silvino E. García Balmaseda.

Caturla's mother: Diana de Caturla y García.

Caturla's birthplace in Remedios: Calle José Antonio Peña #14. The commemorative plaque reads: "En Esta Casa Nació El Genial Músico Cubano Alejandro García Caturla. 7-3-1906 A 1986. P. P. Remedios [In this house was born the Cuban musical genius Alejandro García Caturla. 7 March 1906–1986]." (The "1986" is for the year the plaque was put in place; "P. P. Remedios" probably means it was put there by the citizens [pueblo] of Remedios.)

The García Caturla residence in Remedios: Calle General Carrillo #4, near the Parque José Martí. (The house was built in 1875 by Don José de Caturla Rojas.)

Lorenzo Martín y Garatea.

San Juan Bautista church (eighteenth century) in Remedios.

Teatro Miguel Bru in Remedios.

Caturla (top, second from left) with his Jazz Band Caribe in Havana.

María Muñoz de Quevedo.

Caturla with his Orquesta de Conciertos de Caibarién, 1932.

Septimino Cuevas (Abelardo Cuevas is at far left).

Caturla's publication
of his own music in
Havana, 1925.

Announcement of Caturla's music at the Festivales Sinfónicos, Barcelona, 1929.

Caturla's supplement in
Musicalia, 1930: *Son en Eb.*

Caturla at home, 1929.

Caturla's official portrait, 1929.

This is the last photograph ever taken of Caturla. Havana,
November 1940.

Caturla was shot to death here, at the Calle Independencia. The commemorative plaque reads: "El Pueblo de Caibarién a la Memoria del Gran Músico Remediano Dr. Alejandro García Caturla. 1940–Noviembre 12, 1941 [From the people of Caibarién to the memory of the great Remedian musician Dr. Alejandro García Caturla. 1940–November 12, 1941]." The plaque was installed one year after Caturla's death, on 12 November 1941.

This is the García Caturla family tomb at the Remedios cemetery following Caturla's death.

Caturla's widow, Catalina Rodríguez y Caturla, with Charles White. (Catalina's name was legally changed to include the Caturla family name after the 1959 Castro revolution.) Guanabacoa, Cuba, November 1996.

Cuba—a reaction that was in step with the pending overthrow of Presidente Gerardo Machado. Perhaps it is not coincidental that each of the three Orquesta de Conciertos de Caibarién concerts opened with music that symbolizes freedom and brotherhood: Mozart's Overture to *The Magic Flute*. In any case it was not long after the Vueltas concert that the musical world around Caturla, including PAAC, collapsed:

> The Pan American Association was perhaps a victim of the general chaos in the Western world of the mid-1930's. Already suffering financially, its weak organizational structure could not stand up to the pressures—artistic and otherwise—of the Great Depression. The Association died of neglect. Yet it had fulfilled its goal of stimulating the compositions, performance, and wider appreciation of the instinctive music of the various publics of Americas.[18]

By establishing a chamber orchestra that became Cuba's counterpart to Slonimsky's Chamber Orchestra of Boston and PAAC orchestras abroad (financed for Slonimksy by Charles Ives) Caturla succeeded in fulfilling that part of his goals for the Orquesta de Conciertos de Caibarién, at least temporarily. But more importantly, he succeeded in providing concerts by outstanding young Cuban musicians from the interior in programs of avant-garde music that reflected the ideals of a new generation: these are goals that were clearly stated in the Orquesta de Conciertos de Caibarién's "Profesión de fe." And the inclusion of Afro-Cuban compositions such as *Kid Chocolate* by the young Cuevas and his own *Bembé* at the final concert of the Orquesta de Conciertos leaves one with no doubt that Caturla went beyond these goals by setting paths for future Cuban composers, paths that unfortunately were lost or misunderstood in the chaos of social unrest.

NOTES

1. García Caturla, "Septimino Cuevas," 2.
2. The concert was to benefit the new Biblioteca Pública José Martí in Remedios that his brother, Othón, recently inaugurated.
3. Henríquez, *Correspondencia,* 30 de diciembre 1931, 259–60.
4. Gallardo, "Alejandro García Caturla."
5. From the program notes of the inaugural concert of the Orquesta de Conciertos de Caibarién, 12 December 1932.

6. Portuondo, "Compases de redención." His article was later reprinted in the Remedios journal *El Faro.*

7. Henríquez, *Correspondencia,* 1 de febrero 1933, 265.

8. Santos Ojeda studied piano with César Pérez Sentenat, pianist for the Orquesta Filarmónica de La Habana and close friend of Amadeo Roldán and Caturla.

9. "Bembé," *El Faro,* 15 December 1932, 2. L. Sanchéz de Algibay, "Música," *El Comercio,* 15 December 1932, 3.

The very first performance of Gershwin's *Rhapsody in Blue* in Cuba was by Ernesto Lecuona with the Orquesta Sinfónica de La Habana, under the direction of Gonzalo Roig on 21 April 1929.

10. In a formal *Motion* to the Orquesta de Conciertos, Caturla lashed out at Herberto Romero's group, reminding his orchestra of Romero's disruptive behavior at his concert the previous year with the Septimino Cuevas. Caturla then flatly refused to allow Romero's saxophone quartet to appear on the same program with the Orquesta de Conciertos, accusing them of impoverishing the intellectual atmosphere in Remedios that resulted in a collapse of its cultural climate.

11. In a letter to Cowell (written in English) Caturla informed him that "People are dazzled with the rich work of you" [*sic*]. He enclosed the program for the next "Caibarién Chamber Orchestra" concert, spelling out his band orchestration of Cowell's "beautiful" *Exultation,* originally composed for strings and piano. The letter ended with Caturla's plea to have his only score of *Primera suite cubana,* which Slonimsky had just performed in New York, returned. Earlier Cowell had written to Caturla: "I am delighted that you have an orchestra, and that you have honored me by a performance of my 'Exultation' for strings. This is the first performance of this work in the Western Hemisphere—in America, in other words! It has been played in Berlin, Breslau, Warsaw, Copenhagen, Paris etc. but never here." See Caturla to Cowell, 11 January 1933, and Cowell to Caturla, 7 January 1933, from García Caturla, "Correspondencia inédita."

12. Caturla to Othón García Caturla, 11 de enero 1933, from García Caturla, "Correspondencia inédita."

13. From the printed program of the second concert of the Orquesta de Conciertos de Caibarién, 30 de enero 1933.

14. Caturla to Riegger, 14 de abril 1933, from García Caturla, "Correspondencia inédita." Caturla was familiar with Wallingford Riegger's music through Cowell's *New Music Quarterly.* It was Riegger who returned Caturla's manuscript of *Primera suite cubana,* at which point Caturla discovered Slonimsky's unauthorized edits (cuts).

15. Morenza Abreu, "Kid Chocolate." The only notice found in the Havana press following the Vueltas concert was in *La Voz.* Written by Francisco V. Portela under the column "Musicales," it cited the premiere of *Kid Chocolate* by Cuevas and gave praise to the "worthy artistic endeavors" of Caturla.

16. George Gershwin visited Havana in 1932. Slonimsky conducted Gershwin's *Cuban Overture (Rumba)* and Caturla's *Fanfarria para despertar espiritus apollillados* at the second of his Havana concerts on 30 April 1933.

17. Caturla to Ortiz, 20 August 1933, from García Caturla, "Correspondencia inédita."

18. Deane L. Root, *Yearbook*, 60–61.

Chapter Fifteen

Aftermath of Caturla's Orquesta de Conciertos de Caibarién

Undoubtedly, the success of Caturla's Orquesta de Conciertos de Caibarién—although short-lived—proved to be a profound experience for him. Ultimately, it strengthened his determination to continue his ongoing mission of raising cultural standards of the working class in the interior and possibly opening doors to a conducting career in Havana.

Following the debut of his Orquesta de Conciertos de Caibarién, Caturla wrote to José Antonio Portuondo indicating the direction he wished to follow in his music. Caturla's alliance with Portuondo's political views are apparent in this letter, one that also reflects Caturla's ideals as to the true purpose of the Orquesta de Conciertos de Caibarién:

> Sr. José A. Portuondo
> Santiago de Cuba
> Comrade:
>   . . . My brother has spoken to me many times about you, and we both praise your courageous and fresh poetry—*oriented towards the conscious use of folkloric Afrocuban material*—and I even have in mind to set one of your works to music, as I have done with those of Nicolás Guillén and Emilio Ballagas. [italics mine][1]

As it turned out, Caturla did not set any of Portuondo's "folkloric Afrocuban material" to music (including Portuondo's *Mari-Sabel*). The music alluded to in the letter—*Mulata* from Guillén's *Motivos de Son* and the unfinished *Nombres negros en el Son* (Black names in the

151

Son) by Ballagas—was composed shortly before the inaugural concert of the Orquesta de Conciertos de Caibarién.[2]

The existing music of *Nombres negros en el Son* reflects a new type of orchestration by Caturla that captures sonorities essential to the *Son conjuntos* of that time. Unlike his previous orchestration of *Dos poemas afrocubanos*, for full symphony orchestra, Caturla places the folk poetry of Ballagas in an intimate orchestration, including Afro-Cuban percussion, that evokes the aesthetics of the *Son*: bass clarinet, bassoons (2), claves, *güiro*, horns (2), maracas, oboe, petite timpani, soprano, string bass.

The integrated use of *Son* rhythm (bassoons, bass clarinet, and then voice) against a steady shaking of maracas and syncopated rhythms for petite tympani found therein relate to Afro-Cuban musical elements (see figure 15.1 below).

Whether or not *Nombres negros en el Son* may have been considered for eventual performance by Caturla's Orquesta de Conciertos is unknown. In any case, his setting of Emilio Ballagas's poem was left unfinished, as he was overburdened by work and caught up in the struggle to form his Orquesta de Conciertos de Caibarién. To make matters worse, the state of Cuba's economy was at an all-time low, and Caturla's efforts to remain in Havana—including an advertisement to teach orchestration—brought forth (in his own words) "disastrous results." Caturla summed up his situation in a letter to Carpentier:

> My Dear Alejo:
> [M]y economic situation has worsened noticeably, and I am not lying if I say that I am in the same condition as 99% of the Cuban people, to such an extreme that in order to support myself I have had to return to my law practice.
>   Although . . . for me, Havana exists as an important musical place for premiering my works, it is no longer what it once was.[3]

The other music he alluded to in his letter to José Antonio Portuondo, *Mulata*, was composed in November 1932. *Mulata* is the second and last of Guillén's *Motivos de Son* that Caturla set to music; it bears the subtitle *Poema para voz y piano* (poem for voice and piano). Unlike the first *Motivos* Caturla set to music, *Bito Manué*, the melodic and rhythmic elements of *Mulata* relate directly to elements of

Figure 15.1. *Nombres negros en el Son,* mm. 6–9.

African music. The repetitious chantlike melodic motives at the very beginning (see figure 15.2 below) and drumlike syncopated patterns that enter later (see figure 15.3 below) are but a few illustrations of these elements.

The severe dissonance throughout Caturla's *Mulata,* polytonal at times, express the pain of indignities and mockery found in Guillén's bitter text.[4] It was just this kind of musical language that also reflected Caturla's sense of "blessed rebelliousness" that he previously wrote of to José Antonio Portuondo. And when the Orquesta de Conciertos de Caibarién concerts came to an end, Caturla and his brother, Othón, continued their quest for social reform through the publication of *Atalaya,* their own literary journal.

Figure 15.2.   *Mulata,* mm. 1–12.

Figure 15.3. *Mulata,* mm. 21–30.

NOTES

1. Henríquez, *Correspondencia,* 1 de febrero 1933, 265.

2. Emilio Ballagas (who was born in Camagüey in 1908 and died in Havana in 1954) became widely known for his *poesía afrocubana,* popularized by the well-known mulatto recitalist Eusebia Cosme; Caturla was a close friend of Ballagas and Cosme. Following his studies at the University of Havana, Emilio Ballagas settled in Santa Clara, Cuba, where he became professor of literature and Spanish at the Escuela Normal. Following are some excerpts from *Nombres negros en el Son* by Emilio Ballagas.

Repica por ti mi canto lo mismo que un atabal

. . . .

Rita Barranco, mulata, tu nombre cálido y lindo,

tu voz, tu color . . . envuelven en pulpa de tamarindo.
Rita Barranco, sí, Rita Barranco, no,
de carne tostada al fuego, de carne quemada al sol,
de tersa carne templada al fuego como un bongó.

. . . .

Al tiqui-tí de las claves
las parejas ahondan cielos concéntricos de contacto
y van resbalando lentas sobre las notas del Son
que caen espesas y anchas como gotas de jabón.

[My song is beating for you like a kettledrum.

. . . .

Rita Barranco mulatto girl, your pretty hot name,
your voice, your color . . . wrapped in tamarindo paste.
Rita Barranco yes, Rita Barranco, no,
made of fire-burnt flesh, of sun-burnt flesh,
of glassy flesh tightened by fire like a bongo.

. . . .

To the tick-tack of the claves
the couples make deep concentric skies of contact,
and are slowing down on the notes of the Son
that are falling like thick and wide soap bubbles.]

3. Henríquez, *Correspondencia*, 18 de mayo 1932, 261.
4. Text of *Mulata* by Nicolás Guillén.

> Ya yo me enteré, mulata,
> mulata, ya sé que dise
> que yo tengo la narise
> como nudo de cobbata.
> Y fijate bien que tú
> no ere tan adelantá,
> porque tu boca e bien grande,
> y tu pasa, colorá.
> Tanto tren con tu cuerpo,
> tanto tren;
> tanto tren con tu boca,
> tanto tren;
> tanto tren con tus ojos,
> tanto tren.
> Si tú supiera, mulata,
> la beddá;
> ¡que yo con mi negra tengo,
> y no te quiero pa na!
>
> [I found out that you, mulatta,
> are saying that
> my nose is
> tied like a knot.

And let me tell you
That you are not so far advanced
Because your mouth is pretty big
and your kinky hair is red.
So much bragging about your body,
So much bragging about your mouth,
So much bragging about tus ojos,
If you would know the truth, mulatta,
I have enough with my black woman,
And I don't want you for nothing.]

Chapter Sixteen

Self-Renewal:"To Unite Is the Word of Order"

"STUDENTS UNITE!"

As Cuba was reaching a boiling point of political unrest that eventually led to the collapse of Gerardo Machado's dictatorship (12 August 1933), Caturla and Othón launched *Atalaya* (Watchtower)—a new, progressive periodical—in Remedios in mid-July of that year. Just how daring and courageous they were may be seen in their manifesto against Machado, "Students Unite," which appeared in the first issue. In it Alejandro and Othón García Caturla declared: "Since Machado began his destructive and ignominious reign of tyranny, the student forces find themselves forming a single nucleus." And after quoting José Martí's slogan, "To unite is the word of order," they continued:

> All should be united in these critical moments of the Republic, an initial one of the Revolution, because now begins the Revolution against those who believe that with the shameful departure of the tyrant and the fall of his lackeys, everything has ended. This is the end of the beginning.[1]

CATURLA'S SELF-VINDICATION

Equally assertive was Alejandro's article "Realidad de la utilización sinfónica del instrumental cubano" that also appeared in the first issue of *Atalaya*. In it, Caturla took issue with people in Remedios and elsewhere who labeled him as an "opportunist." He also pointed out proudly in his article that a number of notable composers had adopted his suggestions concerning the use of Afro-Cuban percussion instruments in chamber or symphonic music:

> [W]ith deep satisfaction *I've been vindicated* and the pages of *Musicalia* have grown in stature since my suggestion has become a reality: two notable composers are currently including our typical instruments in their orchestrations, . . . and another has made an analytical study which he'll publish in this section of *Atalaya*. . . . The first . . . is Edgard Varèse and the [second] French Mario Francisco Gaillard and the third: Henry Cowell. [italics mine][2]

After citing Edgard Varèse's *Ionization* (for percussion only—including Cuban percussion instruments) and Gaillard's use of Cuban percussion instruments (influenced by Carpentier), Caturla continued his article by alluding to the influence that Alejo Carpentier (*"mi amigo y colaborador"* [my friend and collaborator]) had had upon these French composers since he moved to Paris, where he was involved with promoting Cuban music. Caturla's article ends with additional evidence that his suggested use of Cuban percussion instruments by classical conductors was now a reality:

> Our percussion instruments are being sold everywhere in musical establishments all over. I saw the director Slonimsky carry from Carreras' window an arsenal of maracas, claves, güiros and even a magical Afro-Cuban drum for which he paid seventeen dollars.[3]

Although short and defensive, Caturla's article set the record straight, leaving his critics (particularly those in Remedios) with much to reconsider.

Among the invited contributors to *Atalaya* to be mentioned are José Antonio Portuondo, Carlos Raggi, Nicolás Guillén, Juan Pérez Abreu, and Edgardo Caturla (physician and uncle of Caturla) of Remedios and others. Writing to Nicolás Guillén, whose provocative poem *Ballada del güije* also appeared in the very first issue of *Atalaya*, Caturla described the impact of his and Othón's new journal:

> [*Atalaya*] . . . has generally been well accepted by the scarce intellectual minority around here—as is natural—; nevertheless, there are reactionary spirits who clamor for six months' arrest for you and three for the directors of Atalaya for including your work. Fortunately they are not the authorities; otherwise we would be heading for Principe or a similar prison, for the crime of offenses against the state.[4]

Although it was short-lived because of the pressing economy and increased professional workloads placed upon the Caturla brothers (Othón, besides being an exceptional pianist, was also in the field of law), *Atalaya* provided a stunning record of their belief in the 1933 revolution and their vision of changes in the social and political climate of Remedios. Among the many cultural elite to whom the Caturla brothers sent copies of *Atalaya* was Fernando Ortiz, then living in Washington, D.C. Caturla's accompanying letter, dated 20 August 1933, reflects the zeal with which he and Othón set out to improve the state of the arts in their district:

> My esteemed D. Fernando:
> My most cordial congratulations to you for the large part that I know you have played in the defeat of the tyranny. . . .
> Here goes the third issue of our magazine Atalaya which my brother Othón and I edit here in Remedios, as a present for you, who takes such an interest in anything related to our culture.[5]

As Cuba's post-Machado leaders faltered, Caturla wrote to his brother (5 September 1933) expressing hopes of a coup that would be recognized by the United States and at the same time put in place an energetic and revolutionary government. After pointing out that reorganizing and cleaning up the army and judiciary power were essentials of the revolution, he continued:

> I believe that now my possibilities for collaborating in the government have been strengthened, even though I have not been an active revolutionary, I do have the required qualifications to work in it: proven honesty and youthful and leftist spirit.[6]

Ultimately, Caturla followed his own path, fighting for justice and social equality in the courts, while composing music that reflected his cause in a daring, progressive style.

THE RETURN OF NICOLAS SLONIMSKY

As previously mentioned, following the final concert of his Orquesta de Conciertos de Caibarién in Vueltas (15 April 1933), Caturla returned to Havana briefly to welcome Nicolas Slonimsky. From Havana, Slonimsky and the Quevedos had wired Caturla, "Accept our sincere congratulations on the success of the concert of new music by the Orquesta de Conciertos de Caibarién."[7] Subsequently, Caturla lost no time in getting to Havana for Slonimsky's concerts.

Caturla received his mangled manuscript of *Primera suite cubana* a short time before Slonimsky arrived in Cuba. In spite of his anger at Slonimsky's unauthorized cuts, Caturla established a high-spirited camaraderie with Slonimsky during his final visit to Havana. Slonimsky presented two concerts with the Orquesta Filarmónica at the Teatro Nacional; one on 23 April and the other on 30 April. As previously mentioned, Caturla's original plan was to have his *Rumba* and Igor Stravinsky's *Rite of Spring* conducted by Slonimsky at these concerts. However, Caturla's *Rumba* was replaced by George Gershwin's *Cuban Overture* (subtitled "La Rumba") at Slonimsky's first concert, and Stravinsky's *Rite of Spring* was abandoned altogether.[8] Following the first concert, Caturla wrote to Henry Cowell (in English): "April 28, 1933: Now I'm in Havana with Slonimsky . . . and in this minute with Antonio and María—'chez elle'. We are remembering—very much—to you [sic]."[9]

Except for the opening composition on the program (J. S. Bach's *Suite No. 2*), the second concert was a showcase of contemporary music that reflected Slonimsky's witty, daring, and flamboyant personality:

Varèse: *Octandre; Ionización*
Schönberg: *Acompañamiento a una escena cinematográfica*
Bliss: *Conversaciones; Fanfarria para un discurso político*
Revueltas: *Colorines*
Copland: *Música para teatro*
Satie: *Fanfarria para despertar un gran mono que duerme sólo con un ojo*
Falla, Milhaud, Goossens, Stravinski, Prokofiev: *Fanfarrias*

From Remedios, after the second concert, Caturla wrote to Cowell again (19 May 1933) describing the two Slonimsky concerts as simply "splendid," adding that there was much discussion about all the works played, particularly the *Fanfares*.[10]

The advance publicity for Slonimsky's two concerts was plentiful, including photos and biographical references (especially in the Havana newspaper *El Mundo*) and notices of the two programs he was to present. Slonimsky's short and final visit to Havana for these concerts was a resounding success. And, like Caturla's concerts with his Orquesta de Conciertos de Caibarién in Vueltas just days before, brought to a close a unique and amazing episode in the development of contemporary music in Cuba.

CUBAN MUSIC: A DEFINITION BY CATURLA AND ROLDÁN

Shortly after Slonimsky's 1933 Havana concerts, Cowell sent several copies of his recently published book, *American Composers on American Music,* to Caturla. Cowell's *American Composers* included two articles by Cuban composers: "The Development of Cuban Music" by Caturla and "The Artistic Position of the American Composer" by Roldán. Caturla and Roldán insisted in their articles, written in 1931, that native composers not imitate European music, if they wanted to "express their inner message to the outer world through music."[11] Other tenets shared by Caturla and Roldán in their articles include the use of "living folklore," new forms derived of Afro-Cuban "native music," and the use of Cuban percussion instruments in symphonic music. While Caturla had already stated these principles in his article "Posibilidades sinfónicas de la musica afrocubana" (*Musicalia* 1929), he repeated them in his article for Cowell's book: "Nothing could be farther from the line of Cuban musical progress than for its composers to drift into an imitation of current European tendencies."[12] This stance coincided with Roldán's view of liberating Cuban music from European influences: "Our efforts should tend toward constant attention to the contemporary movement in the artistic world, from the technical and the aesthetic point of view, and with the final aim of avoiding in our American art any attempt at Europeanization."[13]

Except for some comments on the aesthetics of music that are ambiguous at best, Caturla's short article also expresses the spirit and pride with which he and Roldán created new paths for the future of Cuban music.

CATURLA'S *LA RUMBA*

Caturla's use of African musical elements in his symphonic music reached a climax with *La Rumba.* Completed on 9 August 1933 and dedicated to his brother, Othón, it is a musical setting of the poem *La Rumba* by one of the early Minorista poets, José Zacarias Tallet.[14] Initially, the musical score was composed for soprano and full symphony orchestra, including Afro-Cuban percussion instruments. In respect to the poetry and orchestration, *La Rumba* may be seen as a sequel to Caturla's *Yamba-O* of 1931. The difference lies in the fact that Zacarias Tallet's poetic rendering of Cuba's most popular and most African dance form—rumba—provided Caturla with an ideal text to symbolize, in music, the new era of a post-Machado "Free Cuba" (Caturla appended the phrase *"Cuba Libre"* to his letters at this time). In doing so, he raised the rumba—music associated with the lower working class of Afro-Cubans—to an art form equal to that of compositions such as Maurice Ravel's *La Valse,* thus changing forever the meaning of rumba in the historical context of Cuban symphonic music.

Prior to the completion of *La Rumba,* Caturla visited Havana to negotiate the premiere of this music with Roldán and the Orquesta Filarmónica. Because a suitable soprano to sing the difficult vocal part could not be found, they settled on a version for orchestra alone to be scheduled at a later date. In the meantime Caturla wrote to Henry Cowell:

> I am just finishing a new score for high voice and Orchestra. . . . I should like to have it played first by the PAAC either in New York or California or in any other important city. Do you think Miss Mary Bell would be willing to sing it? As you tell me, she is a good singer [and] I am willing to entrust her with the first performance of it. As soon as I am through with the score I will send it to you. It is entitled La Rumba and its musical shape is something like Bembé, though a little shorter than it.[15]

Clearly, Caturla placed his hopes for a performance of the original version of *La Rumba* (that is, *with* the vocal part) in the hands of Henry Cowell and the PAAC. However, it would be several months before he sent a copy of this music to Cowell, who eventually listed it in his catalog of manuscripts for orchestra and chamber works (*New Music Quarterly*); the performance Caturla envisioned with Mary Bell as vocalist did not materialize. Ultimately, it remained for Roldán and the Orquesta Filarmónica to give the first performance of Caturla's *La Rumba* in an arrangement, as already mentioned, for orchestra alone. The concert took place at the Teatro Nacional in Havana on 31 December 1933. Thus, Caturla's original musical setting of Zacarias Tallet's poem for voice and symphony orchestra met the same fate as his original musical setting of Carpentier's poem *Liturgia (Yamba-O).* Both were premiered as wordless, symphonic compositions with the text of the poem printed in the program.[16]

Unlike *Yamba-O*, Caturla followed the text of Zacarias Tallet's *La Rumba* closely by using rhythmic patterns that matched the poet's onomatopoeic sound groupings and rhythms that worked with the narrative lines as they unfold in the poem. Once started, the succession of musical sections that follow create a rondo-variation form "something like Bembé," as Caturla said. The original score, for voice and symphony orchestra, consists of the following instrumentation:

bassoons (2)	petite clarinette E♭
caisse claire	piano
cencerros	piccolo
clarinette basse B♭	tam-tam
clarinettes in B♭ (2)	timbales cubanos
claves	timpany
contrabasses	triangulo
contrabassoon	trombones (3)
cor anglais	trompettes in C (3)
cors in F (4)	tuba
flutes (3)	viola
güiro	violins (1 & 2)
hautbois (2)	violoncellos
maracas	voice

INTERNAL RELATIONSHIPS OF TEXT AND MUSIC FOUND IN *LA RUMBA*

Following a short instrumental introduction that quickly captures the mood and spirit of a rumba, Caturla establishes the main theme for voice, derived of rhythms from the first stanza of Zacarias Tallet's poem. All instrumental sounds to accompany these lines are in a mid to low range with rhythmic ostinatos played first on the piano, and then doubled by the timpani. The *güiro* has its own independent ostinato and lends an authentic African element to the dark coloration of sounds. The following (see figure 16.1 below) illustrates this theme in the context of Caturla's syncopated rhythmic counterpoint.

Figure 16.1. *La Rumba,* mm. 13–20.

Caturla's rhythmic setting of "Zumba mamá" in figure 16.1 serves as a basis for further development and variation as the music progresses. Of equal importance is his use of call and response—another African element—between voice and trumpet in a contrasting stanza built on the words "Chaqui, chaqui, chaqui, charáqui!" A rhythmic ostinato by the shaking and rubbing of maracas and *güiro* during this passage suggests an atmosphere of ritual related to the rumba, while intensifying the rhythmic counterpoint (see figure 16.2 below):

Figure 16.2. *La Rumba*, mm. 87–92.

Zacarias Tallet brings his poem *La Rumba* to a climatic end with a vivid description of the rumba couple falling to the floor, possessed by spirits as the bongo breaks forth:

> Al suelo se viene la niña Tomasa,
> al suelo se viene José Encarnación;
> y allí se revuelcan con mil contorsiones,
> se les sube el santo, se rompió el bongó,
> se acabó la rumba, con-con-co-ma-bó!
> Pa-ca, pa-ca, pa-ca, pa-ca, pa-ca!
> Pam! Pam! Pam!
> [Tomasa falls to the floor,
> José Encarnación falls to the floor;
> Once on the floor, they writhe in a thousand contortions,

They are possessed by the spirit, the bongó breaks,
The rumba has ended with con-con-co-ma-bó!
Pa-ca, pa-ca, pa-ca, pa-ca, pa-ca!
Pam! Pam! Pam!]

Except for the last two lines, Caturla dramatizes this text by placing in motion a driving pattern of ascending sequences for voice, doubled by trumpets surrounded by the full orchestra in an accelerated crescendo. The sequences are built on the same rhythm used at the beginning for "Zumba mamá," thus completing the overall rondo-variation form. When this exciting effect reaches its climax, the tempo suddenly changes to "lento" as the soprano, doubled by horns, chants in clearly separated syllables "con-con-co-ma-bó!" (see figure 16.3 below). A glissando by full orchestra rushes in on the last syllable to end this remarkable composition.

La Rumba was Caturla's last large-scale symphonic work for voice and orchestra based on Cuban lyric "Afro-Cubanismo" poetry. However, it was not his last effort to elevate popular Cuban musical forms to the level of art.

Figure 16.3.   *La Rumba*, mm. 287–99.

NOTES

1. García Caturla, "Students Unite," 1. Shortly after the overthrow of Machado, "Students Unite!" was reissued in the Remedios newspaper *El Faro* (31 August 1933). The Caturla brothers also contributed articles and reviews to *Atalaya* ranging from literature and poetry to polemics in Cuban history, news of the latest musical events in Havana (María Muñoz de Quevedo's Sociedad Coral, the Filarmónica, and other concerts) and abroad,

and cultural activities such as notices of new acquisitions to the new Biblioteca Pública José Martí of Remedios founded by Othón in late 1931.

2. García Caturla, "Realidad de la utilización," 3.

3. García Caturla, "Realidad de la utilización," 3. Slonimsky later took the Cuban percussion instruments he bought in Havana with him on his European tours.

Ionization is scored for percussion only, including such Cuban percussion instruments as maracas, *güiros,* bongos, claves, and others.

4. Henríquez, *Correspondencia,* 4 de agosto 1933, 270.

5. Caturla to Ortiz, 20 August 1933, from García Caturla, "Correspondencia inédita." Later, Othón dedicated an edition of his own publication *Traditions* to Fernando Ortiz.

6. Alejandro García Caturla to Othón García Caturla, 5 septiembre 1933, from García Caturla, "Correspondencia inédita." Laredo Bru of Remedios (and distant relative of Caturla) served as president of Cuba for a short period during this time.

7. Quevedos to Caturla, 4 April 1933, from García Caturla, "Correspondencia inédita." Caturla shared the contents of this telegram with members of his orchestra pointing out the *"gran efecto y beneficio"* (grand and beneficial effect) of Slonimsky's wire. Writing to Antonio Jiménez (percussionist in the Orquesta), Caturla suggested a performance of Slonimsky's *Suite infantile* at their next concert, planned for August or September, as an expression of gratitude. Slonimsky conducted this music at his previous concerts in Havana in 1931. By 1933 Slonimsky was the leading proponent of Caturla's music throughout the network of the PAAC, including North and South America, Mexico, and Europe.

8. The program for the first concert consisted of Mozart, *Serenata no. 3;* Sibelius, *En saga;* Gershwin, *Obertura Cubana;* Harris, *Obertura Americana;* Mussorgski, *Cuadros en una exposición.*

9. Caturla to Cowell, 28 April 1933, from García Caturla, "Correspondencia inédita."

10. Both Roldán and Caturla composed a short *Fanfare* for the Slonimsky concerts in Havana. The following July (1934), Slonimsky conducted the music of Roldán and Caturla at one of Cowell's concerts at the Hollywood Bowl, including Caturla's *Fanfarria para despertar espíritus apolillados,* a witty miniature (one minute in length and translated by Slonimsky as "Fanfare to Shake up an Old Fogey") and two selections from Roldán's ballet *La rebambaramba.*

11. García Caturla, "The Development of Cuban Music," 173.

12. García Caturla, "The Development of Cuban Music," 174.

13. Roldán, "The Artistic Position of the American Composer," 177.

14. José Zacarias Tallet (1893–1955) became director of the periodical *Revista de Avance* and later editor for the Havana newspaper *El País.* Zacarias Tallet wrote *La Rumba* in 1928; it was published that same year in the

Havana journal *Hatuey.* Shortly before the arrival of Nicolas Slonimsky, Havana celebrated on 31 March 1933 the appearance of Bertha Singerman, an Argentine singer-actress and recitalist. Beautiful and glamorous, her rendition of Zacarias Tallet's *La Rumba* was spectacular. Bertha Singerman captured the Havana press, winning rave reviews in the leading journals. Subsequently, she went on tour in Cuba (including Caibarién and Santa Clara), featuring a recitation of Zacarias Tallet's poem *La Rumba* as the centerpiece of her concerts. Her notoriety for performances of Zacarias Tallet's *La Rumba* became international and in 1934 she recited this poem in a scene of the Hollywood film *Nada más que una mujer* (Fox).

15. Caturla to Cowell, 31 July 1933, from García Caturla, "Correspondencia inédita." Caturla knew of Miss Mary Bell through Cowell's *New Music Quarterly* (to which he subscribed). Mary Bell was sponsored by Henry Cowell to sing the songs of Charles Ives in Hamburg in 1932, as part of the PAAC concerts abroad. Caturla later wrote to Cowell urging him to distribute *La Rumba* among his PAAC conductors and friends, "including Nicolas Slonimsky." Caturla also suggested that he would pay 50 percent of the costs for publishing *La Rumba* if PAAC would cover the rest, adding (in English) "Roldán have said me, and I believe in it, that *La Rumba* is my best work after the *First Cuban Suite* (*Primera suite cubana)*" (Caturla to Cowell, 15 April 1933, from García Caturla, "Correspondencia inédita"). And when Cowell's *New Music Quarterly* recording series began in 1934, Caturla urged Cowell to record his *La Rumba*—a request that went unfulfilled.

16. Caturla wrote to Zacarias Tallet in September of 1933 asking permission to publish his poem *La Rumba* in the program, notifying him that Cowell had promised to perform his *La Rumba* in New York and San Francisco through PAAC. These performances did not come to pass.

Chapter Seventeen

Culmination of a Creative Ideal: *Manita en el Suelo*

During the summer of 1931, while he was involved with the completion of *Yamba-O*, Caturla turned his thoughts once again to ballet. His determination to acquire a ballet libretto from Carpentier was heightened when Roldán's ballet suite *La rebambaramba* was performed that summer with great success as part of a pair of concerts (6 and 11 June 1931) in Paris under the direction of Nicolas Slonimsky. When Carpentier sent a cable of congratulations to Roldán with no mention of Caturla, whose *Bembé* was also enthusiastically received at the same concerts, Caturla expressed his hurt feelings to Carpentier:

> Although Roldán has been graced with your congratulations by cable and I am sure you won't drop me a line, I would be grateful if not to me, you would send to Antonio and María, for publication in *Musicalia* the more important reviews that were published about these two concerts.[1]

Carpentier did send the Paris reviews and subsequently diffused Caturla's hurt feelings.

After having literally begged Carpentier for a ballet text to set to music, Caturla took his most aggressive step toward this goal by writing to Carpentier: "I am prepared to make you a gift of 500 francs for sending me the libretto of our planned ballet *El Embó*. Let us see what your answer is to my offer."[2] Carpentier's response was negative. He was still somewhat despondent over the August 1929 death of Serge Diaghilev, the great Russian ballet

171

producer and choreographer in Paris. Carpentier believed that the
future of ballet had been jeopardized and that writing a ballet libretto then would be a waste of time.[3] He did, however, assure
Caturla that the idea of writing something for him had remained
an obsession since Caturla left Paris in 1928. In place of a ballet,
Carpentier suggested something for the theater that could also be
played in a concert version. Aware that performances of any kind
were difficult to manage at that time, he made the following proposal to Caturla:

> I thought of a piece for puppets, with only one live character, because
> it is easier to stage a piece with puppets than a piece with live singers.
> . . . The possibility of staging it the following way came to mind: next
> to a miniature theater—set up on the stage—Papá Montero sits down
> (the orchestra is also small) on the stage. . . . Papá Montero begins to re-
> cite over the drums, telling the story of "Manita en el Suelo," Iyamba
> [king] of the Ñáñigos, in the Spanish colonial times. . . . The curtain of
> the tiny theater is drawn away and the characters—Juan Indio, Juan
> Odio, Juan Esclavo; the Virgin of Caridad del Cobre, the Moon, the
> Chinaman of the Charade, Eribo, the Spanish Captain General—show
> us how "Manita en Suelo, for revenge, deflated the Moon with a stab."
> . . . It would take, in addition to Papá Montero, some five voices for
> whom easy parts could be written. . . . Do you think there is a possi-
> bility of putting on a concert version of such a thing?
>
> You will have the final say. . . . The idea for this piece came to me a
> long time ago, more than half is already written. . . .[4]

Caturla thought Carpentier's idea of a project with marionettes
was magnificent and proposed to start work on it as soon as he received the libretto. When it arrived (September 1931) he sent a copy
to Antonio de Quevedo asking him to have Hurtado de Mendoza
study its pictorial and scenographic possibilities that Carpentier described so vividly. He also notified Carpentier that the work could
not be completed before January or February of the following year
(1932), because he wanted it to be "impeccable," and wrote to Antonio de Quevedo again: "I hope that by March [1932] I will finish the
concert version of Manita so he [Slonimsky] can offer it as a premiere and as a novelty in our concerts in case those other works of
mine have been played too much."[5]

In the meantime, Carpentier planned to visit Cuba during that
time with hopes of finding a way to have *Manita en el suelo* per-

formed. His approach to having *Manita* produced in Havana was practical. As he pointed out to Caturla, "Although at first glance it may seem very complicated to you, it's so simple that one could stage it even in a place like Remedios."[6] To support this view, he also went on to offer the following advice:

> The puppets can be made with a cardboard tube and some rags. . . . A group of friends can be in charge of the action in a small theater. . . . The costumes are elemental: the only difficult one (the Captain General) can be made with colored paper and with some great mustaches. . . . And there is no backdrop, which is always difficult to obtain, since no painter would decide to put out twenty square yards of decoration.[7]

Apparently, Caturla intended to have the music for *Manita en el suelo* completed by March or April 1932. However, circumstances surrounding him at the time did not permit him to do so. A worsening national economy, commitment to finish his *Primera suite cubana* (dedicated to Nicolas Slonimsky), involvement with establishing his Orquesta de Conciertos de Caibarién, and frustrations with the musicians in Remedios account for most of these unfortunate circumstances. By then, Carpentier had canceled his trip to Cuba.[8] In the meantime, he assured Caturla again that the stage effects for *Manita* were basically simple and offered to send drawings of how to manipulate the puppets. Caturla responded: "I will start full fledged on our *Manita,* for which I have already sketched many ideas and made many notes. I keep with real interest all the notes you have given me about a realization of the staging and its possibilities."[9]

Several years passed before Caturla completed any of the music for *Manita* that he had already sketched. The first evidence of any completed music for *Manita* surfaced in a letter to Henry Cowell dated 12 December 1934. In it he mentioned the possibility of Lydia de Rivera singing the *Cockerl's Elegie* (*Elegía del Enkiko* from *Manita*'s scene III) at one of Varèse's Paris concerts, continuing (in English): "And now I'm enclosing to you this part [*Elegía del Enkiko*] of my Opera for piano and voice. Further I'll send the complete score. Judith Litante or Rudolphine Radil could to sing it [*sic*]. Please to say me [*sic*] soon what do you think about it. . . . Now I'm scoring the third scene."[10] Finishing the music for *Manita* occupied Caturla through 1937, with only a few details of orchestration left incomplete at the time of his premature death in 1940. The only music of

Manita en el suelo published during Caturla's lifetime was a piano version of *Elegía del Enkiko*. He notified Carpentier of this publication the year before his death:

> Manita has been finished for some time now. . . . *Social* which I believe is no longer being published, put in one of its final issues of 1937 a piano version that Conrado [Massaguer] asked for and which I did, of one of the capital numbers of our comic opera. I don't know if it ever reached your hands.[11]

SOME INTERNAL ASPECTS OF THE TEXT AND MUSIC OF *MANITA EN EL SUELO*

The title of the opera refers to Manuel Cañamazo, a famous Ñáñigo who lived during the latter half of the nineteenth century; "en el suelo" is an allusion to Manita's large hands, which almost touched the ground because of his long arms.[12] Carpentier's libretto, consisting of one act and five scenes, is based on a compilation of popular Cuban myths and legends and placed in an imaginary setting that provides for a synthesis of different popular rituals of folklore. Well-known Christian and African legends are juxtaposed against a mixture of rituals, riddles, magic, and miracles, using real and imaginary characters. There is also a deus ex machina at the end of the opera when the Chinaman of the Charade releases a new moon, restoring light and order, creating a "happy ending."

Carpentier's expert use of dialect quickly identifies the ethnicity of specific characters. For example, Papá Montero narrates in an Afro-Cuban folk dialect, the Captain General of Spain sings in perfect Spanish, the three Juans (fishermen) sing *guajira* music (*decima popular*) in the dialect of campesinos, and the Santeros chant in African (Abakuá) dialect.[13]

The most prominent character in *Manita en el Suelo* is Papá Montero, who also narrates the story from the stage. Also a Ñáñigo, Papá Montero was better known than Manita because of his colorful place as a *rumbero* (carouser) in Cuban folklore. Eventually he was immortalized in popular songs and poetry.

Carpentier's libretto ingeniously assimilates all the characters from popular mythology by making the black rooster—Gallo Motoriongo (Enkiko)—the real protagonist, a feature that has been explained as follows:

> The protagonist of Carpentier's *misterio bufo*, however, is neither Manita nor Papá Montero but the omnipresent black rooster, the Gallo Motoriongo (or Enkiko), an indispensable ingredient in the abakuá rituals. . . . The Motoriongo is central to Carpentier's intention of "bringing together for the first time in Cuba all the characters from popular mythology" because it is the nexus he invents to relate the legend of the apparition of the Virgin and her three Juanes with the abakuá and lucumí African-Cuban rituals. Until Carpentier's creative genius brought them together through the interactive role of the rooster, these coexisted only as parts of a living and ever-present whole in the consciousness of every Cuban in touch with popular traditions.[14]

From the point of view of his ideas about scenography, Carpentier felt that *Manita en el suelo* was his finest work; as for the libretto, he described it as "moderno, alerta, teatral y viviente" (modern, alert, theatrical, and lively). Such perspectives reflect his belief that *Manita* should establish an innovative folkloric theater, one that had never before been attempted. The success and artistic worth of *Manita en el suelo*, as he envisioned it, depended on creating "a puppet theater such as a black man would dream up. . . . Everything very popular, very low brow. There is where the real modern art is. Cubist stylization was all very well for *Parade*, in 1917. It's 1932 today."[15]

The stage setting as described by Carpentier is

> decorated with palm leaves, paper flags, etc., typical of Cuban towns on feast days. . . . In the center, there is a small theater with a palm thatch roof, that will be used for the action that requires changes in atmosphere, and will illustrate what Papá Montero narrates. This small theater represents a "bohío" [rustic hut], designed so that the audience can view its interior. The curtain of the small theater is to be decorated with an enlarged and very colorful lithograph of the type usually found on cigar boxes.[16]

Unlike previous collaborations with Caturla, Carpentier's *Manita en el suelo* carried with it specific ideas about the musical setting into which it should be placed. Carpentier shared these ideas with Caturla:

> Since it is a comedy, you can allow yourself all kinds of contrasts: use the *Ñáñigo* element for Manita, the pentatonic scale (Chinese trumpet),

for the Chinaman; the rural and Creole element for the Virgin and the Juans; the style of "great baroque opera" for the ending of all. . . . Don't forget that the storm in scene IV lends itself marvelously to create a conventional and burlesque tempest with distant allusions to the Ride of the Valkyries ("the horses of Santa Barbara, etc."); for the finale I would advise you to use a great "continuous movement" (the chorus of the Civil Guards lends itself for this), in a major key, with fugual entrances, imitations, canons, and your whole bag of tricks. . . . In a parody these tricks have an irresistible effect. . . . Also the Civil Guards—a conservative element—would speak marvelously in a fugal style.[17]

Although Caturla did not fully adhere to Carpentier's suggestions, he did follow some of his overall ideas concerning the musical setting of the libretto. There are, for example, pentatonic passages (without use of the Chinese trumpet) in the music for the Chinaman, *buffo* (comic) elements that parody the Ride of the Valkyries, a *danzón* for the Overture, and the use of other Cuban national forms (*Son, guajira,* etc.) to delineate, musically, the different ethnic groups of Cuban society.

However, Caturla departed from Carpentier's suggestions by relying on his own unique process of assimilating Cuban folk melodies, traditional musical forms, and specific sonorities reflecting Cuban nationalism. For example, the introduction and accompaniment to Papá Montero's opening recitative instantly establishes a strong nationalist spirit by the sounding of claves (and not drums) reiterating the rhythm of the Cuban *cinquillo*. Later Papá Montero transcends his role as narrator by singing *Elegía del Enkiko,* the centerpiece of the opera—vocally and structurally—something Carpentier had not suggested. But it is the scale and musical style of Caturla's *Manita* that differentiates it most from Carpentier's original idea that "one could stage it even in a place like Remedios." Caturla's vocal parts call for eleven singing characters, mixed chorus, male chorus, and an orchestra that exceeds forty instrumentalists, including Caturla's first use of African *batá* drums in the percussion.[18]

The thematic framework upon which Caturla unified the music in *Manita* evolved from a well-known melodic motif found in many types of Cuban folk music. It consists of a triadic figure with an added perfect fourth (indicated with brackets in figures 17.1 through 17.5 below, including permutations). By combining this motif and variations of it against meters and rhythms of different national musical forms, Caturla related the scenes and characters in the opera to

Figure 17.1. *Interludio* between scenes II and III, mm. 1–4.

Figure 17.2. Overture, mm. 65–66.

Figure 17.3. Scene III, *Elegía del Enkiko*, mm. 1–8.

Figure 17.4.   Scene III, *Baile de Santo*, mm. 36–38.

a common musical source. He was also able to combine the music of different ethnic groups in the same way, creating at times syncretic themes and rhythms, which he had by then absorbed into his creative process.[19]

Caturla's highly imaginative use of orchestration to delineate characters and set the mood for changes of scene sharply contrasts the overall recitativo vocal style of the opera. *Elegía del Enkiko* in scene III, for example, opens with muted trumpets and flutes, establishing a dreamlike mood as Papá Montero sings against their rhythmic repetitious sequences (see figure 17.3). The absence of percussion is notable. Clarinets and bassoons eventually join in at times with spacious unisons that create a deeper and darker mood toward the end.

By contrast, *Son de la Virgen* in scene IV is scored only for strings and soprano. Papá Montero introduces this music (after lighting up a cigar on stage) with a recitative accompanied by claves, which are replaced by a halo of quivering strings (a noticeable bow to European tradition), as she sings her *Son*. Melodically, her short (seventeen measures) aria is angular in shape, wide in range and rhythmically, based mainly on rhythmic patterns found in the Cuban *Son* (see figure 17.5).

Caturla's use of ethnic percussion (*instrumentos típicos*) relates directly to those scenes in the opera that involve Afro-Cuban characters and rituals. One of the most dramatic examples of these Afro-Cuban elements occurs in scene III: *Bembé—Baile de Santo*. In this scene the African *batá* drums are joined by timpani and snare drums (*caja platos*) in rhythmic counterpoint against lower strings while

Figure 17.5. Scene IV, *Son de la Virgen*, mm. 1–6.

chantlike passages for the trumpet and voice are heard above. The repetitious rhythms are used to drive the character Candita into a state of trance (see figure 17.4).

The most significant use of ethnic percussion occurs in scene V, during which the claves constantly reiterate the Cuban *cinquillo* against an extended version of a *danzón* pattern played by piano and strings in the lower register (see figure 17.6 below). The effect is similar to that of a rumba, the most popular and collective ethnic dance known in Cuba, and brings together all of the characters at the close of the opera.

There are many brilliant orchestral colors to be found in Caturla's *Manita*, some of which reflect his recent scores (such as *Primera suite cubana* and *La Rumba*) and others the influence of Stravinsky's ballet

Figure 17.6.   Scene V, *Final* (Finale), mm. 1–4.

scores (high-register frenzied tremolos for piano, strings, snare, and triangle for Manita's stabbing of the moon [scene V], for example).

While it is Cuban in essence, *Manita* also stands independently as Caturla's own brand of avant-garde music. It is not surprising that Caturla thought of Henry Cowell, Nicolas Slonimsky, and Edgard Varèse in regard to future performances of *Manita*.

In many ways *Manita en el suelo* may be seen as the culmination of Caturla's ideals—musical and nonmusical. In it, he brought to a climax his art of synthesizing heterogeneous musical elements within an aesthetic context that remained thoroughly Cuban. For it was through Carpentier's libretto that he gathered Cuba's cultural icons and collectively adapted them to a contemporary setting of Cuban musical forms and rhythms in his progressive musical style. While the dissonant, nonlyrical music itself is not of a popular style, it reflects the inner spirit of all sectors of Cuban society. It is music that could only have come from the pen of a native-born Cuban: one who knew and lived in the interior, one who wanted to represent his country with music that came from the very soul of people from the interior, and one who had already dedicated himself to "a national cultural labor" in his music. While earlier Cuban composers such as

José Mauri (*La Esclava,* 1918), Hubert de Blank (*Patria,* 1899) and Eduardo Sánchez de Fuentes (*Yumurí,* 1898) captured a spirit of patriotism in their operas, *Manita en el suelo* has been hailed as the first truly Cuban national opera.[20]

Manita en el suelo is scored for the following orchestration: piccolo, flutes 1 & 2, oboes 1 & 2, English horn, B♭ clarinet, E♭ clarinet, bass clarinet, bassoons 1 & 2, French horns 1-2-3-& 4, trumpets 1 & 2 in C, trombones 1 & 2, tuba, timpani, timbal Cubano, snare drum, bass drum, triangle, tam-tam, claves, *cencerro* (cowbell), maracas, *güiro,* *batá* drums, piano, violins 1 & 2, viola, cello, and bass.

The vocal parts consist of the following:

Papá Montero—tenor
Manita en el suelo—tenor
Captain General of Spain—bass
Chinaman of the Charade—baritone
Juan Odio—tenor
Juan Indio—baritone
Juan Esclavo—bass
El Gallo Motoriongo (rooster)—tenor
Virgin of Caridad del Cobre—soprano
Candita the Crazy—alto
Ta Cuñengue—alto
Mixed chorus (townspeople) and male chorus (civil guards)

NOTES

1. Henríquez, *Correspondencia,* 25 de junio 1931, 217. "Aunque Roldán ha sido agraciado con tu felicitación por cable y a mí estoy seguro que ni una letra me haces, quisiera agradecerte que si no a mí, enviaras a Antonio y a María para publicar en *Musicalia* las críticas más importantes que sobre estos dos conciertos se han publicado."

2. Henríquez, *Correspondencia,* 25 de junio 1931, 218. "Estoy dispuesto a hacerte obsequio de 500 francos para que me hagas y envíes el libro de nuestro pensado ballet *El Embó.* A ver que contestas tú a este ofrecimiento." *Embó* is a charm to bring good luck or rid one of bad luck, or to bring bad luck to another. It was usually a package of wrapped herbs, with perhaps hair or fingernails or other things of the person the charm was intended for.

3. Henríquez, *Correspondencia,* 6 de julio 1931, 362. It is worth mentioning that Carpentier had reason to believe that, prior to his death, Diaghilev was interested in producing Roldán's *La rebambaramba* in Paris. Concerning Caturla's offer of a "gift," Carpentier replied: "I consider it an honor to collaborate with you, and I don't see why I should charge honorariums just because you set my text to music" (Henríquez, *Correspondencia,* 30 de marzo 1932, 375).

4. Henríquez, *Correspondencia,* 6 de julio de 1931, 363. In the Efik sect of the *Ñáñigos,* there were five powers or personalities. Iyamba represented the king. The others were Isue, the bishop; Mocongo, the general; Empego, the scribe; and Enkriknkano, the hunter.

The three Juans are symbolic of the Cuban people in the legend of the Virgin of Caridad del Cobre; the Indian, the Creole, and the Negro. According to the legend, the three fishermen went out to sea, were caught in a terrible storm, and were about to drown. They began to pray, and the Virgin appeared to them, then guided them to safety. The name of the town nearby was El Cobre, and so the Virgin of Caridad del Cobre came to be considered the special protector of the Cuban people. She is generally depicted as a mulatta or mestiza.

The Chinese Charade was a "system" for playing games of chance in Cuba. Though it was played mostly in Havana, it was a sort of underground game and not officially sanctioned. Numbers from 1 to 40, or 1 to 100, were associated each with a symbol—usually an animal or character such as a sailor. Dreaming about a certain animal meant that if you bought a lottery ticket with the related number, you would win. The Chinaman of the Charade was shown as a Mandarin with all the numbers and symbols drawn on his robes.

5. Henríquez, *Correspondencia,* 20 de noviembre 1931, 246. Caturla refers here to his *Bembé,* which Slonimsky had recently performed in Havana and abroad.

6. Henríquez, *Correspondencia,* 16 de agosto 1931, 363. "A pesar de que a primera vista te va a parecer complicado, es tan sencillo que hasta se podría poner en escena en un lugar como Remedios."

7. Henríquez, *Correspondencia,* 16 de agosto 1931, 364. "Los títeres se fabrican con un tubo de cartón, y trapo. . . . Un grupo de amigos puede encargarse de la acción del pequeño teatro. . . . Los trajes son elementales: el único difícil (el Capitán General) se hace con papel de colores, y unos grandes bigotazos. . . . Y no hay telón de fondo, lo cual es siempre difícil de obtener, pues un pintor no se decide siempre a empujarse veinte metros cuadrados de decoración."

8. In the meantime Carpentier engaged in a musical editorial enterprise—*Edition de Musique Hispano Américaine*—to "promote the diffusion of Cuban music in Europe and to re-edit and launch popular works that may suit this [Paris] atmosphere." Reminding him of his "surprising capacity" to write popular music, Carpentier implored Caturla to compose popular Cuban music such as "The Peanut Vendor" and "Mamá Inés," then in vogue and making profits in Europe and elsewhere. "Do something real popular,

creole and tasty . . . you are capable of it, and I repeat, it wouldn't affect the prestige of your symphonic work in the least, since men like Honegger and Milhaud have set the example," wrote Carpentier (Henríquez, *Correspondencia*, 16 de marzo de 1932, 373). There was no response by Caturla to Carpentier's quest for a popular song from his pen.

9. Henríquez, *Correspondencia*, 18 de mayo 1932, 261.

10. Caturla to Cowell, 12 de diciembre 1934, from García Caturla, "Correspondencia inédita." Caturla dedicated the piano vocal score of *Elegía del Enkiko* to Henry Cowell. There is no evidence that either of the two mentioned sopranos sang this music.

11. Henríquez, *Correspondencia*, 2 de julio 1939, 289. The full score of *Manita en el suelo* remains unpublished. A revised copy of the original manuscript completed by Hilario González and Carmelina Muñoz, archivists at the Museo de la Música in Havana, was made available to me in Havana in 1994.

12. Manuel Cañamazo was a famous Ñáñigo who died in 1871 during an assault to liberate students imprisoned at Prado, the same jail where Carpentier was later incarcerated in 1927. It was during his imprisonment that Carpentier drafted his first Afro-Cuban novel, *Écue-Yamba-O*, which deals directly with the underworld of the Ñáñigos.

13. For historical background and discussion of interrelationships of the characters, see Kuss, "The Confluence of Historical Coordinates."

14. Kuss, "The Confluence of Historical Coordinates," 367.

15. Henríquez, *Correspondencia*, 30 de marzo 1932, 374. "[E]l teatro de títeres que soñaría un negro. . . . Todo muy popular, muy arrabalero. Ahí es donde está el auténtico arte moderno. Las estilizaciones cubistas estaban buenas para *Parade*, en 1917. Hoy estamos en 1932."

16. Oramas, "Manita en el suelo," 13–17.

17. Henríquez, *Correspondencia*, 16 de agosto 1931, 364. "Como se trata de algo bufo, te puedes permitir todos los contrastes: usa el elemento Ñáñigo para Manita; el modo pentatónico (trompeta china), para el Chino; el elemento guajiro y criollo para la Virgen y los Juanes; el estilo 'gran ópera barroca,' para todo el final. . . . No olvides que la tempestad de la escena IV se presta a maravillas para hacer una *tempestad* convencional y burlesca, con lejanas alusiones a la Cabalgata de las Walkirias ('los caballos de Santa Bárbara, etcétera'); en el final, te aconsejaría un gran 'movimiento continuo' (el coro de Guardias Civiles se presta a ello), en tono mayor, con entradas fugadas, imitaciones, cánones, y todos los trucos de escuela. . . . En parodia, estos trucos son de un efecto irresistible. . . . Además, los Guardias Civiles— elemento conservador—hablarían a maravilla en estilo fugado."

18. *Batá* are double-headed, hourglass-shaped drums, generally considered in Santería ceremony to be under the protection of, or owned by "Changó," a deified ancestor and god of lightning and thunder. Caturla's use of these drums reflects his theories on the use of Afro-Cuban percussion

instruments in the symphony orchestra to a higher degree than his previous compositions.

19. For a detailed analysis of this process, see Kuss, "The Confluence of Historical Coordinates," 369–75.

20. For details on the history of opera in Cuba, see González, *La Composición operística En Cuba*, 300–547.

Chapter Eighteen

Ranchuelo: Caturla as Defender of Worker's Rights

Palma has sequestered me.

Caturla to J. A. Portuondo

Among the many difficulties Caturla faced in the summer of 1933 was the addition of several municipalities, including Ranchuelo (also within his hometown district of Villa Clara), to his jurisdiction as municipal judge. Because of the new post-Machado reorganization of the judicial court system and an increasing wave of civil unrest, Caturla's judicial duties at Caibarién were already more than doubled. It was during his tenure at Ranchuelo that Caturla verified his lasting reputation as a severe, inflexible, and strict judge. Ranchuelo is the town where Caturla took on a confrontation with the industrialist owners of the tobacco and cigarette company Trinidad & Brothers. He defended the company's workers, passing judgment on all cases involving their rights. On one occasion, when Caturla found out that executives of the Trinidad & Brothers company were organizing a paid demonstration to have him removed as judge in their district, Caturla quickly confronted the mob of demonstrators in time to paralyze their rally. It was a heroic act on his part, one that eventually benefited the workers, but soon jeopardized his personal safety.

During this time, Caturla's music continued to spread abroad. On 4 June 1933, for example, Radiana Pazmor sang *Bito Manué* at a PAAC concert broadcast by station WEVD in New York. She later included two of Caturla's songs, *Mari-Sabel* (Carpentier) and *Bito Manué,* in her program of modern songs in San Francisco (26 September 1933). Also,

Caturla's *Primera suite cubana* was published in Cowell's *New Music Quarterly* before the year was out.

Shortly after the confrontation in Ranchuelo, Caturla finally composed music to Guillén's *Canto Negro* (*Yambambó*), a poem that is rich in onomatopoeic phrases evoking the sound and image of African song and dance.[1] Like *Mulata*, Caturla's *Yambambó* is recitativo in style, opening with a chantlike phrase that serves as a basis for rhythmic and melodic development. The accompaniment for this phrase is based on a rhythmical motive typically found in the Cuban *Son*, surrounded by dissonant polytonal harmonies that capture the exotic images found in Guillén's poem (see figure 18.1 below).

Caturla's use of dissonance in *Yambambó* supersedes what he used in *Mulata*, reaching peaks in chord progressions that at times function as percussion (see figure 18.2 below). Because of such harmonic and rhythmic inventions found in the foregoing examples and elsewhere in *Yambambó*, it may be seen as Caturla's most progressive song.

The first performance of *Yambambó* took place at one of Cowell's New Music concerts in San Francisco, California, on 9 April 1934.[2] Eventually, in 1937, Cowell published *Yambambó*, but in the meantime he published two of Caturla's earlier (1927) short pieces for piano solo: *Preludio Corto* (dedicated to Erik Satie) and *Sonata Corta* (dedicated to Arthur Hardcastle) in July 1934 issue of his *New Music Quarterly*.[3]

Figure 18.1.   *Yambambó*, mm. 1–10.

Figure 18.2. *Yambambó, mm. 49–51.*

As the year drew to a close, Caturla wrote to Cowell, imploring him (in English) to have Slonimsky conduct his orchestral music *La Rumba* or *Yamba-O*, "because they are the best, and genuinely Cuban modern." He then expressed his despair over the state of Cuban modern music: "If you remember what the big public know about Cuban music! Insipid and superficially Lecuona; adulterated Sánchez de Fuentes bad music. Poor Cuba!"[4]

Caturla's efforts to have Slonimsky conduct *La Rumba* or *Yamba-O* were in vain. The next performance of Caturla's orchestral music was a performance by Roldán and the Orquesta Filarmónica of *La Rumba* (the same version he conducted previously). The concert took place in Havana on 28 April 1935 but was not reviewed in the Havana press. Unable to attend because of his judicial duties, Caturla wrote from Ranchuelo thanking Roldán for his support while lamenting the difficulties in having his music performed. He also complained to Roldán about the Havana press, accusing them of a "disregard and lack of respect for a national institution and all efforts on behalf of culture that it has made."[5]

Undaunted by these circumstances, Caturla continually longed to conduct his own music with the Orquesta Filarmónica in Havana. He expressed this to Roldán in a very personal way at the conclusion of the foregoing letter:

May 9, 1935
For a long time now I have been cherishing the idea of conducting the orchestra in one of my pieces since, given my experiences in Caibarién, it doesn't look like I'll do badly in the conductor's role. I'm sharing my thought with you so that you will tell me, with the usual sincerity with which you have obliged our friendship, what you think about it and what the possibilities are that it may happen.[6]

There is no record of a reply from Roldán, but shortly thereafter Caturla was removed from Ranchuelo and assigned a new judicial post at the opposite end of the island from Havana, in the province of Oriente: Palma Soriano, ninety miles southeast of Santiago de Cuba.

PALMA SORIANO

Nestled along the foothills of the Sierra Maestra mountains, Palma Soriano became a prosperous commercial town, mainly because of its sugarcane industry (worked mostly by Haitian immigrants) and commercial trade. It also became a center for gambling and other illegal activities that corrupted local politics. True to his reputation for strictness as a judge, Caturla began to battle the popular "numbers games" in Palma and almost succeeded in eliminating them by simultaneously penalizing bankers and bookies (one of whom was chief of the Rural Guard). In another case, Caturla took on the general manager of Palma's formidable Miranda Sugar Mill, finding him guilty on charges related to violations of labor force laws. As a consequence of Caturla's crackdowns on crime, an attempt was made on his life on 12 December 1936. The incident was reported in the press:

A Palma Judge Attacked with Shotgun

Dr. Alejandro García Caturla escaped miraculously from an attack perpetrated against him, when someone shot at him at point blank range. A shotgun loaded with birdshot was the weapon used in this attack. The crime is shrouded in great mystery.[7]

Further details of the attempted assassination of Caturla in Palma were reported later in *Diario de Cuba*: "Coming to Caturla's house at night, several gunmen rang his front door bell; as the door opened, they blasted their shotgun into the doorway. Fortunately, Caturla was standing behind the unopened half of the double door entrance, escaping fatal injury."

Caturla's tenure in Palma Soriano extended from 16 July 1935 to 8 February 1937. He was no stranger to that part of Cuba because in 1930 he visited his sister Laudelina, then living in Santiago de Cuba. His music was known in Santiago (thanks to the Argentine pianist Ruiz Díaz), and that same year (1930) he proposed a performance of his orchestral music to the newly formed symphony orchestra at the

Conservatorio Provincial de Santiago.[8] But once settled in Palma Soriano, such pursuits vanished—a situation he explained in a letter to José Antonio Portuondo: "The barbarous workload I confront in the Court makes it impossible for me to attend to anything or any enterprise that isn't judicial for now. . . . Palma has sequestered me."[9]

Initially, Caturla arrived in Palma Soriano alone; he was later joined by Catalina Rodríguez (Manuela's younger sister; Manuela was looking after the younger children at home) and several of his children (by 1935, Caturla had eight children by Manuela). Caturla quickly became known as a defender of the rights of lower working class Afro-Cubans in his court and was welcomed in their communities where he occasionally observed their *bembé* ceremonies. Because of these circumstances and his crackdown on officials involved in vice, Caturla was, with few exceptions, estranged from the upper-class society of Palma. His position as a judge also placed certain restrictions on his social life. Such was the case in November 1936 when he kept his distance from Nicolás Guillén, who appeared in Palma under the sponsorship of the "Partido Comunista en la provincia de Oriente." It is not surprising that Caturla's social life in Palma was limited to a small circle of local musicians, including the town's piano teacher Lyda Barbosa, her brother Raphael, the writer and composer Félix B. Caignet, and a few of their friends.[10] Others to be included were his court assistants Lorenzo ("Lordi") Martín y Garatea and Cecil Gordon Mould (stepson of his aunt Olga), both of whom he brought from Remedios.

As his workload increased, leaving practically no free time to compose, Caturla had moments of doubt and despair as to his own fate. He expressed these feelings to Portuondo: "Who knows if in the future better times will return to Cuba and I can dedicate myself to my own thing, which is art. Otherwise I will continue submerged in this career somewhat alien to any manifestation of art."[11] In spite of this, the new and exotic atmosphere of Palma inspired Caturla's creative spirit. He expressed this to Portuondo: "I have many themes and much data written down from Palma. It would not be unlikely that I might do a Palman symphony or something like it."[12]

A "Palman symphony" did not materialize as such; however, Caturla compiled regional themes and rhythms while in Palma, which were eventually used in his opera *Manita en el suelo*. The most significant music Caturla composed in Palma is *Comparsa: Negro Dance*.[13] Dedicated to Fernando Ortiz, *Comparsa* was originally intended for his ballet *Olilé,* a project that was left unfinished. Unlike his previous *Comparsa (Primera suite cubana II),* Caturla captured the boisterous nature of the *comparsa,* a carnival street dance, by combining polyrhythms and bitonal textures with melodic variations on a pentatonic melody that builds to a driving climax of extreme dissonance. Although Caturla did not orchestrate *Comparsa: Negro Dance,* the arrangement he left for piano leaves no doubt that it was intended for orchestra (see figure 18.3 below).

Among other compositions Caturla completed in Palma is *Homenaje a Changó—Preludio* for piano solo.[14] As the title suggests, the music relates to the world of Santería. By then, Caturla had already mastered certain musical aspects of Santería in his opera *Manita en el suelo* (for example, scene III, *Baile de Santo*). African musical elements such as slow chantlike pentatonic phrases accompanied by repetitious polyrhythms, as illustrated in the following example, permeate Caturla's *Homenaje a Changó* (see figure 18.4 below).

Caturla's assignment in Palma Soriano—a period of just a little over one and a half years—was a period of resignation to his fate as a judge and intensification of his musical ideals that were given their greatest form of expression in *Manita en el suelo.* Just days before leaving Palma, Gonzalo Roig conducted a band arrangement of Caturla's *Danza del Tambor* and *Danza Lucumí* in Havana (25 January 1937). Thus the young *juez recto de Remedios* (honest judge from Remedios) left behind in the city of Palma Soriano a reputation of judicial discipline and musical recognition that was never fully understood or appreciated. The attempt on Caturla's life was never fully investigated. And as tensions in Palma increased, Caturla was transferred to another district, Quemado de Güines.

NOTES

1. Like *Bito Manué,* Caturla dedicated this song to Radiana Pazmor. As previously mentioned, Guillén's *Canto Negro (Yambambó)* was published with a dedication to Caturla in Gustavo Urrutia's "black page" of the *Diario de la Marina* (10 May 1930). Guillén's *Canto Negro* was later published in Havana as part of the collection *Sóngoro Consongo "Poemas Mulatos"* in 1931. Here is Guillén's original text (a transliteration follows):

> *Canto Negro (Yambambó)*
> A García Caturla, músico

Figure 18.3. *Comparsa: Negro Dance*, mm. 52–55.

Figure 18.4. *Homenaje a Changó*, mm. 17–19.

Yambambó, yambambé!
Repica el congo solongo,
repica el negro bien negro:
congo solongo del Songo
baila yambó sobre un pie.
Matatomba,
serembe cuserembá
El negro canta y se ajuma,
el negro se ajuma y canta,
el negro canta y se va.
Acuememe serembó,
aé;
yambó,
aé.

Tamba, tamba, tamba, tamba,
tamba del negro que tumba;
tumba del negro, caramba,
caramba, que el negro tumba:
yamba, yambó yambambé!

[Yambambó, Yambambé
Oh, hear the roaring jungle sound.
The black man and his voice resound.
Ah-Oay!
All of the life in the jungle
Dance the yambambó on one toe.
Look! They're singing and they're dancing all around,
All of them fuming and singing.
Look! They're singing and they're dancing all around;
First, hear him sing, then away.
Yambambó, ah-ay, yambambé, ah-oh.
See the loin cloth moving, twisting, turning
Whenever he tumbles;
Wilder and wilder the dance gets, my goodness!!
Good gracious! How he does tumble! Yamba-Yambó
Yambambé, yambambó, Yambambé
And he dances on one toe.]

2. The concert took place at the studio of Doris Barr, a soprano who included *Yambambó* in her program of modern music. For details, see Mead, *Henry Cowell's New Music of 1925–1936*, 279.

3. *Yambambó* was published in *New Music Quarterly*, vol. 10, no. 2, 1937.

4. Caturla to Cowell, 12 de diciembre 1934, from García Caturla, "Correspondencia inédita."

5. Caturla to Roldán, 9 de mayo 1935, from García Caturla, "Correspondencia inédita."

6. Caturla to Roldán, 9 de mayo 1935, from García Caturla, "Correspondencia inédita."

7. "Atacado a tiros un juez de palma," *Diario de Cuba,* 12 de diciembre 1936, 1. "El Dr. Alejandro García Caturla escapo milagrosamente de la agresion de que fue victima cuando le hicieron casi a boca tocante un disparo con una escopeta cargada con perdigones. Esta rodeado de gran misterio este hecho."

8. Through his contacts with *Musicalia* and José Antonio Portuondo, Caturla was in touch with Dulce María Serret, director of the Conservatorio Provincial de Santiago, and her brother Antonio, founder of the first symphony orchestra in Santiago de Cuba. There is no record of a performance of Caturla's orchestral music in Santiago de Cuba at that time.

9. Henríquez, *Correspondencia,* 14 de noviembre 1935, 272.

10. Lydia Barbosa studied piano at the Dulce María Serret conservatory in Santiago; Félix Caignet became famous for his song *Frutas del Caney, Carabalí.*

11. Caturla to Portuondo, 6 de diciembre 1935, from García Caturla, "Correspondencia inédita."

12. Henríquez, *Correspondencia,* 14 de noviembre 1935, 272.

13. *Comparsa: Negro Dance* was later published in Cowell's *New Music Quarterly* in 1939. Caturla made arrangements of it, one for violin and piano and one for cello and piano, as he did with *Danza del Tambor* from *Tres Danzas Cubanas.*

14. Caturla dedicated *Homenaje a Changó* to the pianist Arthur Hardcastle, who had previously performed his music at Cowell's New Music concerts in California.

Chapter Nineteen

Isolation and Premonitions of Death

Shortly after the attempt on his life in Palma Soriano, Caturla was assigned to a new post in Quemado de Güines in the province of Las Villas. His tenure there lasted from 8 February 1937 to 8 August 1938. Smaller and more rural than Palma, Caturla now found himself further isolated from the mainstream of Cuban culture. His single living quarters in Quemado were sparsely furnished and did not include a piano.[1] But he lost no time in finding one at a neighbor's house and on occasion played for gatherings of the local townspeople.

While at Quemado de Güines, Caturla entered a competition for orchestral music of Cuban composers sponsored by the Dirección de Cultura de la Secretaría de Educación in Havana. The competition carried with it a first prize of five hundred dollars and promises of a concert performance of the winning compositions. For the competition, Caturla composed *Suite para orquesta*, in which, for the first time, he utilized Latin American musical themes. He avoided the use of *instrumentos típicos* (Afro-Cuban percussion); apparently, he felt they would compromise his stake in the competition. Some years later he wrote about this to the musicologist Francisco Curt Lange:

> It [*Suite para orquesta*] is not a typically Cuban work, but in my opinion it is more interesting than the Suite de Danzas [*Tres Danzas Cubanas*], and I believe it denotes better my general personality. Brazil and Cuba inspired the two middle movements ("Plantación" and

"Berceuse"), but in order to enter them into the contest, I had to clean them up a bit from "instrumentos típicos" [Afro-Cuban percussion] and say that they correspond to ideas that are universal and not specifically Cuban.[2]

Suite para orquesta is Caturla's final score for large orchestra and consists of four movements: I. Minstrels, II. Plantación, III. Berceuse, IV. Vals. In terms of sonority it is similar to his *Tres Danzas Cubanas* and is scored for the following instruments:

altos	hautbois (2)
arpa	petite clarinet
bass clarinet (1)	petite flauta (1)
bassoons (2)	tam tam
cais	timpani (no coperte) fa mi do re
clarinets (2)	triángulo
contrabasses	trombones (3)
cor anglais	trumpete (2)
cors (4)	tuba
cymbal	violincelles
flauta (2)	violines 1
g. caisse	violines 2

As the deadline for the competition drew close, Caturla decided to also submit his "fiercely Afrocuban" *Obertura Cubana* of 1928. Much to his surprise, the committee chose *Obertura Cubana* for the first prize and gave his *Suite para orquesta* a *Mención Honorifica* (honorable mention). Much to his dismay and that of the other award-winning composers (including José Ardévol and Eduardo Sánchez de Fuentez), the Dirección de Cultura de la Secretaría de Educación in Havana put off awarding the cash prizes. Thanks to Caturla's persistent demands and use of his influential position (including family connections to the president of the Republic of Cuba, Federico Laredo Bru), the cash awards were eventually issued—two years later! In the meantime, Caturla returned home to Remedios. The promised concert of the award-winning compositions never materialized.[3]

While at Quemado de Güines, Caturla visited Havana where he completed *Canto de los cafetales*, a four-part, a cappella mixed chorus, on 21 November 1937. Like his previous a cappella chorus *El caballo blanco*, Caturla based his *Canto de los cafetales* on an anonymous *Son*, this time one that suggests in its text the fear of death. Caturla's choice of this material reflects a premonition of his own death.[4]

> Mamá, la muerte me está rondando,
> y como me vio tan serio
> me dijo que era jugando.
> Ay, mamá,
> y como yo estoy alegre
> me dijo que era jugando.

> [Mamá, death is hanging around,
> And since it saw me so serious
> told me it was for play.
> Ay. mamá,
> and since I am happy
> it told me it was for play.]

Caturla's *Canto de los cafetales* represents his most complex use of musical elements derived of the Cuban *Son*. The most striking musical aspect of *Canto de los cafetales* is the composer's advanced use of polyrhythmic lines that exploit rhythmic "cells," a technique he already applied in previous compositions, including *El caballo blanco*. In *Canto de los cafetales* Caturla reached a peak in mastering the manipulation of counterpoint in such a way as to create a filigree of rhythmic cells that migrate from one line to another, emphasizing the kind of syncopation so characteristic of the *Son*. In the following example, for instance (see figure 19.1 below), the opening text "Mamá" (measure 1) establishes the initial rhythmic cell (contraltos, tenors [tenores], and bass [bajos]), one that displaces the accent to the weak part of the beat. Once reiterated by tenors (measure 2) it is quickly repeated by sopranos, tenors, and basses (measure 3) and then augmented in retrograde by contralto, tenors, and basses (measures 5 and 6).

Other striking musical aspects to be found in *Canto de los cafetales* include textural rhythms that exploit sonority and dynamics, and a harmonic language that evades conventional tonal centers by placing side by side perfect intervals, major/minor triads, pentatonic clusters, and dissonances arrived at through altered seventh chords. Clearly, *Canto de los cafetales* is one of Caturla's most innovative compositions.

Among other compositions completed by Caturla at Quemado de Güines is the song *Berceuse para domir a un negrito* (Lullaby for a

Figure 19.1.   *Canto de los cafetales*, mm. 1–6.

little black boy)—after the poem by Emilio Ballagas.[5] Composed in
May 1938, the poignant *Berceuse* is dedicated to Dr. Guillermo de
Montagú y Vivero, a writer and friend of Caturla. *Berceuse para
domir a un negrito* is yet another variation of the berceuse form in
Caturla's hands. The freely composed African melody is purely
pentatonic, conveying a simplicity and expressiveness befitting to
the poetry (see figure 19.2 below). *Berceuse para domir a un negrito*
may be seen as a companion to his next, and stylistically most
African, song, *Sabás*.

Figure 19.2.   *Berceuse para domir a un negrito*, mm. 3–10.

While in Quemado, Caturla revived the idea of composing music to a set of Guillén's poems—a project that he once started with the poet's *Motivos de Son* but never completed. This time Caturla followed the poet's progressive path by turning to Guillén's *West Indies Ltd.*, a set of twelve poems published in 1934.[6] Caturla began his setting of *West Indies Ltd.* with the second poem in the set, *Sabás*, one of Guillén's most emphatic poems of social protest against racial inequality and poverty, dedicated to Langston Hughes.[7]

Initially, *Sabás* was composed for voice and piano but shortly thereafter, Caturla arranged it for voice and chamber ensemble. *Sabás* is the only song on a Guillén text that Caturla arranged for voice and instruments; it is scored for flute, oboe, clarinet, voice, viola, and cello.[8]

Musically, Caturla identifies Sabás (a legendary beggar) at the very beginning of his song with a short, purely pentatonic, motive based on an Afro-Cuban rhythm. It is played at first by the clarinet (see figure 19.3 below, mm. 1–2). Once established, the Sabás motive permeates most of the remaining music of the song, migrating among the instruments in various combinations as the harmony and rhythm are transformed to express the text (see figure 19.3 below, mm. 3–7 clarinet, oboe, and alto).

The vocal part has its own separate music that is declamatory in style in a syllabic setting. It is superimposed in counterpoint against the Sabás motive and a short, repetitious rhythmic pattern played by pizzicato strings, as if to suggest the sounding of drums (see figure 19.3 below, mm. 4–7).

Caturla's intensified use of *pure* pentatonic motives in the above example and elsewhere in *Sabás* is but one musical aspect that distinguishes it as his most African among his Afro-Cuban songs. Syncopated drumming patterns (already mentioned) and suggested call and response among the instrumental parts are others. *Sabás* is Caturla's last of over twenty songs, a genre that occupied him throughout most of his creative life.

ADOLFO SALAZAR: *LA OBRA MUSICAL DE ALEJANDRO GARCÍA CATURLA*

During his tenure as municipal judge in Quemado de Güines, Adolfo Salazar wrote an essay on Caturla entitled "La Obra musical

Figure 19.3.   *Sabás*, mm. 1–7.

de Alejandro García Caturla." Salazar defended Caturla's position as a composer:

> The reader, I presume, has already realized what the problems are and what *kind* of problems beset a composer in Caturla's situation: an American of Spanish extraction with a background of Latin culture who wants to go in the direction of a Latin American art of strong general ethnic roots and of Cuban roots in particular, which he treats choosing the narrowest path. His music isn't Spanish, or European or merely native but of a recent African procedure.[9]

After establishing a rationale of "resistance to European traditional music" as a common cause among the young Cuban Afro-

Cubanismo composers (specifically Caturla, Amadeo Roldán, and Gilberto Valdés), Salazar points out that the general aesthetic of Caturla's music is the *Son* and its collective use of multirhythms and *instrumentos típicos*. Salazar concludes his essay with a theoretical analysis of Caturla's music subtitled "El 'modus operandi' de A. G. Caturla." The choice of musical examples, details of analysis that lay bare the tenets of Caturla's "recent African procedure" (including his last song, *Sabás*, "del canto negro," as Salazar called it), and Salazar's own opinion less than a decade later that "Caturla's technique was too uncertain" suggests that "El 'modus operandi' de A. G. Caturla" was, to a large extent, based on materials written by Caturla himself.[10] In any case, Caturla stood behind the musical analysis of his music in Salazar's monograph, proudly announcing it to family, friends, and colleagues, including Francisco Curt Lange and the German conductor Richard Klatkovsky.

NOTES

1. Catalina attended to several of his younger children in the adjoining city of Sagua la Grande, close to the northern coast. Manuela was employed by one of Caturla's family members and was not at liberty to join him.

2. Henríquez, *Correspondencia*, 26 de mayo 1940, 305.

3. The concert of prize-winning compositions was to have been a public concert attended by the president (Laredo Bru) and the diplomatic corps. Expressing his views about the proposed concert, Caturla wrote to José Ardévol: "It is my opinion that the performance of my work will be an abomination and may God forgive me if I am unduly prejudiced on this question" (Henríquez, *Correspondencia*, 8 de febrero 1939, 275).

4. *Canto de los cafetales* is dedicated to Judge Berardo Valdés Hernández, a close friend of Caturla's who was killed 18 March 1938 in an automobile accident.

5. The first stanza of *Berceuse para domir a un negrito* is: "Drúmite mi nengre, mi nengre bonito, caimito y merengue, merengue y caimito" ["Sleep my little black boy, my pretty black boy, apple and meringue, meringue and apple"].

6. The collection included *Balada del güije*, a poem that Caturla and his brother, Othón, had published earlier in *El Faro*.

7. Langston Hughes later translated *Sabás* into English for his book *Cuba Libre*. The complete poem *Sabás* by Nicolás Guillén and the English

translation by Langston Hughes from *Cuba Libre* are as follows (© 1948 Ben Frederic Carruthers and Langston Hughes):

Yo vi a Sabás, el negro sin veneno,
pedir su pan de puerta en puerta.
¿Por qué, Sabás, la mano abierta?
(Este Sabás es un negro bueno.)

I looked at Sabás, meek and humble,
begging his bread from door to door.
Why've you always got your hand out, Sabás?
(That Sabás is a good Negro.)

Aunque te den pan, el pan es poco,
y menos ese pan de puerta en puerta.
¿Por qué, Sabás, la mano abierta?
(Este Sabás es un negro loco.)

Although they give you bread, bread's not much
and even less this beggar's bread from door to door.
Why've you always got your hand out, Sabás?
(That Sabás is a stupid Negro.)

Yo vi a Sabás, el negro hirsuto,
pedir por Dios para su muerta.
¿Por qué, Sabás, la mano abierta?
(Este Sabás es un negro bruto.)

I looked at Sabás, hairy Negro,
begging piously to his own defeat.
Why've you always got your hand out, Sabás?
(That Sabás is a dumb negro.)

Coge tu pan, pero no lo pidas;
coge tu luz, coge tu esperanza cierta
como a un caballo por las bridas.
Plántate en medio de la puerta,
pero no con la mano abierta,
ni con tu cordura de loco:
aunque te den el pan, el pan es poco,
y menos ese pan de puerta en puerta.

Take your bread, but don't beg for it.
Take your light. Take the hope that belongs to you,
Like a man grasps the reins of a horse.
Plant yourself in the doorway—
but not with your hand out
or with your stupid wisdom.
Although they give you bread, bread's not much,
and less this beggar's bread from door to door.

¡Caramba, Sabás, que no se diga!
¡Sujétate los pantalones,
y mira a ver si te las compones
para educarte la barriga!

Damn, Sabás, don't tell me you can't!
Tighten up your belt,
and see if you can't find a way
to educate your belly.

La muerte, a veces, es buena amiga,
y el no comer, cuando es preciso
para comer, el pan sumiso tiene belleza.
El cielo abriga.
El sol calienta.
Es blando el piso del portal.
Espera un poco,
afirma el paso irresoluto
y afloja más el freno. . . .

Death sometimes is a good friend,
and not to eat when you must eat
beggar's bread has its beauty.
The sky covers you.
The sun warms you.
The earth is not so hard.
Wait a little,
Strengthen your timid steps
and let up on the reins a bit. . . .

¡Caramba, Sabás, no seas tan loco!
¡Sabás, no seas tan bruto,
ni tan bueno!

Damn, Sabás, don't be so dumb!
Sabás don't be so stupid,
or so good!

8. This idea may have been born when Roldán conducted excerpts of his orchestrated *Motivos de Son* at the regular Orquesta Filarmónica concerts in Havana earlier that year. The concert took place on 28 March 1937, with Do-

lores Pérez Moreno, soprano soloist. On that occasion only two of the eight *Motivos de Son* were performed: *Negro bembón* and *Sigue*. The world premiere of Roldán's *Motivos de Son* for chamber orchestra and soprano solo took place at Town Hall, New York, on 15 April 1934, with Judith Litante soprano soloist.

9. Adolfo Salazar, "La obra musical de Alejandro García Caturla," 20. The most recent of his music that Caturla sent to Salazar was *Sabás*, which Salazar referred to in his essay as "del canto negro."

10. Writing to Caturla, Francisco Curt Lange had the following to say on this point: "Regarding Salazar's essay, here goes a confidential question that responds to my more or less certain nose—the analysis of the works, was it done by you? I am almost certain regarding this. Anyway, having done duty with finality, and having helped him under his signature, everything is justified" (see Henríquez, *Caturla Correspondencia*, 28 de febrero 1940, 393).

Chapter Twenty

The Final Years: Return to Remedios

> Roldán and I were always orphans with no guide. Because of that we had to construct everything for ourselves from A to Z.
>
> Caturla to Francisco Curt Lange

When Caturla's term in Quemado de Güines ended, he returned to the courtrooms of his hometown, Remedios. By then he had been promoted to the rank of *Juez de Instrucción*, a title he cherished.[1] But his circumstances at home had changed. Manuela died of typhoid fever on 30 January 1938 while Caturla was still in Quemado de Güines. His family had expanded to a total of eleven children; the last three were born to Catalina after Manuela died. Also, his duties at the courts in his district were more demanding than ever, and the economic circumstances of his parents had worsened. The atmosphere was also to be clouded by the following circumstances mentioned in a letter Caturla wrote to José Ardévol, one that also reflects Caturla's own sense of fate and resignation:

Accustomed to seeing death at close quarters . . . because of my position as a Penal Judge, I was not taken by surprise by the death of our unforgettable Roldán. For me, . . . it is the third important loss since the first of January, 1938. To begin with, my unforgettable first woman [Manuela], victim of an explosive typhoid, later my intimate friend and colleague, Judge Berardo Valdés Hernández, tragically killed in an automobile accident on the eighteenth of March and now, Amadeo. And all three, when life, as it should have been, was smiling on them.[2]

The sadness of such losses speak for themselves, but Roldán's death also meant the end of performances of Caturla's symphonic music in Havana for the remainder of his life. Shortly before Roldán's memorial concert in Havana, Caturla wrote to Antonio Quevedo: "Roldán (the poor man) . . . May it please God that what has been planned for him may be completed and it does not turn out as it did when he was alive."[3]

The most dispiriting circumstance Caturla was now to endure in Remedios was facing those who had humiliated him in the past, leaving him with emotional scars that had yet to heal. The sensitivity of this issue came to light when Augustín Crespo proposed paying homage to Caturla for his past success at the Dirección de Cultura de la Secretaría de Educación national competition. Caturla responded:

> With real regrets I wish to decline the homage . . . and I want you to excuse me for not opening up my heart to tell you about all the pain I still feel because of the wounds inflicted on me by this community on so many occasions, over a long period of time.
> Silence—on this occasion—would be the best homage you could offer.[4]

Caturla's musical activities in Remedios were restricted to a private world of composing, editing his earlier compositions, and negotiating the performance of his music abroad. Most of his time, however, was taken up by his new position as *Juez de Instrucción*. His days were spent at court and evenings at his parents' large house on the square where he maintained a private office and had access to the family piano. Midday recess and nights were spent at the house he once shared with Manuela, now with Catalina Rodríguez and his children. Overburdened with work in order to support his large family, Caturla declared himself "enslaved" in a judicial career and that he was no longer master of himself. Trips to Havana were now impossible, a predicament that was particularly frustrating when he learned that Carpentier was then visiting the capital.

CARPENTIER'S RETURN: *MANITA EN EL SUELO*

During the summer of 1939 Carpentier was invited to Havana by the Instituto Hispano Cubano de Cultura for whom he delivered a talk on "Las Zonas Inexploradadas del Sonido," a topic of great interest to Caturla. Unable to attend, he wrote to Carpentier, briefly updating him on his circumstances, expressing confidence that María and Antonio Quevedo must have informed him of his activities since the fall of Machado. He wrote Carpentier in the same letter that, apart from a bit of orchestration, their comic opera *Manita* had been finished for some time, and mentioned that he was not sure whether or not Carpentier had seen the piano-vocal edition of *Elegía del Enkiko* (*Manita en el suelo,* scene III) that appeared in one of the final issues of *Social* in 1937.[5] Caturla's letter carried with it an overtone of longing for one of their "unforgettable Montparnasse" talks instead of writing, and ended with the following enigmatic message: "If I can make the trip, you will find me one of these afternoons. If not, it won't be until twelve or fifteen years hence."[6]

Caturla and Carpentier would never meet during the remainder of Caturla's life. In his usual high-spirited manner, Carpentier responded to Caturla's letter with enthusiasm and understanding, evoking the spirit of their former camaraderie:

> Verraco [literally "wild boar," colloquially "you idiot"]:
> When you get sentimental as in your last letter, I feel like insulting you.
> . . . Did you know that one of the main reasons for my trip to Cuba was to see you in Remedios?[7]

After sharing some ideas about his experiments with sound recordings in Paris, some of which he brought with him, Carpentier proposed that Caturla arrange for him to present his talk ("Las Zonas Inexploradadas del Sonido") in Remedios. But more important, as far as Caturla was concerned, Carpentier turned to the subject of *Manita en el suelo* in the same letter:

> I am going to try to present *Manita* in Havana, taking advantage of my acquaintance with Beruff Mendieta, the Mayor. Carlos Enríquez will do the scenography (I've already read him the text). And here I don't know one fucking note of your score.[8]

As it turned out, Carpentier was unable to visit Remedios, and plans for the Havana premiere of *Manita en el suelo* during Caturla's lifetime were doomed.

CATURLA'S LAST COMPOSITIONS

What little time Caturla found for composing at this time was used to complete two small pieces for piano: *Son en fa menor,* subtitled "Piece in Cuban Style in F Minor," and *Berceuse campesina,* subtitled "Pastoral Lullaby—A Pastoral Song in Free Recitative Style," with a dedication to Manuela. They were to be his final compositions, commissioned for publication by Carl Fisher, Inc., in New York.[9]

As a pair, *Son en fa menor* and *Berceuse campesina* contrast one another in form and content, although both reflect Caturla's art of assimilating the Cuban *Son* into his music. Both of these compositions are based on a familiar *Son* rhythmic pattern (see figure 20.1 below), which Caturla manipulates in variation form (*Son en fa menor*) and then as an ostinato upon which the "free recitative" melody (*Berceuse campesina*) is superimposed above (see figure 20.2 below):

Carpentier later described *Berceuse campesina* thus:

> In a composition with a surprising unity of style, he managed a melodic and rhythmic synthesis of the guajiro and the Negro. . . . By placing underneath this melody the rhythm of a Son, he brought off

Figure 20.1.   *Son* rhythmic pattern.

Figure 20.2.   *Berceuse campesina,* mm. 14–17.

a miraculous equilibrium between two kinds of music that had never supported the slightest fusion during previous centuries of conviviality.[10]

While Caturla found little time to compose during the last two years of his life, his music continued to gain recognition in Havana and abroad. The following activities account, in part, for this development. To begin with, José Ardévol performed Caturla's *Primera suite cubana* for the first time in Havana (4 February 1939); second, there were several proposals to have his music broadcast from abroad; and third, the young California composer John Cage solicited new compositions from Caturla for a concert in San Francisco with Henry Cowell.[11] The recognition and spread of Caturla's music abroad was also enhanced by Francisco Curt Lange, an enterprising German musicologist who was dedicated to the cause of having the music of Latin American composers of classical music performed and published.[12]

THE FRANCISCO CURT LANGE CONNECTION

Ironically, the paths of Francisco Curt Lange and Caturla never crossed, although each tried to find the other when Lange visited Cuba in March 1939. Apart from the official aspects of his visit, the main purpose of his trip was to gather examples of orchestral music by Cuban composers, particularly Caturla's, to publish in the supplement of his *Boletín Latino Americano de Música*.[13] As it turned out, Lange returned to Montevideo, Uraguay, without any of Caturla's orchestral scores but took steps to acquire them by initiating a long and fruitful correspondence with him.

Responding enthusiastically to Lange's request for all of his published music, Caturla sent what musical scores he had on hand, lamenting the fact that Lange had not yet heard *Yamba-O, Primera suite cubana,* or *Bembé*.[14] As Caturla explained to Lange, it was music that was "conceived without the prejudicial and deplorable compromises to the general public that have influenced so many temperaments, especially in our tropic [Cuba]."[15]

Because of difficulties in acquiring copies of his own published scores and having new copies of his unpublished scores made, it would take almost a year before Caturla's large orchestral scores reached Lange's hands.[16] In the meantime, their ongoing correspondence led to a unique friendship, one that allowed them to exchange ideas and opinions about music and express grievances concerning their respective careers. For example, Lange and Caturla were highly critical of the liberties Nicolas Slonimsky took in editing and performing Latin American music, including Caturla's.[17] And they were incensed by those who rejected the fact that African musical elements were an integral part of Cuba's music as a whole—a controversial issue that came up at the International Congress of Musicology at New York in September 1939.

Lange looked forward to meeting Caturla at the Congress in New York and fully expected him to be there. Instead, Gonzalo Roig and Eduardo Sánchez de Fuentes appeared as the official Cuban delegates, voicing clear opposition to those composers in Cuba who integrated African musical elements into their music. Dismayed, Lange wrote to Caturla from New York:

> When I saw the delegation from Cuba appear, my soul fell at not seeing you here. Didn't you hear? How can it be explained that you, *the most representative musician of contemporary Cuban music,* was absent from the delegation. [italics mine][18]

Caturla blamed his predicament on the political intrigues among officials in Havana (something Lange was familiar with), whom he believed were conspiring against him. He also informed Lange that "Señor Presidente de la República" (Laredo Bru) did nothing to help him in this matter.

Upon returning home to Montevideo, Lange informed Caturla that plans were being made to have his music performed there and in Buenos Aires as well. Lange was particularly interested in negotiating performances of Caturla's *Yamba-O*.[19] Lange also proposed that he could make arrangements with G. Schirmer in New York to publish piano pieces by Caturla if he was interested—a project that never materialized.[20]

Lange's correspondence lasted practically to the end of Caturla's life, and because of Lange's efforts, Caturla's music gained significant recognition throughout Latin America. While Lange did not find the support he so wished for in Havana, his rare perspective of Cuba could only have been gratifying to Caturla, to whom he wrote the following: "What an attractive island it is! And how much true culture I have found there, although many times it is hidden."[21]

ECHOES OF PAAC

In many ways the role that Francisco Curt Lange played in Caturla's musical life replaced that of Henry Cowell and the Pan American Association of Composers, which collapsed in 1936. And, by the time Francisco Curt Lange contacted Caturla, his correspondence with Cowell and Nicolas Slonimsky had practically come to a standstill. In the meantime, Cowell and Slonimsky were kept busy with Cowell's New Music concerts through 1936, and the publication and recordings of *New Music Quarterly* thereafter. The continuing efforts of Cowell and Slonimsky to engender interest in Latin American music through an international circuit of PAAC concerts were of great value to Caturla. For example, as a result of Cowell and Slonimsky's PAAC concerts of Latin American music in Berlin in 1931 and 1932 respectively, Caturla's music was broadcast twice on German FM radio (12 July and 12 October 1939) by the Berlin Symphony Orchestra under the auspices of the Iberian-American Institute of Berlin (Richard Klatkovsky conducting). Despite the liberties Slonimsky had taken with the performance of Caturla's music and that of other Latin composers (according to Caturla and Lange), Slonimsky did more than any other single conductor to bring Caturla's music to a broad international audience.

The long silence of communication between Caturla and Slonimsky was broken when Caturla responded to Slonimksy's article "Caturla of Cuba" that appeared in the January–February 1940 issue of *Modern Music*. Slonimsky's article provided a colorful program note on the genesis of Caturla's *Yamba-O* and then continued: "*Yamba-O* is, indeed, an extraordinary palimpsest of motives, rhythms, and block harmonies, possibly the freest orchestral work ever to be performed." Turning to Caturla's *La Rumba* (1933), Slonimsky concluded his article: "It is a rumba à la Caturla, with a lilt and an accent all its own, and the rhythms are not shaved down to uniformity. Perhaps his most playable piece, it may even become his *Bolero.*"[22]

Filled with enthusiasm, Caturla wrote to Slonimsky: "Your article about me . . . is *wonderful*. . . . When history does me justice your name will be next to mine. . . . Thank You! . . . I bear witness to my gratitude and my affection."[23]

After urging Slonimsky in the same letter to conduct his music in Boston and New York—preferably on the radio—Caturla petitioned him strongly to conduct *Yamba-O* "with all the Cuban instruments."

Caturla's rationale was that this would be a way for all Americans to better understand his music, which would then "obtain a more prominent position among foreign composers admired in that great nation." Caturla ended his letter further petitioning Slonimsky to arrange for a *New Music Quarterly* recording of "one of my greatest and essentially Cuban accomplishments," *Primera suite cubana*. Left unanswered, Caturla's letter brought to an end his correspondence with Slonimsky, one that had lasted almost a full decade. It would remain for Henry Cowell to respond to Caturla's remaining petitions.

Because of their multifaceted relationship, Caturla's correspondence with Cowell was longer and more constant than it had been with Slonimsky. However, there was a gap shortly after Caturla's arrival in Palma Soriano during the summer of 1935.[24] Cowell resumed his correspondence with Caturla six months following the above letter to Slonimsky, expressing his continued interest in Caturla's music. Caturla responded with enthusiasm, but then expressed anxiety over the *New Music Quarterly* recording of *Primera suite cubana* and *Bembé*. "What's happening with Slonimsky? What is new with the editors of New Music records?" he wrote to Cowell.[25] But to no avail; rising costs of recording suspended Cowell's *New Music Quarterly* recording project for the few remaining weeks of Caturla's life.[26]

As to the issue of having his music performed, Cowell informed Caturla that he was always looking for players of his works, which he found so interesting, adding: "It's very difficult nowadays, since the Senart editions in Paris are not at hand."[27]

Caturla responded by sending Cowell his *Suite para orquesta* and wrote, asking Cowell for his "frank and honest opinion" with hopes of having it performed. Written just three days before his death, once again, Caturla pleaded in the same letter for a *New Music Quarterly* recording of his *Primera suite cubana*—but by then it was a hopeless issue.

NOTES

1. A *Juez de Instrucción* acts as the examining magistrate whose duty is to prepare the necessary evidence prior to submitting a case to the *Audiencia* (Superior Court of the district). A *Juez de Instrucción* does not hold the

power to absolve or condemn anyone, nor does he participate in administering sentences in those cases he has prepared.

2. Henríquez, *Correspondencia*, 6 de marzo 1939. Roldán died of cancer of the face on 2 March 1939 at the age of 38.

3. Henríquez, *Correspondencia*, 9 de marzo 1939, 279. The memorial concert in Havana took place on 2 April 1939, exactly one month after his death, a Sunday morning at 10:00 A.M.

4. Henríquez, *Correspondencia*, 13 de febrero 1939, 277.

5. The following notice also appeared in that same issue of *Social*, written by the editor, Conrado Massaguer—a dedicated admirer and friend of Caturla's: "Alejandro García Caturla, nuestro inspirado compositor, nos ha traído un original inédito, 'Elegía del Enkiko' que para placer de los amantes do la música daremos en nuestro próximo número. García Caturla es uno de nuestros positivos valores como músico de gran talento [Alejandro García Caturla, our noted composer, has brought us an original and unpublished 'Elegía del Enkiko' which we will bring out in our next issue for the pleasure of music lovers. García Caturla is one of our very progressive, and highly talented composers]" ("García Caturla estaría subvencionado," 4).

6. Henríquez, *Correspondencia*, 2 de julio 1939, 289.

7. Henríquez, *Correspondencia*, 3 de julio 1939, 396.

8. Henríquez, *Correspondencia*, 3 de julio 1939, 296–97.

9. These compositions were published by Carl Fisher, Inc., in 1941 as part of their *Masters of Our Day* series for young students. Apparently, the first draft of *Son en fa menor* that Caturla submitted was too advanced for their purposes and had to be rewritten. Isadore Freed of Carl Fisher, Inc., informed Caturla: "I would like for you to find some possibility for simplifying the *Son* a bit and to make some changes that would make the piece easier to read and play (that it wouldn't require three staves for example)." Caturla obliged by submitting a simplified version, which was found acceptable for publication. Caturla's original *Son en fa menor* (written on three staves) is not extant.

10. Carpentier, *La música en Cuba*, 292–93.

11. Apparently Antonio Quevedo was trying to negotiate a performance of Caturla's orchestral music with the NBC radio station in New York, a project that never materialized. However, the German conductor Richard Klatkovsky did negotiate radio broadcasts of Caturla's music from Berlin.

Along with Lou Harrison, Henry Cowell, William Russell, and himself, John Cage was preparing a concert of music for percussion instruments. He asked Caturla to contribute a composition for percussion only, and for loan of the Cuban percussion instruments needed to perform it. Caturla declined Cage's invitation but promised a new composition just for him at a later date (see Henríquez, *Correspondencia*, 15 de marzo 1939, 280).

12. After studying philosophy and architecture in Germany, where he was born at Eilenberg on 12 December 1903, Francisco Curt Lange emigrated to Uruguay in 1924 and settled in Montevideo. He was active there in the field of phonograph recording and publishing. He also became professor of music history and musicology at the University of Montevideo. Eventually, Francisco Curt Lange established the Instituto Interamericano de Música and later published Caturla's two a cappella choruses, *El caballo blanco* and *Canto de cafetales* in the *Editorial Cooperativa Interamericana de Compositores.*

13. The official aspects of Lange's visit were to seek support from Havana officials to sponsor the publication of music by Cuban composers and deliver a lecture at the Instituto Hispano Cubano de Cultura in Havana. Lange's efforts to publish orchestral music by Cuban composers proved to be in vain. He later wrote to Caturla that he found the musical situation in Havana "disastrous."

14. Ironically, Caturla did not have copies of these compositions to send Lange at that time. He promised to send them later, and to provide him with a new version of *Bembé* for twenty-six percussion instruments and piano. The samples of his music that Caturla sent to Lange are *Suite de Tres Danzas,* "the four poems for voice and piano [it may be conjectured that he meant *Dos poemas afrocubanos* on texts by Carpentier and two Guillén songs], *Son in Eb* for piano solo, the arrangements of *Danza del Tambor* for violin and cello and three works for piano" (see Henríquez, *Correspondencia,* 17 de mayo 1939, 284–86). There is no extant copy of Caturla's arrangement of *Bembé* for twenty-six percussion instruments and piano.

15. Henríquez, *Correspondencia,* 17 de mayo 1939, 285.

16. Caturla's publisher, Maurice Senart (*Bembé* and *Tres Danzas Cubanas*), had declared bankruptcy by then; also, retrieving his orchestral scores on loan to the Orquesta Filarmónica in Havana was complicated by Roldán's death. Another complication related to performances of Caturla's Afro-Cuban symphonic music abroad was the availability of Cuban *"instrumentos típicos"* (see Henríquez, *Correspondencia,* 26 de mayo 1940, 304–5).

17. Writing to Caturla from Mexico, Lange reported, "He [Slonimsky] conducted your work very badly (like all the others), and one had to guess. Everything was realized in *grosso modo,* without planes" (see Henríquez, *Correspondencia,* 1 de junio 1939, 384). Caturla responded: "Don't talk to me about Slonimsky's conducting. I just want to say that he was allowed to mutilate the *Primera Suite . . .* in New York" (see Henríquez, *Correspondencia,* 2 de julio 1939, 288).

18. Henríquez, *Correspondencia,* 15 de septiembre 1939, 387.

19. Caturla sent Lange the following instruments for use in performing *Yamba-O*: one pair of maracas, a *güiro,* some claves, and a *cencerro* (cowbell). For practical reasons he was unable to send *timbales de charanga.*

Lange's interest in Cuban music intensified as he was working on a *bibliografía musical cubana* and a *Léxico Latinoamericano de Música.* He asked

Caturla to send him the rhythmic patterns for typical *comparsas* of the Yorubas and *Lucumíes* saying, "You must have a considerable wealth of experience, used in your own compositions" (Henríquez, *Correspondencia*, 15 de enero 1940, 391). He was also fascinated by Carpentier's novel *Écue-Yamba-O* and asked Caturla for information about the author.

20. By then Caturla had already negotiated to publish two piano pieces with Carl Fisher, Inc., New York (*Son en fa menor* and *Berceuse campesina*).

21. Henríquez, *Correspondencia*, 28 de febrero, 1940, 394.

22. Slonimsky, "Caturla of Cuba," 77–80. Much of the content in Slonimsky's article had already been covered in Salazar's essay, "La obra musical de Alejandro García Caturla," including a comparative reference of Caturla's *La Rumba* to the music of Maurice Ravel.

23. Henríquez, *Correspondencia*, 8 de febrero 1940, 295.

24. Before the summer of 1935 came to an end, Caturla received the latest *New Music Quarterly* recording including Cowell's *Suite for Woodwinds* (woodwind quintet for flute, oboe, clarinet, French horn, and bassoon). He wrote to Cowell, saying, "Your *Suite for Woodwinds* is marvelous! Delightful! Dreamily [*sic*], bucolic . . . my congratulations!" (Caturla to Cowell, 19 de agosto 1935, from García Caturla, "*Correspondencia* inédita"). Before closing, Caturla reminded Cowell that he too wanted to have his music issued on *New Music Quarterly* recordings. Caturla had written to Cowell the previous year that he wanted to have *Bembé* or *Primera suite cubana* recorded on *New Music Quarterly* records. For details on the *New Music Quarterly* recording of Cowell's *Suite for Woodwinds*, see Rita Mead, *Henry Cowell's New Music of 1925–1936*, 309–10.

25. Caturla to Cowell, 9 de septiembre 1940, from García Caturla, "Correspondencia inédita."

26. Shortly after Caturla's death, Cowell's *New Music Quarterly* recordings were resumed under the auspices of Bennington College, Vermont. It was here that Henry Brant recorded Caturla's *Preludio Corto* for the *New Music Quarterly* recordings, followed by a recording of *Yambambó* with Radiana Pazmor.

27. Cowell suggested that Caturla might pursue further publication of his scores through Elkan Vogel, Inc. (Philadelphia), Senart's former U.S. representatives. Apparently, Elkan Vogel, Inc., had expressed interest in publishing Caturla's *Bembé*, a project that did not materialize.

Chapter Twenty-one

Caturla's Legacy:
A New Perspective

With prize money from the 1938 Dirección de Cultura de la Secretaría de Educación national competition still unpaid in April 1939, Caturla assumed a legal position in this matter by drafting a letter on behalf of himself and the other prize winners, José Ardévol and Eduardo Sánchez de Fuentes. Caturla's letter is a brilliant piece of diplomacy, one that eventually brought forth the desired results. Addressed to the secretary of education in Havana, Caturla wrote:

> It is lamentable that, having held the cited contest on a date so remotely long ago, still the Section that should act in this matter . . . hasn't made the mentioned prizes effective; a delay that has been cause for commentary in the daily press, since the State cannot declare itself insolvent and given the seriousness of the same, shouldn't use pretexts to delay carrying out an obligation of this kind.[1]

After advising the secretary to forget about the announced concert performance of the prize-winning compositions, Caturla reminded him that "future contests will not have any kind of stimulus" without the prize money being disbursed as promised. The prize money was finally sent on 15 May 1940.[2] In the meantime, Caturla responded to an inquiry by Eduardo Sánchez de Fuentes concerning disbursement of the prize money. After explaining that he had been given a runaround by government officials, Caturla assured him that by writing to the president (Laredo Bru), he would have the issue resolved.[3]

In the meantime, Caturla's new rank of *Juez de Instrucción* brought with it a renewed sense of responsibility and commitment to sustaining high standards in his courtrooms. "I must study hard in order to carry out my new charge with honor. . . . I don't want to be a bureaucratic judge," he wrote to Judge Filberto Rodríguez Conde.[4] But Caturla knew by then that his judiciary career was dangerous and insecure. He expressed this perspective to a magistrate of the Supreme Court in Havana, from whom he asked confidential information as to the future of judicial power:

> I believe I have served Cuba loyally and honestly, exposing myself almost constantly to losing my life; but we all remember how the Judiciary has been treated in the past. . . . I would like to know if once more vengeance and passions will control the well being of Judges and Magistrates and the peace and future of their families.[5]

While serving in his district as *Juez de Instrucción*, Caturla continued fighting for the judicial cause that concerned him most: juvenile delinquency. For example, he averted a prison sentence for a juvenile in Remedios who committed "an imperfect homicide," placing him under house arrest instead.[6]

Perhaps the most dramatic documentation of Caturla's reputation as a judge is to be found in a letter written to him from the prisoners in the jail of Santa Clara, Cuba. The letter is also an exposé of the state of corruption in the penal system that flourished in Cuba at that time.

> Dr. Alejandro García Caturla
> Judge of Justice
>   All the prisoners of this penal establishment agree that you are our salvation; because you are, as we have observed, a true Judge, one who has not stained the "toga." . . .
>   You are the just Judge . . . you are a prestigious and worthy Judge who knows how to immerse himself in truth. . . .
>   [All] of us have placed our hopes in you . . . we ask you for justice against an evil one who tortures us and tramples on us daily with his cruelty and ambitions.[7]

The letter ends with an emotional plea by the prisoners for Caturla to visit them, expressing hope that he will take action on their behalf. There is no evidence that Caturla visited the prisoners in Santa Clara, but their plight was just the type of injustice he openly and fiercely opposed.

It is not surprising that, later, Caturla confronted the local judicial system by placing charges against several national police in his own district. Subsequently, he discovered a plot designed by members of the Cuban army and the national police for his assassination. As a result, Caturla appealed to the minister of national defense for a guarantee of safety for himself and his family—but to no avail.[8] One month later, Caturla applied to the Cuban government for a renewal of his license to carry a firearm. His application concluded with the following statement:

> The revolver is of Colt brand, 32 caliber, identified by the number 95429 and I attest that I am the son of Diana and Silvino, of white race, *single*, with education and native resident of this city, [street address] Calle pastor Valera Number 58. [italics mine][9]

Within hours after Caturla wrote the application, he was shot to death at point-blank range in the streets of Remedios by a local, hardened criminal by the name of José Argacha Betancourt. The tragedy took place on 12 November 1940, not far from the San Juan Bautista church on a side street leading to the Remedios post office. News of the shocking event spread quickly. The Havana press carried the following headlines the next day: "Muerto a Tiros en Remedios el Juez García Caturla [Judge García Caturla Killed by Shots in Remedios]" (*El Mundo*),[10] and "Un escolta de la cárcel dió muerte a juez de Remedios [Jail Escort Kills Judge in Remedios]" (*Diario de la Marina*).[11]

The ambiguous circumstances surrounding Caturla's death are as follows: Several days prior to his assassination, Caturla was called to serve as substitute judge at the provincial *Audiencia* in Santa Clara. Judge Fernando Arsenio Roa, his former classmate at the University of Havana, was called in to substitute for Caturla in Remedios. During Caturla's absence, Judge Roa was faced with a case in Remedios dealing with a well-known criminal who was arrested for severely beating a young woman. Because she was unable to appear in court, Judge Roa decided that the woman had to be examined at home by two forensic doctors the following morning. Meanwhile, Caturla returned from Santa Clara earlier than expected and took over the case. However, as *Juez de Instrucción*, Caturla would have no role whatsoever in sentencing. Little did he know that the criminal charged in this case would be his own executioner: José Argacha Betancourt.[12]

The day after Caturla's return from Santa Clara, Argacha Betancourt gunned him down and then fled, in fear for his life, to a nearby army barracks, where he was found and arrested. It is not clear whether Argacha Betancourt fully understood Caturla's role in his pending case. Thus his motive for committing such a crime remains unclear. Fear of Caturla's strictness as a judge? A preconceived plan supported by criminal elements in the district? Revenge? Such were some of the rumors circulating in Remedios. In any case, Argacha Betancourt was tried and found guilty of killing Alejandro García Caturla, a crime that shocked the entire island. Argacha Betancourt was sentenced to life in prison.[13]

POSTHUMOUS RECOGNITION

Of the many written tributes made to Caturla following his death, one of the first was by Pedro Sanjuán. Entitled "El discípulo indisciplinado" (The undisciplined pupil), he made no attempt at a eulogy, but did give recognition to the natural force of Caturla's talent 'likening it to a bursting dike' that gave birth to a new musical era. Sanjuán's short article offers a personal view of Caturla seen through the eyes of a European. In it he compared Caturla's creative instincts to those of Moussorgsky and came to the following conclusion: "Moussorgsky achieved what he wanted. García Caturla also would have done so if, instead of burying his life in the monotony of a limited environment, he could have given freedom to his ideals in more ample and hospitable panoramas."[14] Compared to the many tributes to Caturla that followed, Sanjuán's article stands out as the most unsympathetic.

Sanjuán's "El discípulo indisciplinado" was quickly followed by Nicolás Guillén's tribute to Caturla entitled "El crimen de todos" (It was everyone's crime), published the next day in the same Havana journal, *Tiempo.* "Cuban culture owes a great deal to García Caturla. . . . We have lost one of Cuba's strongest leaders in our folklore, a rich and powerful force. . . . The sad reality of his death—and his life—should set an example so that Cuba will give great recognition and love to her artists."[15] Only a Cuban such as Guillén, with roots and artistic talent, could have written such lines. In his article Guillén also took issue with Cuba's bureaucratic system for "burying Caturla in a corner of the island." Guillén continued by chiding the country for priding itself in being cultured, without having provisions at its disposal to assist men of Caturla's caliber.

While Sanjuán and Guillén paid tribute to Caturla within days of his assassination, it would be at least a year before others, closer to Caturla during his lifetime, did the same. And when they responded, it was from a broader, more universal perspective than that of Sanjuán or Guillén. Such was the case with Alejo Carpentier and María Muñoz de Quevedo, both of whom were in Havana at the time of Caturla's death.

Of these two, María Muñoz de Quevedo was the first to pay homage to Caturla. She did so by publishing in *Musicalia* her personal literary portrait of him, entitled "Alejandro García Caturla." The familylike relationship that Caturla and María Muñoz shared accounts for the maternal way in which she warmly refers to him in her portrait as "un muchacho grande"; this relationship also enabled her to capture a rare glimpse of Caturla's character when writing, in the same article, of his return from his first trip abroad (Paris, quoted in chapter 5).

Continuing in her article, María Muñoz de Quevedo also commented on Caturla's "spiritual affinity" with people of color in Cuba, a relationship that caused a widespread stir during his lifetime. But she was quick to add that, for Caturla, this did not mean composing music that was an imitation or pastiche of their music. Having published, performed, and critiqued Caturla's music, she summarized his accomplishments in the field of orchestral and vocal music from an authoritative point of view.[16]

She brought her article on Caturla to an end by stating: "Su muerte es doble, porque perece el hombre y termina una escuela" ["The assassin committed a double murder: one of a man and one of a school"].[17]

Carpentier observed the first anniversary of Caturla's death by publishing an article written for the Remedios journal *El Huracán*. Also entitled "Alejandro García Caturla," he addressed the issue of Caturla's integrity as a man and artist. Carpentier points out in his article that Caturla had no interest in financial gain from his compositions; and the desperate economic conditions in which Caturla worked qualified his compositions as "heroic gestures" of "mystical elevation." After characterizing Caturla as the type of composer whose music was "impelled by a primordial necessity for creation," Carpentier continued: "Alejandro García Caturla, whom we evoke on the first anniversary of his assassination, belongs to that incredible race of heroes that has given us a few composers of international stature." Having drawn a concise and vivid comparison of Roldán the professional musician, to Caturla the judge, in his article, Carpentier concluded:

> Caturla's life is a magnificent example of the struggle for an ideal. An ideal that has remained unstained. . . . A year after his death, the figure of Alejandro García Caturla has grown larger in our devotion. His soul now occupies the place it had always deserved in the musical production of our young continent.[18]

News of Caturla's death brought forth an outpouring of respect by musicians from Europe, Latin America, and the United States. Richard Klatkovsky, for example, paid tribute to Caturla on Berlin FM radio with a five-minute period of silence followed by performances of Caturla's music. Also, Francisco Curt Lange reprinted María Muñoz de Quevedo's article "Alejandro García Caturla" in his *Boletín Latino*, and Henry Cowell paid homage with a short article in *Modern Music* entitled "Roldán and Caturla of Cuba."[19]

CATURLA'S LEGACY

> For each new age is obliged to find a touchstone, postulate its relation to a continuing tradition, and leave to the future to make of it what it can.
>
> Glen Watkins, *Pyramids at the Louvre*

Caturla's touchstone was simply truth; truth as he interpreted it in relation to his ideals. Caturla left an enlightened spirit of patriotism for future generations; a spirit dedicated to progress; a spirit inspired by the humanitarian ideals of social equality and visions of a better future for the peoples of Cuba. Musically, Caturla became a symbol of national pride, courage, fierce independence, and innovation for future generations. Because his life was cut short so abruptly, Caturla left no paths—only ideas to be further developed by future generations.

The composer in Cuba who perceived Caturla's spirit most intuitively during his lifetime and did most to ignite a new era of Cuban music was José Ardévol. Inspired by Caturla's ideas of a new Cuban national music, Ardévol established in Havana the Grupo de Renovación Musical in 1942. Ardévol explained the aims of this group:

In all, the main accomplishments of the composers of the group have been the incorporation of our music into the great universal forms and a treatment less direct and typical of the stylistic Cuban elements than that which had predominated in Roldán and Caturla—that is to say, more expression of "national, rather than proper folklorism."[20]

From that point on, the names of Caturla and Roldán became touchstones for each new generation of Cuban composers. Finally, it was Leo Brouwer, Cuba's most innovative composer of the "movimiento de 'Vanguardia Musical,'" who accurately identified Caturla as one of the *"real maravilloso de Nuestra América"* composers.

A NEW PERSPECTIVE

Owing to his participation in the 1929 Barcelona Festivales Sinfóni-cos, becoming a member of Henry Cowell's Pan American Association of Composers (PAAC), and his own efforts as an entrepreneur, Caturla's name became increasingly well known internationally during the years 1929–35. By then, Caturla could boast that he was one of the most frequently performed Latin composers at Cowell's New Music concerts—a truism. Parallel to Cowell's support was that of the German musicologist Francisco Curt Lange, who spread Caturla's name in Latin America through his *Boletín Latino Ameri-cano de Música*, published in Montevideo, Uruguay. Carlos Chávez and Silvestre Revueltas also spread Caturla's name in Mexico City prior to his death. One of the first lexiconists to document Caturla after his death was the German musicologist Otto Mayer-Serra, who in 1947 included Caturla in his *Música y Músicos de Latino América*, published in Mexico in 1947.

Following the collapse of Cowell's PAAC, *New Music Quarterly*, and New Music concerts, Caturla's name, along with countless other members of PAAC, rapidly disappeared from international publica-tions, concert programs, and radio broadcasts. Caturla's death and the following political lockdown of World War II placed his name in near oblivion for almost two decades. Subsequently, Fidel Castro's revolution of 1959 brought with it a rediscovery of Caturla's music, most of which would be kept at the Museo Nacional de la Música, es-tablished in Havana in 1971. Eventually (1975), the Museo de la Música Provincial "Alejandro García Caturla" was established in Remedios at the grand house of his parents, and a new generation of

Cuban composers and historians initiated a Caturla renaissance. While Caturla's name and music once again resounded in the concert halls of Havana and elsewhere on the island, the world beyond Cuba was, by and large, shut out. Cuba's national recording studios, EGREM, flowed with recordings of music by Caturla and Roldán, accompanied by countless articles and educational publications intended to designate Caturla's legacy as part of Castro's revolution.

Since the premiere of Caturla's opera *Manita en el suelo* in Havana by the Cuban National Ballet in 1979, annual concerts to commemorate Caturla have, by now, become a tradition in Havana, Remedios, and other cities (Camagüey, Santiago de Cuba) on the island. More recently, I attended (in 1996) a piano solo and vocal competition sponsored by the Museo de la Música in Havana and dedicated to the performance of Caturla's music in honor of his ninetieth birthday. A stunning amount of Caturla's unknown and unpublished music was presented on this occasion. The foregoing references to the status of Caturla's name in Cuba today represent but a fraction of efforts being made by Cubans throughout the island to perpetuate and honor one of their most significant national composers.

Recent indications that Caturla's name is regaining some of its lost international recognition are intriguing. For example, the release by Vanguard recordings in 1964 of two Caturla songs (*Bito Manué* and *Juego santo*) in a stunning performance by Phyllis Curtain, and later Argo's release of *Tres Danzas Cubanas* for orchestra in an excellent performance by Michael Tilson Thomas with the New World Symphony may be viewed as signals that interest in, and demands for, the music of composers such as Caturla and Roldán are increasing. Both these composers were an integral part of a series of concerts at Lincoln Center in New York in 1997, sponsored by the Juilliard School of Music; these concerts were announced as "Focus! The Cowell Circle." One of the most recent and exciting presentations of the "unknown" Caturla came about in 1999, when the Griffin String Quartet of New York gave the North American premiere of his four *Piezas para cuarteto de cuerdas* (*Preludio, Pieza en forma de Giga, Pieza en forma de Vals, Pieza en forma de Danza cubana*), composed in 1926–27. This event was sponsored by the Fleisher Collection at the Free Library of Philadelphia, and I'm proud to say I organized and recorded it myself.

Names directly related to Caturla and his times, such as Ernesto Lecuona and Fernando Ortiz, have also become more familiar in the

United States than previously. The recent "Fernando Ortiz Symposium on Cuban Culture and History" sponsored by City University
of New York in March 2000 and the recent announcement of a
recording and publication of the complete piano works of Ernesto
Lecuona are examples. With interest in Cuban music and musicians
of Caturla's era at an all-time high, here and abroad, one eagerly
awaits full-scaled performances of his larger and important works,
including the original version of *Yamba-O* (originally entitled *Liturgia*) scored for double chorus with megaphones and full symphony
orchestra, orchestrated songs such as *Sabás* on a text by Nicolás Guillén, and, obviously, performances of his puppet opera *Manita en el
suelo* . . . time will tell.

NOTES

1. Henríquez, *Correspondencia*, 14 de abril 1939, 281–82.
2. Among the many who benefited from his prize money (actual amount:
$495) were his brother, Othón, and other family members, including his sis-
ter Bertha and his aunt Olga. Liquidating accumulated debts accounted for
some of the remaining money while the bulk of it was used to purchase a
refrigerator for his parent's house.
3. Concerning the disbursement of the prize money, Caturla also wrote to
José Ardévol: "I have written to the President of the Republic [Laredo Bru],
with whom I am linked by bonds of parentage and friendship, so he may intercede with the Secretary of Education in the payment of our prizes" (Henríquez, *Correspondencia*, 6 de abril 1939, 277).
4. Henríquez, *Correspondencia*, 25 de abril 1939, 282–83. Judge Filberto Ro-
dríquez Conde was serving in the same district as Caturla (Villa Clara). By
then Caturla had already published an article entitled "Acción Personal y
Trabajo Sobre Justicia Correccional" in the September 1937 issue of *Repertorio Judicial* (Havana).
5. Henríquez, *Correspondencia*, Caturla to Dr. Pedro Cantero, 10 de febrero
1940, 296–97. During this time, Cuba was engaged in a constitutional assembly to reorganize the government. The assembly adopted a new constitution
loosely modeled on the U.S. constitution and other Spanish models in October
1940; Fulgencio Batista became the legal president of Cuba on 10 October 1940.
6. Henríquez, *Correspondencia*, 26 de febrero 1940, 297–98. The following
May, Caturla wrote to Francisco Llaca y Argudin, Esq., magistrate of the
Supreme Tribunal in Havana, informing him of his intentions to send an article about tutelary measures for delinquent or dangerous minors, for publication in *Repertorio Judicial* (Havana). Eventually, Caturla's article "Sobre la

acción personal" was published in 1940. For the full text of this article see: Henríquez, Antonieta Maria. *Alejandro García Caturlo*, 244–46.

7. Henríquez, *Correspondencia*, 1 de enero 1940, 388. The prisoners' letter continues with a litany of grievances against "the Boss" of the prison; the inmates had reason to believe he had connections with the Cuban army. Among other things, they accused him of selling their food allotments to finance his gambling habits. Their complaints ranged from unjust corporal punishment and denial of visitations to extortion.

8. When Caturla's mother, Diana, found out there was a plot against her son, she went directly to Santa Clara to implore the authorities, specifically one Colonel Gómez, to protect him. The Colonel's response implied that Caturla was plotting against the army, and that this was known at the army headquarters. The Colonel then cynically asked Diana if her son Alejandro wanted a couple of bodyguards from the army. Later, Caturla reportedly said to Catalina Rodríguez: "I would rather let them kill me." For details, see Martín Farto, "Entrevista con la viuda de García Caturla."

9. Henríquez, *Correspondencia*, 12 de noviembre 1940, 308–9.

10. *El Mundo*, 13 de noviembre 1940. *El Mundo* carried a portrait photo and biographical summary on the front page directly under the headlines. The editor points out that "His [Caturla's] life was marked by a shadow of fatalism that was expressed in the two attempts on his life, the last of which was fatal." The first line to Caturla's *Canto de los cafetales* ("Death is looking for me to take me to the cemetery Oh! Mamá") was included in the biographical sketch.

11. *Diario de la Marina*, 13 de noviembre 1940.

12. "Argacha was used by unscrupulous politicians in their electoral campaigns in which they tried to obtain votes by persuasion, self-interest or fear. Using their influence, it was said in the town, he had managed to get the accusation brought against him reduced to a simple assault against persons, with very light punishment" (from a letter by Fernando Arsenio Roa to me, dated 20 August 1993).

13. Under Cuban law at that time, the maximum term for life imprisonment was thirty years. Numerous attempts were made by Argacha Betancourt's connections to have him pardoned. In each case the townspeople of Remedios successfully petitioned the local authorities to block such an appeal. Following his prison term, he moved to the district of Mantanzas where his life came to a natural end.

14. Sanjuán, "El discípulo indisciplinado," 8.

15. Guillén. "El crimen de todos."

16. Some of the main points in her summary include:

1. A documentation of Caturla's international success (references to Cowell, Slonimsky, and others).

2. Caturla's development of an uncompromising musical language that was "fiercely" nationalistic because of its Afro-Cuban musical elements and was at times "chaotic" (Rumba, Bembé as examples).
3. Caturla's creation of a new style of choral music containing "dangerous dissonances" and many voice crossings.
4. Caturla's freedom of creative style based on Afro-Cuban musical elements that set him apart from Roldán, whose music was more conventional because of his academic schooling.

17. Muñoz de Quevedo, "Alejandro García Caturla," 14.

18. Carpentier, "Alejandro García Caturla."

19. One is at a loss to understand the errors and lack of content in Cowell's article. The opening sentence, for example, erroneously states that "Amadeo Roldán and Alejandro García Caturla, both Cubans, died unexpectedly in their prime *during the year 1940*" [italics mine]. Other information in Cowell's short article does not coincide with his previous writings about Caturla.

20. "En conjunto, los principales aportes de los compositores de Grupo han sido la incorporación a nuestra música de las grandes formas universales y un tratamiento menos directo y típico de los elementos estilísticos cubanos que el que había primado en Roldán y Caturla—es decir, más expresión "nacional que propiamente folklorismo." Members of the Grupo de Renovación Musical include Harold Gramatges, Edgardo Martín, Julián Orbón, Argeliers León, Hilario González, Derafín Pro, and Gisela Hernández.

Catalog of Compositions by Alejandro García Caturla

ABBREVIATIONS USED IN THIS CATALOG

a	alto [instrument]	dbn	double bassoon
A	alto [voice]	ded	dedicated to
acc.	accompaniment,	el	electric
	accompaniment by	el-ac	electroacoustic
accdn	accordion	elec	electronic
amp	amplified	eng hn	english horn
b	bass [instrument]	ens	ensemble
B	bass [voice]	fl	flute
bar	baritone	glock	glockenspiel
	[instrument]	gui	guitar
Bar	baritone [voice]	hmn	harmonium
B-Bar	bass-baritone	hn	horn
bc	basso continuo	hp	harp
bn	bassoon	hpd	harpsichord
C	contralto	inst(s)	instrument(s),
cel	celesta		instrumental
chit	chitarone	kbd	keyboard
chmb	chamber	mand	mandolin
cimb	cimbalom	mar	marimba
cl	clarinet	Mez	mezzo-soprano
clvd	clavichord	mic	microphone
cont	continuo	mod	modulator
Ct	countertenor	movt(s)	movement(s)
db	double bass	nar	narrator

ob	oboe	synth	synthesizer
obbl	obbligato	t	tenor [instrument]
orch	orchestra, orchestral	T	tenor [voice]
org	organ	timp	timpani
orig	original, originally	tpt	trumpet
perc	percussion	tr	treble [instrument]
pf	piano	Tr	treble [voice]
pic	piccolo	trbn	trombone
prep pf	prepared piano	unacc.	unaccompanied
rec	recorder	v, vv	voice, voices
s	soprano [instrument]	va	viola
S	soprano [voice]	vc	violincello
S,A,T,B	solo voices	vib	vibraphone
SATB	chorus	vle	violone
sax	saxophone	vn	violin
spkr	speaker	ww	woodwind
str	string(s)	xyl	xylophone

ORCHESTRA

1925   *Pequeña suite de conciertos.* I–Minuet, II–Danza del duende
       Tres preludios para orquesta (pf manuscript; orch. incomplete).
       I–Jardines en quietud, II–Después de la lluvia salió la
       luna, III–Fuegos artificiales
       Poema de ambiente cubano (pf manuscript; orch. incomplete).

1926   *Allegro noble,* concerto for violin and orchestra (first move-
       ment only)
       Impresiones Cubanas (pf manuscript; orch. incomplete). I–El
       Pinar del Rio, II–Guajireñas

1927   *Poema de verano* (pf manuscript; orch. incomplete)
       Son en do menor (pf manuscript; orch. incomplete)
       Serenata del guajiro (pf manuscript; orch. incomplete)
       Serenata pastoril (pf manuscript; orch. incomplete)
       Obertura cubana (pic 2fl 2ob eng hn 2cl bcl 2bn contra bn 4hn3
       tpt 2trbn t timp trgl tdr cymb bdr tam-t cel pf vn va vc db)

1929   *Tres danzas cubanas.* I–Danza del tambor, II–Motivos de danza,
       III–Danza lucumí (pic 2fl 2ob eng hn 2cl bcl 2bn 4hn 3tpt
       3trbn t 2timb trgl tdr cymb bdr tam-t pf hp cel vn va vc db)

1931   *Yamba-O* (orig. *Liturgia* with double male chorus, mega-
       phones, and orch) (pic 3fl 2ob eng hn scl 2cl bcl 2bn contra

bn 4hn 4tpt 4trbn t 2charanga 3timp tdr cymb trgl bdr
claves *güiro* marac *cencerro* tam-t vn va vc db)
Rumba (revised version of earlier *Obertura cubana*, 1927)

1933   *La Rumba* (orig. Soprano and orch. on text by Zacarias Tallet).
Orchestral version: pic 3fl 2ob eng hn scl 2cl bcl 2bn contra
bn 4hn 3tpt 3tbn t timp timbales trgl tdr cymb bdr marac
claves *güiro cencerro* tam-t pf vn va vc db
Fanfarria para desperatar espíritus apolillados (pic 2cl bn 2hn
2tpt tbn timp sdr cymb bdr pf)

1937   *Suite para orquesta.* I–Minstrels, II–Plantación, III–Berceuse,
IV–Vals

CHAMBER ORCHESTRA

1929   *Bembé* (fl ob cl bcl bn 2hn tpt trbn pf tdr cymb bdr tam-t)
Desolación-impromptu (fl eng hn cl bcl bn va vc)

1931   *Primera suite cubana* (fl ob eng hn cl bcl bn hn tmp pf)

1932   *Nombres negros en el son* (incomplete; on text by Ballagas) (v
ob bcl tpt 2bn 2hn dbs 2timp clave marac *güiro*)

CHAMBER MUSIC

1924   *Berceuse* 2vl pf
Impromptus I–Lamento, II–Leyenda, III–Balada y pequeño scherzo vl pf

1925   *Valsette* (fl vn vc pf)
Danza del amor salvaje (fl 2vn vc pf)
Minuet (fl cl 2vn vc db pf)
Melodía disonante (vc pf and sax pf)

1926   *Concierto de cámara.* I–Preludio, II–Aria (fl ob cl bn hn vn
va vc db pf)
Berceuse (str quint pf)

1926   *Romanza* (vl pf)
Serenata exótica (ded. Jascha Heifetz) (vl pf)

1926–27 *Piezas para cuarteto de cuerdas.* Preludio, Giga, Vals, Minuet, Pavana, Danza cubana, Son, Momento musical

1927   *Improvisación*
Desolación (vl pf)

Canzonetta (vl pf)
Pieza en mi menor (vl pf)
Serenata pastoril (vl pf)
Elegía liturgia (vl pf)
Gavota (vl pf)
Danza del tambor (vc pf)
Serenata vehemente (vn va vc 2cl bn)
Berceuse (2cl 5sax)
Tres piezas para violín, cello y piano. I–En modo de Minuet,
　　II–En modo de Pavana, III–En modo de Danza cubana
Danza del tambor (sax septet)
Cuarteto de cuerdas. I–Allegro
1928　*Minuet a l'antica* (vl pf)
　　Balada romántica (ded. Amadeo Roldán) (vl pf)
　　Canto guajiro (vl pf)
　　Danza del tambor (vl pf)
　　Quinteto (str quart pf). I–Oriental, II–Cubana, III–Danza
　　　　Negra, IV–Allegro non troppo
1937　*Comparsa* (from ballet *Olilé*) (vl pf and vc pf)
　　Canto de los cafetales (orig. a cappella SATB) (str quart)

BALLET

1929–30　*Olilé (El Velorio).* Orig. libretto (Afro-Cuban poem), full
　　symphony orchestra

OPERA

1934–37　*Manita en el suelo.* Chamber opera in one act for puppets.
　　Full symphony orchestra, chorus, and Afro-Cuban and
　　African percussion (*batá* drums). Libretto by Alejo Car-
　　pentier.

OPERETTA

1924　*El Lucero.* Two acts. Piano vocal. I–Preludio, II–Rondel de
　　Bomabalín, III–Entrada de Teodoro y Dúo de Teodoro y
　　Lucero, IV–Balada del molino, V–Angelus

CINEMA

1923   *Recuerdos del Sheik*. Poema sinfónico for a Rudolf Valentino
film. Piano score with orchestrations indicated.
Kaleidoscopio. For theater orchestra (teatro Campoamor)

BAND

1925   *Berceuse*
1927   *Poema de verano*
1929   *Tres danzas cubanas*. I–Danza del tambor, II–Motivos de
danza, III–Danza lucumí
Suite para banda. I–Preludio, II–Vals, III–Danza

ORGAN

1924   *Preludio en mi menor*

PIANO SOLO

1922   *Las tardes de Campoamor (danzón)*
1923   *El olvido de la canción (danzón)*
Tu alma y la mía (danzón)
Ay mamá, yo te vi bailando (danzón)
El saxofón de Cuco (danzón)
Laredo se va (danzón)
Tócala con limón (danzón)
Cine Méndez (danzón)
1924   *Mi mamá no quiere que yo baile el son* (danzón)
Quiéreme camagüeyana (danzón)
Carolyn (fox-trot)
No quiero juego con tu marido (Danza cubana no. 1)
La viciosa (Danza cubana no. 2)
La no. 3 (Danza cubana no. 3)
Serenata del guajiro
Preludio en fa menor
1925   *Nadie se muere de amor (danzón)*
Doña Francisquita (Danzón)

Cuentos musicales. Escenas infantiles: I–Baladita del niño en la
cuna, II–El baile del gnomo Pinocho, III–Scherzito de la
lluvia en los cristales, IV–La luna me besa por la ventana,
V–Fuegos artificiales de juguete, VI–La balada del amor
bandolero, VII–Dr. Gradus ad Parnassum, VIII–Alba radiante, Sol! Sol!, IX–El caballo encantado, X–Berceuse

Danza Negra

Danza Lucumí

Tres Preludios. I–Jardines en quietud, II–Después de la lluvia
salió la luna, III–Fuegos artificiales

Preludio-vals

1926   *Piano easy jazz music* (ragtime)
1927   *Son en do menor*
       Toccata en Do menor
       Pieza en forma de son
       Preludio Corto no. 1 "Mi vida será siempre triste"
       Preludio Corto no 2 "Tu amor era falso"
       Preludio Corto no. 3 "Un sueño irrealizable"
       Sonata Corta
       Vals corto
       Tres grandes preludios
       Sonatina
       Elegía liturgica
       Pavana
       Canzonetta
       Momento musical
       Pieza en forma de Vals
       Pieza en forma de Minuet
       Pieza en forma de Danza cubana
       Pieza en forma de Giga
       Monsieur l'agriculteur (Pieza satírica)
       Danza del tambor
1928   *Primera Comparsa*
       Canon a 2 voces
       Fuga libre a 2 voces
       Gaviotas
1930   *Son en Mi b*
       Comparsa (ded. Fernando Ortiz)
1936   *Preludio* Homenaje a Changó
1937   *Berceuse* Para dormir a un negrito
1938   *Berceuse campesina*
1939   *Son en fa menor*

SOLO VOCAL MUSIC

1924   *Y si él volviera un día* (v pf orig. text)
       La promesa (lied v pf on text by Juana de Ibarbourou)
       La deshilachada (tango milonga v pf orig. text)
       Como te amaba mi corazón (criolla-bolero v pf orig. text)
       Bajo mis besos (ded. Carpentier) (bolero v pf orig. text)—
1925   *Ansia* (bolero v pf orig. text)—
       Vidita (bolero v pf orig. text)
       Serenata de mayo (lied v pf on text by Julio Herrera y Reissig)
       Serenata de otoño (lied v pf on text by Julio Herrera y Reissig)
       Pebetita (tango v pf orig. text)
1926   *Labios queridos* (Berceuse a lo guajiro) (lied v pf orig. text)
       Una lágrima (criolla-ballada v pf on text by Luis Urbina)
1927   *Ave maría* (bar 2vn va org)
       La leyenda de la rosa (Vals S chmb orch orig. text)
1928   *El simbolo* (lied v pf orig. text)
       Canto de esperanza (lied v pf orig. text)
       Tarde tropical (lied v pf on text by Rubén Darío)
       Mi vida (madrigal v pf orig. text)
       Mi amor aquel (criolla v pf on text by Rosario Sansores)
       Ingratitud (criolla-bolero v pf orig. text)
1929   *Sonera* (v pf orig. text)
       En el Batey (vocaliso) v pf—
       Mari-sabel (v pf orig. text)—
       Dos poemas afrocubanos (v pf on text by Carpentier)
1930   *Bito Manué* (v pf on text by Guillén)
1933   *Mulata* (v pf on text by Guillén)
       Yambambó (v pf on text by Guillén)
1934   *Elegía del Enkiko* (aria from *Manita en el suelo*) (v pf on text by
         Carpentier)
1937   *Berceuse para dormir a un negrito* (v pf on text by Ballagas)
       Sabás (v pf on text by Guillén)

VOCAL MUSIC WITH ORCHESTRA

1928   *Liturgia* (on text by Carpentier) (pic 2fl 2ob eng hn 3cl bcl 3bn
       4hn 4tpt 2trbn btrbn tuba 3timp tamtam trgl cymb bdr
       bongos claves gangarias pf male chorus I male chorus II
       [both w megaphones] vn va vc db)

1930   *Dos poemas afrocubanos* (on text by Carpentier). S & Orch. (orig. v & pf 1929; pic 2fl 2ob eng hn 2cl bcl 2bn contra bn 4hn 3trbn t timp tam-t cymb bdr trgl sdr claves S harp vn va vc db)

1933   *La Rumba* (orig.) S & Orch. (on text by Zacarias Tallet) (pic 3fl 2ob eng hn scl 2cl bcl 2bn contra bn 4hn 3tpt 3tbn t timp timbales trgl tdr cymb bdr marac claves *güiro cencerro* tam-t pf S vn va vc db)

1937   *Sabás* (on text by Guillén) (v fl ob cl va vc)

A CAPPELLA CHORUS

1929   *Tú que robas mi cariño* (S I II Mez S Contralto)
1931   *El caballo blanco (Son)* (SATB)
1937   *Canto de cafetales (Son)* (SATB)

Principal publishers: Carl Fisher, *New Music Quarterly* (Cowell), *Edition Salabert* (col. Senart), Otto Mayer-Serra (*Música y Músicos de Latino America*), *Musicalia, Social,* Instituo Interamericano de Musicología (Montevideo), EGREM (Editora Musical de Cuba). Manuscripts are stored at the Museo Nacional de la Música, Havana.

Bibliography

BOOKS

Aguiarre, Mirta. "El Cincuentenario de Motivos de Son." Introductory essay in *Nicolás Guillén Motivos de Son*, edited by Eliana Dávila, 5–22. Havana: Editorial Letras Cubanas, 1980.

Aguilar, Luis E. *Cuba 1933*. Ithaca, N.Y.: Cornell University Press, 1972.

Alén Rodríguez, Olavo. "Cuba." In *The Garland Handbook of Latin American Music*, edited by Dale A. Olsen, and Daniel E. Sheey, 116–33. New York: Garland Publishing, Inc., 2000.

Amira, John, and Steven Cornelius. *The Music of Santería: Traditional Rhythms of the Batá Drums*. Crown Point, Ind.: White Cliffs Media Company, 1992.

Asche, Charles Byron. "Cuban Folklore Traditions and Twentieth Century Idioms in the Music of Amadeo Roldán and Alejandro García Caturla." Ph.D. diss., University of Texas at Austin, 1983.

Béhague, Gerard. *Music in Latin America*. Englewood Cliffs, N.J.: Prentice Hall, 1979.

Ballagas, Emilio. *Júbilo y Fuga: Poemas*. Havana, Cuba: La Cooperativa, Virtudes, 1931.

Boulware-Miller, Patricia Kay. *Nature in Three 'Negrista' Poets: Nicolás Guillén, Emilio Ballagas and Luis P. Matos*. Ann Arbor, Mich.: University Microfilms, 1978.

Brouwer, Leo. *La música, lo cubano y la innovación*. Havana: Editorial Letras Cubanas, 1982.

Cañizares, Dulcila. *Gonzalo Roig*. Havana: Editorial Letras Cubanas, 1978.

Carpentier, Alejo. *La música en Cuba*. Havana: Editorial Pueblo Y Educación, 1989.

Chase, Gilbert. *A Guide to the Music of Latin America*. New York: AMS Press, Inc., 1972.

Cobb, Martha K. *The Black Experience in the Poetry of Nicolás Guillén, Jacques Roumain, Langston Hughes.* Ann Arbor, Mich.: University Microfilms, 1974.

Collaer, Paul. *Darius Milhaud.* San Francisco: San Francisco Press, 1988.

Cowell, Henry, ed. *American Composers on American Music: A Symposium.* Stanford, Calif.: Stanford University Press, 1933.

———. *Charles Ives and His Music.* New York: Oxford University Press, 1955.

Dávila, Eliana, ed. *Nicolás Guillén Motivos De Son: Música de Amadeo Roldán, Alejandro García Caturla, Eliseo Grenet, Emilio Grenet. Edición Especial 50 Aniversario.* Havana: Editorial Letras Cubanas, 1980.

Ellis, Keith. *Cuba's Nicolás Guillén.* Toronto: University of Toronto Press, 1983.

Euba, Akin. *Essays on Music in Africa.* Vol. 2, *Intercultural Perspectives.* Bayreuth, Germany: Elékoto Music Centre Lagos, 1989.

Feijóo, Samuel. *El Son Cubano: Poesía General.* Havana: Editorial Letras Cubanas, 1986.

———. *El Negro en la Literatura Folklorica Cubana.* Havana: Editorial Letras Cubanas, 1987.

Galán, Natalio. *Cuba y Sus Sones.* Valencia, Spain: Luis Santángel, 1983.

García-Carranza, Araceli. *Biobiliografía de Alejo Carpentier.* Havana: Editorial Letras Cubanas, 1984.

García Caturla, Alejandro. "Correspondencia inédita" (file of unpublished letters). Museo de Música de La Habana.

———. "The Development of Cuban Music." In *American Composers on American Music: A Symposium,* edited by Henry Cowell, 173–74. Stanford, Calif.: Stanford University Press, 1933.

Gómez, Zoila. *Amadeus Roldán.* Havana: Editorial Arte y Literatura, 1978.

———, ed. *Alejo Carpentier: Ese Músico que llevo dentro.* 3 vols. Havana: Editorial Letras Cubanas, 1980.

González, Hilario. "Alejo Carpentier: precursor del 'movimiento afrocubano'." In *Alejo Carpentier: Ese Músico que llevo dentro,* edited by Zoila Gómez, vol. I, 11–20. Havana: Editorial Letras Cubanas, 1980.

González, Hilario, and María Antonieta Henriquez, eds. *Museo Alejandro García Caturla (catálogo de obras de A. G. Caturla).* Havana: Conselo Nacional de Cultura Delegación Provincial, 1975.

González, Jorge Antonio. *La Composición Operística En Cuba.* Havana: Editorial Letras Cubanas, 1986.

Gray, John. *Blacks in Classical Music: A Bibliographical Guide to Composers, Performers, and Ensembles.* New York: Greenwood Press, 1988.

Grenet, Emilio. *Popular Cuban Music.* Havana: Ministerio de Educación, Dirección de Cultura, 1939.

Guillén, Nicolás. *Prosa de Prisa: Cronicas.* Santa Clara: Universidad Central de las Villas Dirección de Publicaciones, 1962.

Henríquez, María Antonieta, ed. *Alejandro García Caturla Correspondencia.* Havana: Editorial Arte y Literatura, 1978.

——. *Alejandro García Caturla*. Havana: Unión de Escritores y Artistas de Cuba, 1998.

Hughes, Langston. *Journals 1920–1937*. Yale University, Beinike Library Rare Books & Archives. JWJ MSS Hughes.

Janney, Frank. *Alejo Carpentier and His Early Works*. London: Tamesis, 1981.

Kuss, Malena. "The Confluence of Historical Coordinates in Carpentier/Caturla's Puppet Opera *Manita en el suelo*." In *Musical Repercussions of 1492*, edited by Carol E. Robertsonk, 355–80. Washington, D.C.: Smithsonian Institution, 1992.

Leon, Argeliers. *Del Canto y el Tiempo*. Havana: Editorial Letras Cubanas, 1984.

Lezcano, José Manuel. "Afro-Cuban Rhythmic and Metric Elements in the Published Choral and Solo Vocal Works of Alejandro García Caturla and Amadeo Roldán." Ph.D. diss., Florida State University School of Music, 1991.

Linaras, María Teresa. *La música y el pueblo*. Havana: Editorial Pueblo y Educación, 1974.

Lozano, Eduardo. *Cuban Periodicals in the University of Pittsburgh Libraries*. Pittsburgh: Pittsburgh University Libraries, 1991.

Manion, Martha L. *Writings About Henry Cowell: An Annotated Bibliography*. Number 16. Brooklyn, N.Y.: I.S.A.M. Monographs, 1982.

Martín Farto, Miguel. *Las parrandas remedianas*. Havana: Editorial Letras Cubanas, 1988.

Márquez, Robert, and David Arthur McMurray, trans. *Guillén: Man Making Words. Selected Poems of Nicolás Guillén*. Havana: Editorial Arte y Literatura, 1973.

Martín, Edgardo. *Panorama histórico de la música cubana*. Havana: Universidad de La Habana, 1971.

Martinez Escobar, Manuel. *Historia de Remedios*. Santa Clara, Cuba: J. Montero, 1944.

Martinez, Orlando. *Ernesto Lecuona*. Havana: Unión de Escritores y Artistas de Cuba, 1989.

Mayer-Serra, Otto. *Música y Músicos de Latino America*. Mexico City: Editorial Atlante, SA, 1947.

Mead, Rita. *Henry Cowell's New Music of 1925–1936*. Ann Arbor: University of Michigan Research Press, 1981.

Morgan, Robert P. *Twentieth-Century Music*. New York: Norton, 1991.

Olsen, Dale A., and Daniel E. Sheey, eds. *The Garland Handbook of Latin American Music*. New York: Garland Publishing, Inc., 2000.

Orovio, Helio. *Diccionario de la música cubana*. Havana: Editorial Letras Cubanas, 1981.

Ortiz, Fernando. *La africanía de la música folklórica de Cuba*. Havana: Ministerio de Educación, 1950.

——. *Los Bailes y el Teatro de los Negros en el Folklore de Cuba*. Havana: Editorial Letras Cubanas, 1981.

Ramperstad, Arnold. *The Life of Langston Hughes.* New York: Oxford University Press, 1986.

Roldán, Amadeo. "The Artistic Position of the American Composer." In *American Composers on American Music: A Symposium,* edited by Henry Cowell, 175–77. Stanford, Calif.: Stanford University Press, 1933.

Root, Deane L. *Yearbook for Interamerican Musical Research.* Texas: University of Texas at Austin, 1978.

Rubin, Jane Gregory, ed. *Miscelanea II of Studies Dedicated to Fernando Ortiz.* New York: InterAmericas Society of Arts and Letters of the Americas, 1998.

Salazar, Adolfo. *Music in Our Time: Trends in Music Since the Romantic Era.* New York: Norton, 1946.

Sánchez Cabrera, Maruja. *Orquesta Filarmónica de La Habana. Memoria (1924–1959).* Havana: Ministerio de Cultura, *Editorial Orbe,* 1979.

Sánchez-Gutiérrez, Carlos Daniel. "The Cooked and the Raw: Syncretism in the Music of Silvestre Revueltas." Ph.D. diss., Princeton University, 1996.

Sardinha, Dennis. *The Poetry of Nicolás Guillén.* London: Beacon Books, 1976.

Saylor, Bruce. *A Descriptive Bibliography of Henry Cowell.* Number 16. Brooklyn, N.Y.: I.S.A.M. Monographs, 1977.

Slonimsky, Nicolas. *Music of Latin America.* New York: Da Capo Press, 1972.

———. *Perfect Pitch.* New York: Oxford University Press. 1988.

Stevens, Halsey, paper. "Critical Years in European Musical History, 1915–1925." In *International Musicological Society Report of the Tenth Congress Ljubljana,* 1969, edited by Dragotin Cvetko, 216–47. RILM 70-02902.

Stukenschmidt, H. H. *Twentieth Century Music.* London: Weidenfeld and Nicolson, 1969.

Suchlicki, Jaime. *Historical Dictionary of Cuba, Second Edition.* Lanham: Scarecrow Press, 2001.

Thomas, Hugh. *Cuba: The Pursuit of Freedom.* New York: Harper & Row, 1971.

Tiro, Frank. *Jazz: A History.* New York: Norton, 1977.

Valdés Cruz, Rosa. *La Poesía Negroide En America.* Long Island, N.Y.: Las Americas Publishing Co., 1970.

Varèse, Louise. *Varèse: A Looking-Glass Diary.* New York: Norton, 1972.

Watkins, Glenn. *Pyramids at the Louvre: Music, Culture, and Collage from Stravinsky to the Postmodernists.* Cambridge, Mass.: The Belknap Press of Harvard University Press, 1994.

ARTICLES

Álvarez Sanabria, Carlos. "Una Originalidad Escandalosa." *El Caiman Barbudo* (April 1975): 25.

Ardévol, José. "La Rumba, Movimiento Sinfónico de Alejandro García Caturla." *La Gaceta de Cuba,* 1 April 1972, 22.

———. "El músico: Homenaje a Alejandro García Caturla." *Nueva Revista Cubana* (March 1962): 23–25.

Belvaines, Marcel. "*Bembé* de Caturla." *Le Menestrel,* 21 December 1929.

Capote, María Helena. "Por las calles de Remedios en busca de Caturla." *Mujeres* (October 1975): 58–68.

Carpentier, Alejo. "Adolfo Salazar." *El Nacional* (December 1958).

———. "Alejandro García Caturla 1906–1949." *El Huracán,* 11 Diciembre 1941. Reprinted in *El Mundo,* November 1960.

———. "Carpentier Escribe Sobre García Caturla." *Signos* (January 1978): 71–98.

———. "Caturla en Paris." *El Mundo,* November 1960.

———. "Dos Festivales de Música Cubana y Americana." *Carteles* (July 1931): 210–15.

———. "Erik Satie, Profeta y Renovador." *Social* (September 1927): 318–24.

———. "El Neoclasicismo en la música contemporánea." Part I. *Musicalia* (June 1928): 3–5.

———. "El Neoclasicismo en la música contemporánea." Part II. *Musicalia* (July 1928): 45–47.

———. "Homenaje a la Memoria de Alejandro García Caturla: El Hombre." *Neuva Revista Cubana* (November 1962): 5–22.

———. "La Música Cubana en Paris." *Carteles* (September 1928): 544–50.

———. "La Rebambaramba." *El Mundo,* November 1960.

———. "Las Nuevas Ofensivas del Cubanismo." *Carteles* (December 1929): 533–37.

———. "Los Problemas del Compositor Latinoamericano. I & II." *El Nacional,* March and April 1946.

———. "Martí, Estudiante de Música." *El Nacional,* March 1953.

———. "Panorama de la Música en Cuba. La Música Contemporánea." *Revista Musical Chileana* (December 1947): 272–84.

———. "Silvestre Revueltas." *El Nacional,* October 1952.

———. "Sóngoro Cosongo . . . en Paris." *Carteles* (September 1932): 563–67.

———. "Un Compositor Cubano y un Éxito en Paris." *Carteles* (July 1929): 24–27.

———. "Un Revolucionario de la Música: Edgar Varèse. Para Alejandro García Caturla." *Social* (June 1929): 97–102.

———. "Una Obra Sinfónica Cubana." *Social* (February 1926): 9–12.

Caturla de la Maza, Olga. "Recuerdos de Alejandro García Caturla." *Pro Arte Musicale* (April 1960).

Cowell, Henry. "Compositores Modernos de los Estados Unidos." *Musicalia* (November–December 1928): 124–27.

———. "Roldan and Caturla of Cuba." *Modern Music* (January 1941): 98–99.

———. "The 'Sones' of Cuba." *Modern Music* (January–February 1931): 45–47.

Downes, Olin. "Stokowski Offers Novel Items Here." *New York Times,* 6 January 1932, 25.

Fernández de Castro, José Antonio. "Yamba-O." *Orbe* (October 1931): 15.

Fiejóo, Samuel. "Roldán y Caturla." *Gramma* (April 1979): 4.

Gallardo, Conchita. "Alejandro García Caturla." *El País,* 3 December 1932.

García Caturla, Alejandro. "Breve nota sobre *Yamba-O.*" From composer's unpublished orchestral score. See *Works by Latin American Composers* in the Edwin A. Fleisher Collection of Orchestral Music, the Free Library of Philadelphia.

———. "Charles E. Ives 4a Sinfonia." *Musicalia* (January–February 1929): 190–91.

———. "Cowell Conferences." *El Faro,* 22 January 1931.

———. "Festivales Sinfónicos Ibero-Americanos." *Musicalia* (November–December 1929): 103–6.

———. "Notes From Abroad." *Musicalia* (November–December 1929): 104.

———. "Posibilidades sinfónicas de la música afrocubana." *Musicalia* (July–August 1929): 15–17.

———. "Profesión de Fe." From the program notes of the inaugural concert of the Orquesta de Conciertos de Caibarien, 2 December 1932.

———. "Realidad de la utilización sinfónica del instrumental cubano." *Atalaya* (15 July 1933): 2.

———. "Septimino Cuevas." *El Faro,* 18 November 1931.

———. "Students Unite!" *Atalaya* (15 July 1933): 1.

González, Hilario. Datos biográficos y Catálogo de obras de AGC. Catálogo de la Inauguración del Museo Provincial de Música "Alejandro García Caturla," Museo Nacional de la Música, La Habana (1975).

———. "*La Rumba* de Alejandro García Caturla." *Boletín de Música* (1971).

Gramatges, Harold. "Anniversario de la muerte de Caturla." *Boletín de Música,* (November 1970).

Guillén, Nicolás. "El crimen de todos." *Tiempo,* 15 November 1940.

———. "No Hay Poesía Negra, Ni Mucho Menos El Llamado Afrocubanismo." *Vanguardia* [Columbia] (4 July 1945): 1.

Hall, D. "New Music Quarterly Recordings—a Discography." *Journal* [Assoc. of Recorded Sound Collections] (1984): 10.

Henríquez, María Antonieta, and Hilario González. "Alejandro García Caturla: Portador de un fuego nuevo." *Bohemia* (March 1986): 14–19.

———. "Visión de Caturla." *Revolución y Cultura* (March 1986): 50–55.

Ichaso, Francisco. "Caturla: *Tres Danzas Cubanas.*" *Revista de Avance* (15 March 1930): 95.

Loyola, José. "La música contemporánea Cubana." *Ritmo* (January 1983): 11–15.

Martín, Edgardo. "Las canciones de Caturla." *Boletín de Música* (March–April 1976): 9–25.

Martín Farto, Miguel. "Entrevista con la viuda de García Caturla." *Signos* (December 1978): 99–107.

———. "Música de parrandas." *Revolución y Cultura* (December 1984).

Martin, Linton. "Stokowski Offers New Year's Concert." *Philadelphia Inquirer*, 3 January 1932, 3.

Martínez, Lara, and Melvin Dej. "Caturla: el hombre sin fronteras ni prejuicios." *Poder del Pueblo* (Remedios) (March 1980): 27–30.

Massaguer, Conrado W. "García Caturla en la Exposición de Barcelona." *Social* (February 1930): 26.

———. "García Caturla estariá subvencionado en Berlin o en Bruselas si Cuba no fuera la Madrasta de sus artistas." *Social* (November 1937): 4.

———. "Garcia Caturla y un comentario elogioso de una revista norte Americana." *Social* (August 1931): 15.

———. "Lydia Rivera." *Social* (October 1930): 21.

Morenza Abreu, Juan. "Kid Chocolate—The Free Negro; Bembé—The Black Slave." *El Faro*, 18 April 1933.

Mosquera, Gerardo. "Modernidad y Africanía—Wilfred Lam in His Island." *Third Text—Cuba* (1992): 43–69.

Muñoz de Quevedo, María. "Alejandro García Caturla." *Musicalia* (January–February 1941): 8–14.

———. "Critica a Amadeo Roldán." *Musicalia* (September–October 1928): 104–9.

———. "Critica a Alejandro García Caturla." *Musicalia* (November–December 1928): 144.

———. "Sociedad de Música Contemporánea—Profesión de fe." *Musicalia* (January–March 1930): 19–21.

Oramas, Ada. "Manita en el suelo: Por primera vez a escena." *Revolución y Cultura* (October 1979): 13–17.

Ortiz, Fernando. "El estudio de la música afrocubana." Part I. *Musicalia* (November–December 1928): 115–19.

———. "El estudio de la música afrocubana." Part II. *Musicalia* (January–February 1929): 169–174.

"Pedro San Juan for New Music Concert." *The Argonaut* (San Francisco), 11 October 1930, 6.

Pérez Sentenat, César. "Amadeo Roldán, se no muere!" *Musicalia* (January–February 1941): 12–14.

Piñeiro Díaz, José. "Cronología 80 aniversario de Rita Montaner." Booklet. Ministerio de Cultura. Museo Nacional de la Música (1968).

———. "María Muñoz de Quevedo centenario de su nacimiento (1886–1986) y cincuenta y cinco aniversario de la fundación de la Sociedad Coral de La Habana." Ministerio de Cultura. Museo Nacional de la Música (1986).

Portuondo, José Antonio. "Compases de redención." *Diario de Cuba*, 2 January 1933 (later reprinted in *El Faro*, 19 January 1933).

Quevedo, Antonio. "Orquesta Filarmónica—*Dos Danzas Cubanas*, de Alejandro García Caturla." *Revista de Avance* (December 1928): 364.

Robbins, James. "The Cuban *Son* as Form, Genre, and Symbol." *Latin American Music Review* 11 no. 2 (December 1990): 183–99.

"Roldán, Caturla, Yo. . . ." *Bohemia* (March 1966): 54–55.

Salazar, Adolfo. "La obra musical de Alejandro García Caturla." *Revista Cubana* (January 1938): 5–43.

———. "Musicas Negras" *Nuestra Música* (Month 1952): 134–56.

Sanjuán, Pedro. "El discípulo indisciplinado." *Tiempo,* 13 de noviembre 1940, 1–2. Reprinted in *Signos* (January 1978): 108–9.

———. "Notes on *Liturgia Negra.*" *Eschig* (1939).

Slonimsky, Nicolas. "Caturla of Cuba." *Modern Music* (January–February 1940): 76–80.

———. "Music in Cuba." *The Musical Record* (August 1933): 90–93.

Urrutia, Gustavo. "Ideales de una Raza: Espíritu De Raza." *Diario de la Marina,* 12 October 1930.

Valdéz, Carmen. "Alejandro García Caturla." *Revolución y Cultura* (November 1977): 28–34.

Vásquez, Omar. "Inaugurada la casa de la música Alejandro García Caturla." *Gramma* (August 1985): 4.

Index

Index of Caturla's Works

About the Author

Charles W. White (Diploma, Staatsakademie Für Musik, Vienna; M.M., Music History, Temple University, Phila., Pa.; Ph.D., Musicology, Bryn Mawr College, Pa.). Although he made his debut as a classical pianist in Vienna and subsequently completed a doctoral dissertation in nineteenth-century music, Charles White has concentrated on twentieth-century Latin American music since the 1980s. He has been chairman of the Fine Arts Department at La Salle University, Philadelphia, Pa., since that time. His publications include articles on Cuban music in *Latin American Music Review, The New Groves Dictionary of Music and Musicians, Heterophonia,* and other journals. He was awarded two grants from the National Endowment of the Humanities, one of which focused on the life, times, and music of twentieth-century Cuban nationalist composer Alejandro García Caturla. Interviews with family, friends, and colleagues of Caturla's still living in Cuba and the United States followed. He also undertook several recording sessions of Caturla's music and presented multimedia programs of this composer's life and music in Havana (UNEAC Festival 1991–92) and Philadelphia (La Salle University and Free Library of Philadelphia).